Meeting Ethnography

T0331285

This volume asks and addresses elusive ontological, epistemological, and methodological questions about meetings. What are meetings? What sort of knowledge, identities, and power relationships are produced, performed, communicated, and legitimized through meetings? How do—and how might—ethnographers study meetings as objects, and how might they best conduct research in meetings as particular elements of their field sites? Through contributions from an international group of ethnographers who have conducted "meeting ethnography" in diverse field sites, this volume offers both theoretical insight and methodological guidance into the study of this most ubiquitous ritual.

Jen Sandler is a lecturer in the Department of Anthropology at the University of Massachusetts Amherst, USA.

Renita Thedvall is a researcher at the Stockholm Centre for Organizational Research at Stockholm University and Stockholm School of Economics, Sweden.

Routledge Studies in Anthropology

For a full list of titles in this series, please visit www.routledge.com

28 Islam, Standards, and Technoscience
In Global Halal Zones
Johan Fischer

29 After the Crisis
Anthropological thought, neoliberalism
and the aftermath
James G. Carrier

30 Hope and Uncertainty in Contemporary African Migration
Edited by Nauja Kleist and Dorte Thorsen

31 Work and Livelihoods in Times of Crisis
Edited by Susana Narotzky and Victoria Goddard

32 Anthropology and Alterity
Edited by Bernhard Leistle

33 Mixed Race Identities in Australia, New Zealand
and the Pacific Islands
Edited by Farida Fozdar and Kirsten McGavin

34 Freedom in Practice
Edited by Moises Lino e Silva and Huon Wardle

35 Indian Classical Dance in a Transnational Context
Dancing on Empire's Stage
Sitara Thobani

36 Truth, Intentionality and Evidence
Anthropological Approaches to Crime
Edited by Yazid Ben Hounet and Deborah Puccio-Den

37 Meeting Ethnography
Meetings as Key Technologies of Contemporary
Governance, Development, and Resistance
Edited by Jen Sandler and Renita Thedvall

Meeting Ethnography

Meetings as Key Technologies
of Contemporary Governance,
Development, and Resistance

**Edited by Jen Sandler
and Renita Thedvall**

Routledge
Taylor & Francis Group
NEW YORK AND LONDON

First published 2017
by Routledge
711 Third Avenue, New York, NY 10017

and by Routledge
2 Park Square, Milton Park, Abingdon, Oxon OX14 4RN

Routledge is an imprint of the Taylor & Francis Group, an informa business

British Library Cataloguing-in-Publication Data
A catalogue record for this book is available from the British Library

Library of Congress Cataloging-in-Publication Data
A catalog record for this book has been requested

ISBN: 978-1-138-67769-2 (hbk)
ISBN: 978-0-367-87569-5 (pbk)

DOI: 10.4324/9781315559407

Contents

Acknowledgements								vii

Introduction: Exploring the Boring – An Introduction
to Meeting Ethnography							1
JEN SANDLER AND RENITA THEDVALL

1 Mapping International Development Relations
   through Meeting Ethnography						24
   NANCY KENDALL AND RACHEL SILVER

2 Learning to Meet (or How to Talk to Chairs)				46
   SIMONE ABRAM

3 Argentinean *Asamblea* Meetings as Assemblage:
   Presence in Emergence						69
   SUSANN BAEZ ULLBERG AND KARIN SKILL

4 How to Avoid Getting Stuck in Meetings: On the
   Value of Recognizing the Limits of Meeting
   Ethnography for Community Studies					88
   JAPONICA BROWN-SARACINO AND MEAGHAN STIMAN

5 Meetings All the Way Through: United States
   Broad-based Reform Coalitions and the Thickening
   of American Democracy						106
   JEN SANDLER

6 Small Places, Big Stakes: Meetings as Moments
   of Ethnographic Momentum						126
   CHRISTINA GARSTEN AND ADRIENNE SÖRBOM

7   **Meeting to Improve: Lean[ing] Swedish Public Preschools** 143
    RENITA THEDVALL

    Conclusion: The Meeting and the Mirror 158
    HELEN B. SCHWARTZMAN

    Notes on Contributors 179
    Index 183

Acknowledgements

This volume has been a collaborative project not only between an organizational anthropologist from Sweden (Thedvall) and an activist anthropologist from the United States (Sandler), but also with the many participants in the three workshops we organized between 2013 and 2015. We extend them our sincere gratitude, and have attempted to acknowledge each of their contributions to this volume more specifically through the Introduction. Of the participants not represented in this volume, we especially would like to thank Don Brenneis, whose support for the project has been invaluable. We also would like to thank two external reviewers for the project, whose insights improved our thinking and contributed greatly to the final product.

The volume would not have been possible without the people in the workshops. We are extremely grateful for the financial support that enabled these workshops to take place. Stockholm Centre for Organizational Research (Score), Stockholm University, and Stockholm School of Economics and the Department of Social Anthropology at Stockholm University funded the first workshop in June 2013. The second workshop in June 2014 was made possible by the generous support of the Institute for Social Science Research at the University of Massachusetts Amherst. The third workshop was a larger event that took place over the course of three days, and it was made possible by the generous support of the Riksbankens Jubileumsfond, The Swedish Foundation for Humanities and Social Science, with support from the Institute for Social Science Research and the Department of Anthropology at UMass Amherst.

Finally, we would like to thank Helen B. Schwartzman, both as a person for her extraordinary support of this project and for her book, *The Meeting*, which brought us together.

Introduction: Exploring the Boring

An Introduction to Meeting Ethnography

Jen Sandler and Renita Thedvall[1]

Introduction: Meetings as the Doxa of Everyday Life

The meeting is arguably the most important and under-theorized phenomenon that ethnographers encounter. Whether in policy organizations or local communities, labor halls or religious institutions, schools or corporations, among activists or social workers or anarchists, ethnographers often find that meetings are where the action is. In meetings power is produced and enacted, dynamics of identity and hierarchy are negotiated, and organization is produced, determined, and challenged. Meetings are a ubiquitous part of many contemporary contexts, and what takes place in meetings matters for many more.

Yet, there has, for a long time, been little sustained critical ethnographic inquiry into the meeting itself. Helen Schwartzman's seminal work, *The Meeting* (1989), in which she called attention to the taken-for-grantedness of meetings in ethnographic writing, has remained a notable exception. Meetings are part of the doxa of everyday life; we take them for granted to the point that there has been insufficient concerted effort to theorize them or to strategize fieldwork within and around them. Of course, this is precisely the province of anthropology: to interrogate the familiar, to learn from the richness of everyday experience.

Why have meetings largely been ignored by the scholars whose role it is to make the "familiar strange"? Some possible obstacles to taking meetings seriously as objects of ethnographic inquiry have likely been the personal aversion to anticipated tedium, the dread and loathing of meetings that so many academics experience in their own day-to-day lives, and an internalization of the popular trope of meetings as a waste of time or a distraction from "real work." Hence, ethnographers have reported on meetings as simply a naturalized setting of fieldwork, sometimes affording them uninterrogated status and other times avoiding thick description of them entirely.

The purpose of this volume is to explore meetings as both ethnographic objects in themselves and as sites of ethnographic inquiry of diverse issues and practices—what we have called *meeting ethnography*.

DOI: 10.4324/9781315559407-1

It is high time that ethnographers give meetings focused attention. When we began this project, we set out to ask and address elusive ontological, epistemological, and methodological questions: What are meetings? What sorts of knowledge, identities, and power relationships are produced, performed, communicated, and legitimized through meetings? How do—and how might—ethnographers study meetings? But the process of collaboration of which this book is an artifact has led to more productive insights than we expected. Examining meetings as tools for both ethnographic fieldwork and anthropological thought has enabled us, along with our collaborators in this volume and beyond, to see myriad contemporary shifts in global and local governance, development, and resistance in new ways, through their everyday manifestations in and around the meetings of activists, bureaucrats, citizens, civil servants, corporate players, politicians, and international development actors.

At the outset, this meeting ethnography project was not an attempt to generalize an organizational form across wildly diverse contexts. It was developed as quite the opposite: a thoroughly comparative endeavor thinking across diverse silos of ethnography, including the study of organizations, movements, and development processes, as well as across geographic regions. Throughout this process, we have attempted to understand what meetings are by inviting ethnographers who have used meetings as sites for ethnographic inquiry to talk about what they are and how they work in their contexts. We came, rather late in this three-year project, to an initial conceptual ontology of meetings—what meetings are across sites, not simply methodologically but as near-ubiquitous phenomena. Our theory is a result of the collective intermittent work of a large group of scholars, only some of who are represented in the chapters of this volume. We try to represent more of these scholars' voices in this introduction in order to give a sense of how, over time and space and through our own meetings, the grist and structure for our theoretical understanding was crafted.

In this introduction, we contextualize this meeting ethnography project within earlier treatments of meetings in related fields. We then share some of what this project has looked like collectively, as well as where it has led us conceptually. The rest of the volume details particular ethnographers' efforts to grapple with meetings in diverse field sites of governance, organization, and resistance/activism. In the final chapter, Helen B. Schwartzman concludes the volume by discussing and analyzing the chapters in relation to her understanding of meetings.

The Salience of Meetings

The "in-person meeting" interaction itself remains an undeniably large part of the everyday lives of academics, activists, bureaucrats, laborers, managers, NGO staff and clients, professionals, and politicians. It did not have to be this way. In fact, one might have expected that in-person meetings would have become an anachronism over the past two decades. To be sure, there are many virtual meeting platforms, and a veritable explosion of methods for what might be called "non-meeting," including the migration of many corporate and transnational meetings to digital platforms and the development of many technologies for interaction without real-time or face-to-face interaction (social networking, SMS, shared document and database platforms, workflow platforms, etc.). Communication without meeting has certainly increased through these technologies. Yet, despite this increase, in-person meetings do not seem to have waned.

Why has the in-person meeting not become largely supplanted by digitally-based communication technologies and virtual meetings? Wasson (2006) explains that virtual meetings are different from in-person meetings, because taking part in a virtual meeting means participating in two interactional spaces at the same time. Virtual meetings encourage other types of (anti-) communicative behaviors, such as leaving the room now and then, or openly, plain to see for the other meeting participants, and working on other matters on your computer while the real-time meeting is going on. Perhaps, as the technologists would have it, we have simply not developed the correct technology to stem meetings. Or, perhaps, meeting face to face itself serves as an abiding functional technology.

It is not hard to find evidence for the salience of both in-person meetings and the virtual variety. A vast list of contemporary professional "how to" books, with titles such as *Meeting and Event Planner for Dummies*, *Boring Meetings Suck*, and *The Hamster Revolution for Meetings*, as well as an extensive literature in the management field, suggests great demand for technological innovations to make corporate and bureaucratic meetings more pleasant, productive, and efficient (e.g., Nelson and Economy 1995; Kloppenborg and Petrick 1999; Rogelberg et al 2007; Cohen et al 2011). These innovations include such ideas as daily stand-up meetings, clear agenda/assessment/follow-up protocols, improvement group meetings (Womack et al 1990), quality improvement team or problem solving team meetings (Deming 1986), and team learning meetings (Sense 1994). Such meeting-intensive processes, and management ideas about them, have logically affected the way ethnographic inquiry is conducted on organizational work in corporations, state bureaucracies, and transnational organizations (e.g., Thedvall 2006; Garsten and Nyqvist 2013).

Meetings also have particular significance for global governance with the rise of neoliberal global capitalism. In particular, shifts in the site of regulatory governance from nation-states to large NGOs and INGOs follow from the reduced role of states in transnational governance issues, the deregulation of markets, and the increased role for the private sector. As documented by Boström and Tamm Hallström (2010), West (2012), and Besky (2014), these regulatory NGOs require meetings to enact their multi-stakeholder models. Thus, dynamics of neoliberalization, and decentralization of state governance and service provision to local levels, are not merely visible in meetings; to a large extent, they are shaped and negotiated through new configurations of meetings.

Maintaining and shifting power, in other words, seems to require an ever-stronger focus on meeting forms. The implicit and explicit focus on meetings is also evident in all manner of local and transnational projects geared toward liberation, resistance, social movements, and social reform. Inside the global justice movement, and in countless national and local community movements, activists in fact pay great attention to the form and function of meetings as chronicled by Francesca Polletta (2002), Jen Sandler (2008, 2011), David Graeber (2009), Christoph Haug (2010, 2013), and Maple Razsa (2015). Polletta (2002) characterizes participatory democracy and American social movements as an "endless meeting," suggesting how we may think anew about social movements, democracy, and strategic choice, and showing us how the deliberative model works through meetings. Graeber (2009) gives a detailed ethnography on the global justice movement and how they mobilize resistance and protest through series of meetings. Haug (2013) develops a framework for understanding meetings within the global justice movement, a hybrid of organization, institution, and network—three different forms of social order. He argues that it is the meeting arena that synchronizes the activities of actors.

In sum, we contend that across diverse sites and silos of organization, development, and activism, the salience of meetings to contemporary human life cannot be overstated.

The History of Meeting Ethnography

This volume claims a topical, though not necessarily theoretical, kinship with a line of inquiry that emerged in the 1960s, particularly in Goffman's (1959, 1963) work on social gatherings. Goffman had a particular interest in communicative behavior as "frontstage" and "backstage" behavior. He defined meetings as social encounters with a central situational focus (Goffman 1963: 80). Ethnographic studies on meetings from the 1960s and 70s focused on the form of decision-making in meetings, such as F. G. Bailey's (1965) writings on decision by consensus or majority rule, distinguishing between two ideal types where arena councils make majority rule decisions and elite councils make consensus decisions. In the 1971 volume *Councils in Action* edited by Audrey Richards and Adam Kuper decision-making and political process were discussed in a number of councils. Richards and Kuper were inspired by Bailey and concluded that although it was difficult to use the typology by connecting one type of meeting with one type of decision-making, the aspects of consensus and majority vote in relation to arena and elite councils were nonetheless useful. Richards and Kuper also contributed to Bailey's model by adding "unauthoritative decisions," such as failure to reach any resolution, which are typical for arena councils lacking effective sanctions. These volumes are illustrative (not exhaustive) accounts of the structural-functionalist ethnographic approaches to meeting-intensive settings that could be found in the 60s and 70s.

In the 1970s and 1980s, ethnographic studies on meetings and events could also be found within sociolinguistics. For example, drawing on Dell Hymes's (1972) term *speech events*, Judith Irvine (1979) discussed political meetings as communicative events since they were determined by a degree of formality in the speech register. Fred Myers focused on speech at meetings among the Australian aborigines Pintupi and argued that the meeting worked as a mediator between two central and dialectically related values among the Pintupi: relatedness and autonomy (Myers 1986: 432). Fred Myers and Donald Brenneis explained speech events as ". . . reproducing the mechanisms that make power possible" (1984: 4). Brenneis has also focused in later work on the construction of social scientific knowledge through peer review and academic meeting settings on the United States National Research Council (1994, 2009). He reads such events as "at the intersection of text and talk," characteristic of bureaucratic discourse. Such work also recalls Deidre Boden's (1994) sociological work on the "business of talk" in organizations.

We would not have been able to get from these mostly structuralist accounts to our own post-structuralist understanding of meetings without Helen Schwartzman's (1987, 1989) classic study of meetings in an American mental health center. Schwartzman went beyond previous literature by questioning the assumption that meetings are all about making decisions in service of power structures and ideology. She argued instead that meetings are what generates and maintains the organization. This argument allowed her to examine the components of meetings, whether it be power, speech, format, or tools, and their relationships in particular sociocultural settings. She drew on the work of organizational theorists Cohen, March, and Olsen's *garbage-can theory* (1972) to argue that decisions are the result of particular problems, solutions, and participants coming together at a particular point in time—thrown into the "garbage can." Schwartzman added to this argument by maintaining that the meeting is the actual garbage can. In this way, she diverted from Cohen, March, and Olsen's task-focused approach by arguing that it was the meetings, not the decisions, that should be the center of attention for our studies. She argued for the salience of "meetings as a form with many effects on our behavior" (Schwartzman 1989: 314). Schwartzman also brought in power and control in way that Cohen, March, and Olsen disregard, arguing ". . . it is the meeting and how it produces and reproduces power relations and systems of control that should be the subject of attention" (Schwartzman 1989: 239). Schwartzman viewed meetings as disciplining individuals, organizations, and sectors.

Our reading of the intellectual trajectory is that the creative conceptual space that Schwartzman's seminal study might have opened up was quickly foreclosed by a scholarly rush to account theoretically for the "new" information age: networks, flows, movements. Fortunately, the tide seems to have turned back in recent years within organization studies (e.g., Peck and Towell 2004; Jarzabkowski and Seidl 2008; Allen et al 2015), in political science (e.g., Adams 2004; Tepper 2004, Hall and Löfgren, 2016), in sociology (e.g., Polletta 2002; Åkerström 2011, 2013; Haug 2013; Haug et al 2013; Roumbanis, 2016), and in anthropology. In anthropology, Simone Abram's (2003) examination of rituals in town hall councils and committee meetings in Norway is one such example. Abram argues that town hall council and committee meetings in Norway serve as arenas for the enactment of transnational flows of policy ideas and concepts, such as "holistic future visions," "client focus," and "reorganisation for better services," transforming them into local practice.

Other examples can be found in our own work (Thedvall 2005, 2006, 2008, 2013; Sandler 2008, 2011, 2015; Sandler and Apple 2010). Thedvall has, for example, studied meetings in the European Union as *rituals of legitimation* (2006, 2008). The decision in EU meetings does not become legitimate because of the accuracy and reliability of the decision, but through the structural processes of following the rules concerning who may participate in the meetings, who may be president, who sets the agenda, when and where the participants meet, what they will discuss, how they will discuss it, and the correct way to arrive at a decision. The ritual process makes the policy process trustworthy and justifiable. The rules and regulations deal with opposition from the member states and the Commission by disguising the conflicts in ritual compromises, thereby conferring legality on the decision. Jen Sandler's (2008, 2011, 2015) studies of three distinct U.S. social reform movements reveal epistemic practices that are visible largely through each movement's meetings. Sandler shows how policy coalitions instantiate particular reform epistemologies through practices of organizing knowledge production in community-based meetings.

Other recent anthropological work on meetings is the aforementioned Wasson's (2006) examination of how virtual meetings are different from "in-person meetings," and particularly what it means to participate in two interactional spaces at the same time. She describes how these types of meetings have started to blend, making in-person meetings more like virtual meetings in the way the participants behave. Morais (2007) has studied meetings between a client and advertising agency in the United States, where advertising ideas are presented, discussed, and selected. He emphasizes the importance, to the ability to negotiate, of an individual's command of the unwritten rules and understanding of subtle verbal and nonverbal behavior. Shore's (2008) study of religious camp meetings in the United States focuses on the camp meeting as a theater of family memory and identity building. Graeber (2009) shows ethnographically the importance of meetings within activist movements, attempting to give an account of the social experimental zones that meetings give rise to— creative spaces for developing ideas about what social world their efforts should bring about.

Inspired by sociologist Wilbert van Vree's book (1999) about the development of modern meeting behavior Gregory Duff Morton (2014) examines the meetings within Brazil's MST (Movimento dos Trabalhadores Sem Terra) landless movement, arguing that such modern meetings are defined by their qualities as universal opportunities to speak and participate. According to Morton, the modern meeting is characterized by speech that is plain, direct, and available to everyone: *equally available speech acts.* Nyqvist (2015) studies annual general meetings (AGMs) in corporations, which have the main purpose of legitimizing and building trust in the corporation and its leading actors. Yarrow (2017) writes about meetings as spaces for the alignment of various forms of expert knowledge within the national heritage agency of historic Scotland. Adam Reed (2017) explores the relationship between meetings and organizational ethics in an animal protection charity in Scotland, and Hannah Brown and Maia Green (2017)[2] argue for the centrality of meetings in contemporary developmental regimes by the example of aid in Kenya's health system. There seems now to be no shortage of attention to meetings as important field sites for anthropologists.

Still, given the explosion of contemporary ethnographies within and about meetings, the tenor of meeting ethnographies in recent decades has often taken *the meeting*, in its simultaneous ubiquity and specificity, for granted. Taking the meeting form's specificity for granted is precisely what Schwartzman's work showed us three decades ago that we cannot do if we are to understand organizations in everyday, meaning-making form. We believe that the comparative project resulting in this volume shows the possibilities that emerge when we refuse to take for granted the meeting's ubiquity, across/within/between contexts.

The ubiquitousness of meetings presents ethnographers with a conceptual apparatus and methodological orientation for exploring human interaction across traditional domains of anthropology (religion, medical, policy, education, organizations, activism/resistance, development). And while there are certainly dangers of limiting one's ethnographic fieldwork to meeting settings (which Brown-Saracino and Stiman explore in this volume in relation to community studies), meetings nonetheless might provide an organizing framework for producing forms of knowledge that cut across domains, that move with particular social actors and/or actants (such as documents or other objects), that move from one meeting-intensive site to another, and that ultimately enable the multiple and local to speak with and to the particular and global.

The Meetings from Whence This Book Emerged

Meetings are not simply the subject of this book, its *raison d'etre*. Meetings have also played an important role in bringing about this volume, and have given rise to a broader network and project. Our general starting point was a desire to develop a project toward which both of our experiences as ethnographers had pointed. We proceeded to create meetings for others to join us in thinking through these issues, bringing their own fieldwork experiences in and insights into meetings to a common table. We have found that our meetings on meeting ethnography have required us to confront the question of ontology of meetings in a much more detailed manner.

The most obvious way of thinking about what meetings are is to consider them as communicative/deliberative/productive rituals or events. Such a conceptualization hearkens to classical anthropological projects, and has clear methodological implications. If the meeting ought simply to be brought out of the shadows and studied as an important, ubiquitous contemporary ritual, there is a somewhat seamless connection to a century of cultural anthropological inquiry. Schwartzman situated her own examination of the meeting in this way, connecting classic cultural anthropology of the event, ritual, and deliberative political process to what was then cutting-edge organizational anthropology, and thereby encouraging a turn toward the "everyday" meeting practices of organizations. Thirty years later, it remains an important point: meetings may be understood as rituals of legitimation (Thedvall 2006, 2008) or ritualistic trust-building events (Nyqvist 2015). Still, this is not all they are.

Reading over jottings from our first meeting ethnography meeting in Stockholm in the summer of 2013,[3] it is clear that over the course of the daylong discussion ontological questions came to the fore. Are meetings the same symbolically and functionally for the Wall Street women Melissa Fisher studies as they are for Lambros Roumbanis's scientific peer reviewers? What makes a meeting in Lean Preschools the same conceptual phenomenon as the World Economic Forum's meetings? (see Thedvall, and Garsten and Sörbom, this volume). We played with the usefulness of taxonomies of meetings, organizing our understanding of different meetings based on their scales, purposes, publicity/exclusivity, formality/informality. We asked whether meetings are best thought of as a particular communication-dense form of event, or as a way of structuring power. We asked about the boundaries of the meeting—what happens afterward, what happened before, what are its externalities? We grappled for language to talk about this thing across vast expanses of geography, institution, power, and scale. The ontological questions provided the greatest traction, but a day was not enough to move together.

In our subsequent meeting ethnography meeting in June 2014 at UMass Amherst,[4] a mostly different group of ethnographers landed on somewhat different questions. After a morning exploring one another's work, we tried to map themes and interests. We oscillated between the assertion that meetings do not contain anything near the full variety of a community's experience and expression (an early version of Brown-Saracino and Stiman's chapter, this volume) to the notion in other papers by Julie Hemment, Felicity Aulino, and Laurel Smith-Doerr that meetings in diverse university settings and projects contain rich structural, artifactual, and communicative phenomena—micro-manifestations of power, identity, and habituated action. Nancy Kendall's and Elif Babul's distinct examinations of meetings in development NGO contexts suggested that there was a great deal to understand about the role of meetings in producing or articulating dynamics of global/local power and knowledge. Across sites, we again found productive traction in ontology: it was impossible to access comparative knowledge from meeting ethnography if we could not even state with any clarity what meetings are. We also discovered that most of us were unable through our individual projects to go deeper into that question, to plumb the taken-for-granted of the meeting in helpful ways, without the uncomfortable tensions wrought of comparison. We left determined to go deeper, both individually through chapters written for this edited volume and as a collective, comparative project.

Finally, we come to our most recent and longest meeting ethnography workshop, October 2015 at UMass Amherst.[5] A dozen participants spent three days discussing longer drafts of papers (including many of the chapters in this volume). There was a refreshing dynamism to the discussions, as concepts from a discussion of one paper were woven and developed through discussions of another paper in an utterly different meeting-rich context. Perhaps because it was the third meeting, or perhaps because we were a slightly larger group working with longer papers over greater time, the participants quickly began to develop a tentative collective, conceptual, and citational universe. There were concepts that kept coming back: the churn of people through sites marked by meetings (invoked by Simone Abram and elaborated by Nancy Kendall and Rachel Silver), the meeting as a form of play/play of forms (invoked by Helen Schwartzman and elaborated by Don Brenneis), the status of language and artifact. We spent most of our time as a fairly stable group. Participants presented their projects, both within the group and in a public seminar. Assigned discussants helped elaborate the group's engagement with each paper, and dialogue began to coalesce.

Then, on the third and final day, the discussion became particularly rich, heated, and productive. We share some of that discussion below, through an ethnographic reconstruction of a crucial dialogue within this meeting ethnography project in an attempt to take our own meetings seriously.

On the final day of the three-day seminar, the participants had availed themselves of coffee and pastries by 9 a.m. They were seated around a large conference table in a sunny room at UMass Amherst on a Saturday afternoon. Jen Sandler's paper (a draft of Chapter 5, this volume), was presented, one of the last of the conference. Sandler's paper involved an analysis of 1–1 community organizing meetings as central to the U.S. urban social reform coalition work she had studied. She suggested that while such coalitions included a wide variety of meetings, purposeful 1–1 meetings were a key component of the meeting-saturated culture. Adrienne Sörbom, one of the assigned discussants to the paper, reminded us that the literature on meetings defines meetings as including at least three people. She asked if perhaps 1–1 meetings should not be considered meetings. "After all, they are not formalized, they are like chats, just two people talking."

This was the starting point for a fruitful final-day conversation on the ontology of meetings, which we had not before discussed directly. We decided to try to include a bit of the conversation in the volume, a sort of a meta-text on meetings seen through our elaborated jottings on a particular meeting, as a way to show our gratitude to all of the workshop participants for what became an important starting point for this part of the introduction. What follows is thus an edited ethnographic anecdote describing approximately an hour of the conversation that took place on that day. We present this anecdote to bring the reader into our discussions, and to show something of the dynamic interchanges that we have found over these past few years of thinking through the meeting.

Sörbom's challenge to the 1–1 as a meeting immediately garnered responses. Simone Abram, via Skype, agreed with the critique, saying, "Well, they aren't really part of the explosion of bureaucratization in the twentieth century, are they? The 1–1 flattens the idea of the meeting. It evades the universality of the form, which is what is important about meetings."

The conversation pivoted, as Nancy Kendall took up Sörbom's challenge by offering another example to broaden the question of what the conceptual boundaries of "the meeting" should be. Kendall explained that when two people pass each other on the path in Malawi, they greet one another. If they stop, they may later say, "We have met." Are they meeting? What is this "meeting" concept supposed to mobilize? Would it include their interaction? What would it mean to include or exclude it?

Gregory Duff Morton said no, meeting on the path is not a meeting. He made the connection back to his concept from his paper the day before, and in his previous research (Morton 2014), which elaborates a notion of the meeting as an equally available speech act. Morton's concept of the meeting is a space to which everyone ostensibly has equal access to question, and this concept for him originates historically in the eighteenth century with the tension between the birth of parliamentary democracy and the Quaker meeting. This concept of the meeting speaks ultimately to the legislative state. Morton argued for a notion of the meeting as a democratic project—as in some sense the democratic project. An informal meeting on a path in Malawi should in that sense be considered under a different purview than one with this more particular genealogy, Duff argued.

"No," Celeste Alexander interjected. "I disagree." Morton, a bit taken aback, said "No? No to what, to the equal accessibility—or?" "I just disagree," Alexander said again. She went on to argue that we needed to be careful about drawing clean-cut distinctions here, as there are also long-standing histories of interaction and potentially shared genealogies. She was concerned that we might slip into reifying typologies of "Western" and "non-Western" meetings, which could have the inadvertent effect of delegitimizing meetings in the Malawian context, 1–1 or otherwise. She cautioned that these things are always in flux, and that the histories are more intermingled than is often acknowledged.

This moment of the meeting opened up a space for considering Morton's analytic in a new light, as perhaps both more relevant and more historically contingent. Just as important, when Alexander said, "No," the dynamic of our meeting shifted. Suddenly the group seemed capable of speaking about the stakes of the project of understanding the meeting, and in a more richly comparative manner.

Morton easily acknowledged the importance of the historicity of his project, clarifying the breadth and specificity of what the equally available speech act concept could include. He then noted that what he appreciated about Sandler's description of 1–1s as meetings is that this is how community organizers think of them. Morton argued that these meetings ought to be considered meetings, and that doing so expands the notion of what we are all doing in our field sites, at least within activist and movement contexts. He pointed out that it was the intention of the organizers that mattered, the emic conception of the meeting as doing something. Morton contended that we need to map the native ideology of meetings in form and content.

Sandler then returned to the concept of speaking to the legislature by noting that it was not exactly the coalition actors' intention to speak to power that was at work in the 1–1 meetings she described. It was more about intention to build a powerful relationship, to "have met," as perhaps Kendall had said of the women on the path, and the possibility of that "having met" to do something as yet undefined. Didn't that accord with what Kendall is saying, Sandler asked, hopeful. Kendall said that no, it does not, because the village women having met does not in fact "do something" in the way we have been discussing.

Renita Thedvall, as the chair of this component of the meeting, jumped in and said, "Jen and I've been talking about intentionality. Meetings are instruments for action with intent. Of course they are. But meetings in themselves are also action where the ethnographically interesting parts are not necessarily planned or intentional."

Christina Garsten took up this notion of the ambiguity of intentionality. Garsten noted that the 1–1 meeting is challenging because, in a way, she and Sörbom had counted such meetings as well; many of the meetings that surrounded the WEF were individual networking meetings, and these were meetings that everyone could agree mattered. She wondered whether Jasanoff's concept of arenas for articulation might help illuminate what meetings are in these contexts – that they are ways of making the meeting tellable, legible.

Sörbom said, "Yes, this makes sense in the context of how Haug describes arenas of infrastructure in social movements as well." She worked herself toward reversing course: all right, the 1–1s in Sandler's paper might count as meetings, but we have to draw the line somewhere. The meeting on the path is not a meeting. Or, if it is, it's not one we would care about.

And yet Kendall's question stood, almost haunting the group: since we could now ask the question about the boundaries of the meeting, it must be asked: What do we make of the encounter of the women passing on the path? Why and how should a distinction be drawn without, as Alexander had noted, somehow reifying the binary colonial project? The group was stuck. There were murmurs. Restless discomfort and trailing-off sentences persisted for a few minutes.

Then Kysa Nygreen (whose paper had also addressed urban community organizing that takes place largely through meetings) cut into this space, saying, "What I like about the 1–1 meeting concept is that I cannot have a 1–1 as just myself. I have to have an organization behind me, a movement or a project. A 1–1 only makes sense as a meeting in reference to a community of practice."

"Ah!" Everyone stopped murmuring, suddenly seeming to focus together, to alight on the same project. "Yes," Sandler said, "and the people I work with have a term for that! Some community organizers call it 'credentialing,' the act of saying who you are in relation to your organization, movement, whatever larger entity you represent that locates you in that meeting."

Nygreen further assented: "Right, you're never just a person talking; in a meeting you have to represent something."

"Yes," Don Brenneis said. "That's important: communities of practice, credentialing, representing."

Thedvall was excited: "This is central! I'm appreciatively taking notes."

Helen Schwartzman continued, "But then the important question becomes: what makes it flip? We need to locate it in relation to credentialing. How the meeting is constructed in interaction. How do you accomplish meetings?"

"OK. But in my own village," Kendall said, "I spend fifteen minutes every day waiting for and riding the bus into campus with a faculty colleague. We talk about the weather, our children, and, often enough, we end up bitching about the university. Later, I might be talking about a topic of bureaucratic importance and might invoke our discussions by saying, 'I was meeting with a colleague and she said . . .'. So, was that a meeting?" Susann Baez Ullberg broke in and reminded us that we have to remember the importance of temporality. "It's possible to construct the intention post-hoc," she said.

Sandler then gave a counter-example: "OK, yes. But let's say when you meet a student on the street, not on campus, and you desperately try to make it not a meeting. You talk about the weather, everything *but* your shared project that would invoke your distinct roles . . .".

Brenneis noted, "Yes—and there are distinctive linguistic markers for the making of a meeting out of that moment: 'by the way . . .' and suddenly you are talking about their paper—then you are in a meeting!"

There were murmurs of assent and recognition, and a few more sentiments voiced parsing the examples. In the end, Kendall maintained the establishment of a boundary to the meeting: "They are not meeting, the women who pass one another on the path. I'm sorry, they're just not. It does not speak to the development apparatus. Power, however defined, does not care about their having met." Perhaps in that moment Kendall was agreeing with Morton: meetings are acts that speak to the legislature, to contemporary governing power whether in state or NGO-laden form. And the meeting on the path does not. This conceptualization might be understood not so much as a re-inscription of colonial narratives, but an articulation of their continued relevance.

This discussion had begun as a disagreement over what might easily have remained the technical semantics of the meeting: Does a meeting need to include three people, as 1970s organizational theorists said, and as is often reiterated by those who take the meeting as their "unit of analysis"? Does it need to be planned and organized according to official structures? However, due perhaps to the work of this particular meeting context, this semantic disagreement became the catalyst for a discussion about the politics of our work, the ethical dimension of meetings, the status of the colonial project in contemporary anthropology. It became a discussion about meetings as arenas for articulations, as infrastructure of social movements, as equally available speech acts, as communities of practices, as constructed in interaction. And with the help of each of our conceptual and fieldwork concepts, from credentialing and representation to linguistic markers and the possibility of constructing the intention post-hoc, we came closer to the elusive ontology of the meeting.

We share this ethnographic anecdote from our meetings-on-meetings to show the collective work of how our theory was developed. We suspect that most new concepts and frameworks ultimately emerge at least in part out of a series of rambling dialogues that unfold in some sort of meetings. Given the topic, we wanted to make visible some of the messy, productive, interpersonal conceptual work that a series of meetings accomplished for our project. Now, we turn to the theoretical framework itself, to our current comparative understanding of what a meeting is and does.

An Analytical Framework for Understanding What a Meeting Is

Before the workshop chronicled above, we elaborated on meetings as a political technology in the Foucauldian sense. Following the conceptual framing of the anthropology of policy (Shore and Wright 1997, 2011), we thought of meetings as policy mechanisms. We considered how they might be ways of controlling the epistemic boundaries of meeting participants on the one hand, and might serve as a space for production of mechanisms of resistance and governance on the other. We also used the concept of technology in the more prosaic sense: meetings as a tool to think with, meeting ethnography as a tool for revealing certain knowledge, as a technique for knowing both as a researcher and as a practitioner of meetings. In the end, after all our meeting-meetings, we did not think the concept of technology made it clearer what a meeting is; it obfuscated and flattened our conversations rather than deepening and clarifying them. We decided to use the technology concept solely in its more everyday commonsense rather than in its Foucauldian or Latourian sense: meetings are, for ethnographers, a valuable tool to think with. They are a methodological tool to understand something about organizations, social movements, development, or whatever social process one is focused on understanding deeply. Meetings are not necessarily a side act, nor are they necessarily the main event; methodologically, paying attention to meetings and to what *particular* role they play helps get us there. Meeting ethnography, as we are coming to define it, is a technology for ethnographic inquiry.

Having relegated technology to the methodological, we then turned back to ontology. Spurred on by our conversations about the workshop interactions abstracted above, our reading of Haug's article (2013), and the infrastructure debate within anthropology (e.g., Larkin 2013), we began considering meetings as infrastructure. Infrastructure brought something that technology did not: the concept of practices of circulation. In Larkin's influential article on infrastructure (2013), he puts forward the need for anthropologists to understand infrastructure as systems, but at the same time keep our dynamic approach focusing on contingency and practices. We became particularly inspired by a sentence in the conclusion where Larkin notes that infrastructure is both architecture and practices of circulation (2013: 339).

Infrastructure enabled us to maintain within the concept of the meeting a notion of the formal, replicable, invisible structuring elements and the practices of circulation of ideas, instruments, documents, etc., in the meeting that so many of the participants in this project find compelling as they examine how meetings are "learned" and navigated (Abram, this volume), used to exploit (Kendall and Silver, this volume), used to exclude (Garsten and Sörbom, this volume), and used to disseminate and inculcate practices (Thedvall, this volume). It was a tempting framework. Infrastructure points to the circulation within and through financial instruments, management models, budgets and accounting, and of course within and through electric wiring or water pipes (cf. Larkin 2013). Why not meetings? It answered some questions. The concept pointed to the material, technological, mediating function in interesting ways that resonate with some of the ways ethnographers consider meetings. But, as with most analytical frames, it soon became clear to both of us that infrastructure made certain vital aspects of our collaborative project invisible, inarticulable. It was not only that infrastructure does not say enough. In the end, the concept of infrastructure seemed to hide (as physical infrastructures themselves often do) what we were trying to get at. Instead of considering the meeting as infrastructure, we want to use the notions of the *architectural* and *practices of circulation*, and forego the overarching concept of infrastructure. We then add a third dimension: that of the meeting as a *maker*.

We understand meetings as *architectural* for an organization, network, or an activist movement in the same way as a pipe can be for water, or crossbeams can be for a building. Meetings as an architectural construct carry ideas, practices, documents, language, and discussions, and the architec-tural/structural components of meetings determine, structure, configure, and affect ideas, practices, documents, language, discussions, decision-making processes, and subjects and subjectivities. The way issues can be articulated in meetings, the time frame of meetings, and the regulatory framework sur-rounding meetings serve as an architecture that has material, cultural/ideolog-ical, and productive (in the Foucauldian sense) effects in terms of what can be decided, how resistance may be performed, how discussions end. However, beyond "infrastructure," there is an aesthetic design element to the meeting's structuring dimension that is captured by the term *architecture*. Pipes and beams can be exposed or hidden, can be composed of distinct materials for pragmatic as well as aesthetic reasons; they are functional and also aesthetic. And both dimensions of architecture are ultimately productive.

We also want to use the concept *practices of circulation* to get away from the strictly architectural dimension and to focus on what goes on in meet-ings themselves. Through meetings, there is an actual circulation of (again) ideas, documents, language, and discussions, power, resistance, decision-making, etc. Meetings are not simply the containers through which these things move; they are themselves practices of circulation where ideas take form or power is worked out. Our understanding of practices of circulation relates to what Nygreen in our meeting called "communities of practice," as an anchoring concept for the interpersonal communicative function, distin-guishing a meeting from other forms of interaction. Practices of circulation also speaks to Abram's (2003) notion of meetings as arenas for enactment of transnational flows of policy ideas and concepts, also invoking Jasanoff's "arenas of circulation." Still, the notions of architecture and practices of circulation are not sufficient to capture what a meeting is.

There is something missing from these concepts, an energy that comes through many of our interlocutors' work on meetings that is not captured by either. Indeed, there is something that animates meetings as important possibility laden with opportunities—no matter how many memes of bore-dom they may inspire in social media—in many of our day-to-day lives. As people engaged in organization, governance, and activism, we do not look to meetings as a mode of engagement simply because they are architecture or because they entail circulations of practices. We also, and particularly when we desire change of some kind, look to meetings because they can make things happen.

Meetings also operate as *makers*. Meetings are not only the architecture but also the architect. Irrespective of intention, meetings make certain pro-cesses possible and close other directions of development. Meetings are mak-ers of governance, resistance, discipline, development, re-articulations, as we believe will become evident in the chapters to come in this volume. Meeting, as a way of interacting, is what enables people to impose projects of collec-tive reason and interaction upon others. Meeting is what produces structural violence, and it is what produces liberation. Meeting is a flexible intervention, used and deployed in some contexts to affect change to how power works and who benefits, to structures of control, or to aspects of the organization. Thus we come full circle, in a way, back to Foucault (meetings are also productive), and ultimately to Latour (meetings are also actors, producers, actants). But we prefer the relatively unladen concept, which resonates for us and fills the ontological gap: in addition to *architecture* and *practices of circulation*, meetings are *makers*, making willing revolutionaries and endlessly improvement-oriented workers and rule-internalizing bureaucrats.

From the Theoretical to the Methodological: This Volume

A thorough exploration of the methodological challenges of meeting ethnography is beyond the scope of this volume. But we came to this topic out of methodological frustrations, and we imagine many scholars may pick up this book in the same spirit. The technical challenges of doing meeting ethnography become ever more urgent with a fuller recognition of the salience of the meeting in contemporary life. So we would like to introduce the chapters in this volume by describing how each contributor grapples with meetings as both site and object of study in the field. It is our hope that the reader might engage with their own meeting ethnography challenges by moving toward the object itself, by engaging the meeting directly, as this volume's contributors have done.

The first methodological challenge of meeting ethnography is the actual data collection. There are many concrete data collection challenges for ethnographers working in meeting-intensive settings. Meetings are often extraordinarily data-intensive events, particularly since the (often many, sometimes simultaneous) "meetings-before-the-meetings" and post-meeting "debrief" sessions are often as crucial as the formal meetings themselves. In social movements, organizations, and development settings there may be six to twelve hours of meetings each day. Anthropologists tend to follow their organizations, movements, or processes for years, or at least many months. Furthermore, there are so many different aspects that are possible to focus on that one ethnographer is seldom enough if one wants to capture them all, which Kendall and Silver show interestingly in their chapter (Chapter 1, this volume) on development partner meetings in Malawi. Their chapter explores how relations of power and authority are produced in the international development arena through partner meetings, and the consequences of these relations on the central actors in international development. The chapter illustrates three different analytic approaches to meeting ethnography where they in one observation focus on documenting relations of inequality and their effects on the policy agendas that emerged from these meetings; in another on the performative, even ritualistic, moments in meetings; and in the final observation on taking word-for-word notes enabling a more focused discourse analysis. In their chapter, Kendall and Silver discuss an observational approach and describe its rationale, strengths, and weaknesses.

Abram's chapter (Chapter 2, this volume) also shows that meetings are not only data-intensive events for the ethnographer. Participants in meetings have to be aware not only of the issues discussed but also the performative, sometime ritualistic, form of the meetings. She describes two instances of learning how to 'do' meetings where tacit and coercive norms are made explicit, which provide the exceptions to the rule of meeting-practices as tacit, learned, normative assumptions about 'proper' practice. Abram argues that the skills and knowledge needed to be effective at running municipal meetings are rarely contained in the written rules and regulations pertaining to municipal procedures. On the contrary, participants learn from each other in the meeting context, learning in the process how to interpret, manipulate, and bend whatever formal rules exist.

The fact that meetings are extraordinary data-intensive events is also evident in Baez Ullberg and Skill's chapter (Chapter 3, this volume), when they walk us through the assemblage of heterogeneous elements like books, ideas, skills, activists, experts, technologies, documents, the constitution and the police force, places, historical events, and discourses assembled through social labor at Argentinian *asamblea* activist meetings. In Argentina the *asamblea*, both as a social actor and as a meeting form, has emerged as a figure of and for grassroots political mobilization, claiming social change, and demanding justice. The Argentinian *asambleas* bear transnational traits of contemporary collective action, yet they also feature particular discourses and practices related to the Argentinian and Latin American political settings and historical continuities.

The second challenge we want to bring forward when conducting ethnography in meeting-intensive sites is named most explicitly in Brown-Saracino and Stiman's chapter (Chapter 4, this volume) where they use examples from a study of four gentrifying places in a large city in the United States, a study of queer women's migration to small U.S. cities, and an ethnography of second homeownership in a Maine tourist village to discuss the benefits and limits of meeting ethnography for community studies. What are the limits of meeting ethnography? This, of course, has to do with what meetings are in a particular research site or for a particular research question. Where do meetings occur? Who attends and who does not attend meetings? The relevance and particular usefulness of meeting fieldwork is in no way universal. One should certainly not "get stuck in" meetings or take refuge in any ease of conducting fieldwork in meeting settings versus other spaces. But neither should one take the meeting format, norms, interactions, symbols, language, and artifacts for granted. Just because meetings are already structured, already coded, already "boring" does not justify declaring them less salient or "real" sources of field data than less formal or structured sites. The particular structure functions for the context outside the meeting, and vice versa: How? Why? By whom?

Sandler's chapter (Chapter 5, this volume) presents in some sense the inverse of Brown-Saracino and Stiman's chapter. While they ask, "What are the limits of meeting ethnography?" Sandler's chapter implicitly asks, "What is the potential of ethnography to capture the meeting-saturated cultures of urban reform coalitions?" Sandler walks us through several meeting forms that not only characterize but produce and describe urban reform coalitions. She introduces the notion that meeting ethnography includes fieldwork not only inside but also about and around meetings, and she uses an understanding of meetings that includes intentional 1–1 organizing meetings, as well as the many pre-meeting meetings and post-meeting debrief meetings. The result is not an endless meeting of deliberative interaction like what Polletta (2002) describes, but a complex political project that *is* the development of knowledge and relationships developed among and between elites and activists in and through diverse meetings. But if reform coalition meetings are in fact "all the way through" as Sandler contends, what does that mean for the task of ethnographic fieldwork and analysis? The methodological implications, such as the simple need to attend—let alone capture in any substantial way—any reasonable fraction of the myriad simultaneous pre- and post-meetings surrounding a meeting, are overwhelming.

The third methodological challenge is access. While the challenge of meeting ethnography for community studies might be that community meetings are a site that is too easy, too comfortable for ethnographic fieldwork (Brown-Saracino and Stiman, this volume), the challenge of ethnography in organizations of global capital and global governance poses the opposite problem of access. Garsten and Sörbom's chapter (Chapter 6, this volume) addresses this problem in relation to their chapter on the World Economic Forum in Davos and how their problem of access made them aware of all the important meeting activities that were going on around the "meeting proper," and also made visible boundaries and the process of constructing the meeting. We would urge ethnographers studying power to recognize the vital importance of meetings and what is going on around meetings, and to exert a certain fearlessness and courage in their attempts to gain access to both the formal and informal meetings of powerful organizations. For some organizations and processes, difficult-to-access meetings are some of the only occasions for participant observation of the processes of production of inter-subjective meaning, policy, and power. Ethnography is the key method for getting beyond epiphenomena of public document analysis to examine how power and meaning is constructed in real time. One of us (Sandler) stepped back from a pilot project on philanthropy in educational policy when she was unable to gain access to major foundations' day-to-day meetings. The other (Thedvall) has spent years seeking access. Garsten and Sörbom have jumped fences and attempted to charm armed guards in order to gain access. We would suggest that meetings of global capital and global governance warrant this level of seriousness. In such settings, ethnographic data from meetings is crucial to the development of a more sophisticated understanding of how power works, for meetings in their various states of formality and informality are where the powerful do much of their work.

The question of access to meetings even as part of the staff or accepted participant observer in an organization is always present since the meeting in itself has particular boundaries that might demand agreed access. One of us (Thedvall) has elaborated on the particularities of doing fieldwork in European Union committee meetings and the negotiations that had to take place before every entry. Thus, her fieldwork was characterized by what she has called *punctuated entries* (Thedvall 2013) into the field that corresponded to the meeting dates. Doing fieldwork in meetings meant that the excitements and anxieties of entering a field were repeated at every entry. In Thedvall's chapter (Chapter 7, this volume) she again was subject to punctuated entries into different meetings, but this time in a Swedish municipality where she studied the introduction and use of the management model Lean in Swedish public preschools. In the Lean management model meetings are central to performing Lean. The Lean model takes place in meetings with particular names determined by the model such as "improvement group" meetings or "board [whiteboard] meetings." Seeing Lean through its meetings reveals shifts in the preschool staff's labor as they fit their knowledge and work practices into tools and aesthetics of the Lean management model. Studying Lean meetings through ethnography enables Thedvall to pinpoint the kind of framework the Lean management model brings and in what ways it is set to impact organizations such as preschools in relation to how it is handled by staff.

While we decided to organize this volume according to methodological approaches and themes described above, it is possible to read and to use the chapters in many different ways. For those who intend to teach with this volume, you might consider thematic pairings: Abram, Sandler, and Thedvall each view meetings as different types of political/institutional instruments. Brown-Saracino and Stiman's warning about the context outside community meetings might be contrasted nicely with Baez Ullberg and Skill's note that it is meetings that constitute an assemblage of community, artifact, and movement. A similar contrast can be drawn around treatments of the meeting as a site of global agendas, as both Garsten and Sörbom's chapter and Kendall and Silver's chapter promote quite different analyses of the role of meetings in speaking to, about, or for global/local articulations.

This Introduction and Helen Schwartzman's Conclusion are both offered to provide bookends of historical background, theoretical framing, and comparative analysis of the chapters within the volume. Schwartzman's analysis in the Conclusion, in particular, demonstrates the virtue of comparison in this (re-)emerging field as, essentially, a methodological tool for engaging precisely the conceptual challenges that have emerged from this project as a whole.

We are grateful for the willingness of so many generous colleagues, old and new, to join together in the meetings that have structured this project, circulated the artifacts and discourses assembled herein, and ultimately made this volume. We hope that others will find the act of "exploring the boring" as unexpectedly exciting as we have, and we look forward to the many theoretical, methodological, and comparative challenges of meeting ethnography in the years to come.

Notes

1 The authors contributed equally to the writing of this introduction, and to the editing of the volume overall.
2 Articles cited from a special issue on meetings in the *Journal of the Royal Anthropological Institute* (JRAI) edited by Hannah Brown, Adam Reed, and Thomas Yarrow also feature articles by Simone Abram, Catherine Alexander, Gillian Evans, Alberto Corsín Jiménez and Adolfo Estalella, Bernard Keenan and Alain Pottage, Nicholas Lamp, Morten Nielsen, and Annelise Riles.
3 Participants included Susann Baez Ullberg (Swedish National Defence College), Melissa Fischer (New York University), Christina Garsten (Stockholm University), Anette Nyqvist (Stockholm University), Lambros Roumbanis (Stockholm University), Jen Sandler (UMass Amherst), Adrienne Sörbom (Södertörn University), and Renita Thedvall (Stockholm University).
4 Participants included Felicity Aulino (UMass Amherst), Elif Babul (Mount Holyoke College), Don Brenneis (University of California Santa Cruz), Japonica Brown-Saracino (Boston University), Julie Hemment (UMass Amherst), Nancy Kendall (University of Wisconsin-Madison), Jen Sandler (UMass Amherst), Helen Schwartzman (Northwestern University), Laurel Smith-Doerr (UMass Amherst), and Renita Thedvall (Stockholm University).
5 Participants were Simone Abram (Durham University), Celeste Alexander (Princeton University), Susann Baez Ullberg (Swedish National Defence College), Don Brenneis (University of California Santa Cruz), Japonica Brown-Saracino (Boston University), Christina Garsten (Stockholm University), William Girard (Amherst College), Krista Harper (UMass Amherst), Nancy Kendall (University of Wisconsin-Madison), Gregory Duff Morton (Brown University), Kysa Nygreen (UMass Amherst), Jen Sandler (UMass Amherst), Helen Schwartzman (Northwestern University), Rachel Silver (University of Wisconsin-Madison), Adrienne Sörbom (Södertörn University), and Renita Thedvall (Stockholm University).

References

Abram, Simone. "Anthropologies in policies, anthropologies in places: Reflections of fieldwork 'in' documents and policies." In *Globalisation: Studies in Anthropology*, edited by Thomas Hylland Eriksen, 138–157. London: Pluto Press, 2003.

Adams, Brian. "Public meetings and the democratic process." *Public Administration Review* 64(2004): 43–54.

Åkerström, Malin. "Möteskultur i ungdomsvården." *Socialvetenskaplig tidskrift* 18(2011): 186–205.

Åkerström, Malin. "Curiosity and serendipity in qualitative research." *Qualitative Sociological Review* 9(2013): 10–18.

Allen, Joseph A., Nale Lehmann-Willenbrock and Steven Rogelberg. *The Cambridge Handbook on Meeting Science*. Cambridge: Cambridge University Press, 2015.

Bailey, F. G. "Decisions by consensus in councils and committees." In *Political Systems and the Distribution of Power*, edited by Michael Banton, 1–20. London: Routledge, 1965.

Besky, Sarah. *The Darjeeling Distinction: Labor and Justice on Fair-Trade Tea Plantations in India*. Berkeley: University of California Press, 2014.

Boden, Deidre. *The Business of Talk: Organizations in Action*. Cambridge: Polity, 1994.

Boström, Magnus and Kristina Tamm Hallström. *Transnational Multi-Stakeholder Standardization: Organizing Fragile Non-State Authority*. Northampton, MA: Edward Elgar, 2010.

Brenneis, Donald. "Discourse and discipline at the National Research Council: A bureaucratic bildungsroman." *Cultural Anthropology* 9(1994): 23–36.

Brenneis, Donald. "Anthropology in and of the academy: Globalization, assessment and our field's future." *Social Anthropology* 17(2009): 261–275.

Brown, Hannah and Maia Green. "Meeting development targets: Performing aid effectiveness in Kenya's health system." Special issue edited by Hannah Brown, Adam Reed and Thomas Yarrow. *Journal of the Royal Anthropological Institute* (2017).

Cohen, Melissa A., Steven G. Rogelberg, Joseph A. Allen and Alexandra Luong. "Meeting design characteristics and attendee perceptions of staff/team meeting quality." *Group Dynamics: Theory, Research and Practice* 15(2011): 90–104.

Cohen, Michael D., James G. March and Johan P. Olsen. "A garbage can model of organizational choice." *Administrative Science Quarterly* 17(1972): 1–25.

Deming, Edwards W. *Out of the Crisis: Quality, Productivity and Competitive Position*. Cambridge: Cambridge University Press, 1986.

Garsten, Christina and Anette Nyqvist. *Organisational Anthropology: Doing Ethnography in and among Complex Organisations*. London: Pluto Press, 2013.

Goffman, Erving. *The Presentation of Self in Everyday Life*. London: Penguin Books, 1959.

Goffman, Erving. *Behavior in Public Places: Notes on the Social Organization of Gatherings*. New York: The Free Press, 1963.

Graeber, David. *Direct Action: An Ethnography*. Baltimore: AK Press, 2009.

Hall, Patrik and Karl Löfgren. "Innovation policy as performativity – The Case of Sweden." *International Journal of Public Administration* (2016). http://dx.doi.org/10.1080/01900692.2015.1107740.

Haug, Christoph. Discursive Decision-Making in Meetings of the Global Justice Movements: Cultures and Practices. PhD Diss., Berlin: Freie Universität Berlin, 2010.

Haug, Christoph. "Organizing spaces: Meeting arenas as a social movement infrastructure between organization, network, and institution." *Organization Studies* 34(2013): 705–732.

Haug, Christoph, Dieter Rucht and Simon Teune. "A methodology for studying democracy and power in group meetings." In *Meeting Democracy: Power and Deliberation in Global Justice Movements*, edited by Donatella della Porta and Dieter Rucht, 23–46. Cambridge: Cambridge University Press, 2013.

Hymes, Dell H. "Models of the interaction of language and social life." In *Directions in Sociolinguistics: The Ethnography of Communication*, edited by John Gumperz and Dell Hymes, 35–71. Oxford: Basil Blackwell, [1972] 1986.

Irvine, Judith T. "Formality and informality in communicative events." *American Anthropologist* 81(1979): 773–790.

Jarzabkowski, Paula and David Seidl. "The role of meetings in the social practice of strategy." *Organization Studies* 29(2008): 1319–1426.

Kloppenborg, Timothy J. and Joseph A. Petrick. "Meeting management and group character development." *Journal of Managerial Issues* 11(1999): 166–179.

Larkin, Brian. "The poetics and politics of infrastructure." *Annual Review of Anthropology* 42(2013): 327–343.

Morais, Robert J. "Conflict and confluence in advertising meetings." *Human Organization* 66(2007): 150–159.

Morton, Gregory Duff. "Modern meetings: Participation, democracy, and language ideology in Brazil's MST landless movement." *American Ethnologist* 41(2014): 728–742.

Myers, Fred. "Reflections on a meeting: Structure, language, and the polity in a small-scale society." *American Ethnologist* 13(1986): 430–447.

Myers, Fred and Donald Brenneis. *Dangerous Words: Language and Politics in the Pacific.* New York: New York University Press, 1984.

Nelson, Robert B. and Peter Economy. *Better Business Meetings.* Willowbrook, IL: Irwin Professional Publishing, 1995.

Nyqvist, Anette. "The corporation performed: Minutes from the rituals of annual general meetings." *Journal of Organizational Ethnography* 4(2015): 341–355.

Peck, Edward, Pauline Gulliver and David Towell. "Why do we keep on meeting like this? The board as a ritual in health and social care." *Health Services Management Research* 17(2004): 100–109.

Polletta, Francesca. *Freedom Is an Endless Meeting: Democracy in American Social Movements.* Chicago: University of Chicago Press, 2002.

Razsa, Maple. *Bastards of Utopia: Living Radical Politics after Socialism.* Bloomington, IN: Indiana University Press, 2015.

Reed, Adam. "An office of ethics: Meetings, roles and moral enthusiasm in animal protection." Special issue edited by Hannah Brown, Adam Reed and Thomas Yarrow. *Journal of the Royal Anthropological Institute* (2017).

Richards, Audrey and Adam Kuper, eds. *Councils in Action.* Cambridge: Cambridge University Press, 1971.

Rogelberg, Steven G., Cliff S. Scott and John Kello. "The science and fiction of meetings." *MIT Sloan, Management Review* 48(2007): 18–21.

Roumbanis, Lambros. "Academic judgment under uncertainty: A study of collective anchoring effects in Swedish Research Council panel groups." *Social Studies of Science* (2016). doi:10.1177/0306312716659789.

Sandler, Jen. *What Works? Who Decides? Scientific Evidence, Local Governance and the Politics of Knowledge in Social and Educational Reform.* PhD Diss., ProQuest Digital Dissertations, 2008.

Sandler, Jen. "Re-framing the politics of urban feeding in U.S. public schools: Parents, programs, activists, and the state." In *School Food Politics: The Complex Ecology of Hunger and Feeding in Schools Around the World*, edited by Sarah A. Robert and Marcus B. Weaver-Hightower, 25–45. New York: Peter Lang, 2011.

Sandler, Jen. "As the tide turns on the violence of US neoliberal education: Un-organized white-led activism, from abstract critique to nonviolent resistance." *Landscapes of Violence* 3(2015), 7.

Sandler, Jen and Michael W. Apple. "A culture of evidence, a politics of objectivity: The evidence-based practices movement in educational policy." In *Handbook of Cultural Politics in Education*, edited by Zeus Leonardo, 325–340. New York: Routledge, 2010.

Schwartzman, Helen B. "The significance of meetings in an American mental health center." *American Ethnologist* 14(1987): 271–294.

Schwartzman, Helen B. *The Meeting: Gatherings in Organizations and Communities.* New York: Springer Science, 1989.

Sense, Peter. *The Fifth Discipline: The Art and Practice of the Learning Organization.* London: Random House Books, [1994] 2006.

Shore, Bradd. "Spiritual work, memory work: Revival and recollection at Salem Camp Meeting." *Ethos* 36(2008): 98–119.

Shore, Cris and Susan Wright. *Anthropology of Policy: Critical Perspectives on Governance and Power.* London: Routledge, 1997.

Shore, Cris, Susan Wright and Davide Però. *Policy Worlds: Anthropology and the Analysis of Contemporary Power.* New York: Berghahn Books, 2011.

Tepper, Steven. "Setting agendas and designing alternatives: Policymaking and the strategic role of meetings." *Review of Policy Research* 21(2004): 523–542.

Thedvall, Renita. "The meeting as a shaper of the decision-making process. The case of the EU Employment Committee." Score working paper series: 2005:1, 2005. www.score.su.se.

Thedvall, Renita. *Eurocrats at Work: Negotiating Transparency in Postnational Employment Policy.* PhD Diss., Social Anthropology, Stockholm University. Stockholm: Stockholm Studies in Social Anthropology, 58, 2006.

Thedvall, Renita. "Rituals of legitimation: Organising accountability in EU employment policy." In *Organizing Transnational Accountability: Mobilization, Tools, Challenges*, edited by Magnus Boström and Christina Garsten, 131–146. Cheltenham: Edward Elgar Publishing, 2008.

Thedvall, Renita. "Punctuated entries: Doing fieldwork in policy meetings in the EU." In *Organisational Anthropology: Doing Ethnography in and among Complex Organisations*, edited by Christina Garsten and Anette Nyqvist, 106–119. London: Pluto Press, 2013.

van Vree, Wilbert. *Meetings, Manners and Civilization: The Development of Modern Meeting Behaviour.* London: Leicester University Press, 1999.

Wasson, Christina "Being at two spaces at once: Virtual meetings and their representation." *Journal of Linguistic Anthropology* 16(2006): 103–130.

West, Paige. *From Modern Production to Imagined Primitive: The Social World of Coffee from Papua New Guinea.* Durham: Duke University Press, 2012.

Womack, James P., Daniel T. Jones and Daniel Roos. *The Machine That Changed the World: The Story of Lean Production.* New York: Rawson Associates and Macmillan, 1990.

Yarrow, Thomas. "Where knowledge meets: Heritage expertise at the intersection of people, perspective and place." Special issue edited by Hannah Brown, Adam Reed and Thomas Yarrow. *Journal of the Royal Anthropological Institute* (2017).

1 Mapping International Development Relations through Meeting Ethnography

Nancy Kendall and Rachel Silver

Introduction: Meetings and International Development Aid

The field of international development offers significant and exciting ethnographic challenges. This chapter explores the strengths and limitations of meeting ethnography in revealing how relations of power and authority are produced through international development discourses, policies, and practices, and the consequences of these relations on the central actors in international development: international "donors,"[1] recipient country governments, non-governmental organizations (NGOs, often involved in development project implementation), and end recipients.

Scholars of international development studies have demonstrated that deep inequities exist between development aid funders and recipients (e.g., Mkandawire 2010); aside from the ethical implications of these inequities (Samoff 1999; Odora Hoppers 2001), over time, a consensus has formed that such inequities harm both the efficiency and the effectiveness of development aid (Kharas 2007; Esser 2014). Much of this literature is based on an analysis of the political economic relations of aid, in which disparities in resources are understood to both represent and fuel disparities in power and authority.

Ethnographers have provided new insights into relations of power and authority in development aid through their careful analysis of the unintended consequences of development aid on its intended beneficiaries (see, e.g., Elyachar 2005; Englund 2006). These ethnographies have shown how, in practice, relations of power among development recipients and funders are more multiplex, changing, partial, and fragmented (Li 1999; Mosse 2004) than political economic studies revealed.

Despite the insights generated by existing research about how power "works" in development, there are important lacunae in current research paradigms. The study of development is fundamentally a study about fully globalized and yet utterly personal relationships and flows of resources across levels of social scale, institutional types, and political economic arrangements. Biases within anthropology about what constitutes "real fieldwork," difficulties with gaining access to "study up" in funding

DOI: 10.4324/9781315559407-2

institutions, and the extensive resources necessary to conduct quality multi-sited ethnography have resulted in a relatively widespread practice of utilizing discourse analysis and limited interview data to represent development funders, while conducting more extensive ethnographic engagement with communities or groups of people designated as recipients of international development funding or programming. This yields very different kinds of data and different understandings of development practice as daily experience across levels of social organization. As a result, there is often a methodological, and accompanying analytic, disconnect between accounts of development funder policy and discourse, and accounts of international development-as-practice.

This disconnect poses a methodological obstacle to understanding power and its working across the levels of social, institutional, and financial organization that constitute the field of international development. It does so in large part by obscuring the experiences and meaning-making of the diverse set of professionals who constitute the global international development apparatus (Chabbott 2013). In particular, current research seldom engages the cadre of mid-level NGO workers and civil servants whose translational work between international funders and the recipients of aid is required for the development apparatus to function (Olivier de Sardan 2005; Mosse and Lewis 2006). Without an understanding of these actors' practices, the constitution and consequences of power in the field of development remain illegible.

Studying Through

There has been discussion and debate for decades about how, and how best, anthropologists might study "down," study "up" (Nader 1972), "follow" (Marcus 1995), and study "through" (Wright and Reinhold 2011) complex sites of global(izing) power, such as the international development arena. These new ethnographic methodologies attempt to "reframe anthropological 'strategies for knowledge' so as to grasp the contribution of local sites to large-scale processes of transformation" (Wright and Reinhold 2011: 87).

Sutton and Levinson (2001) and Ortner (2006) have argued that a practice approach provides a more generative frame for conceptualizing how discourse and practice constitute relations of power. Discourse as/in practice approaches allows us to study through the field of international development with a stable conception of the mutual constitutions of discourse and practice across levels of social scale. As such, this approach provides a methodological and analytic framework for studying through the development process, from elite planners and funders, through to "middle figures" (Hunt 1999) who are expected to implement development aid, to the end recipients of these efforts, and back again.

Yet, as noted above, studying through is seldom achieved in current ethnographies of international development. Discursive data often stand in as the "framing," top-down, developmentalist rationality, which is contrasted with the practical consequences of this framing on recipients' daily practice (see, e.g., Ferguson 1994; Katz 2004; Kendall 2007; cf. Bebbington et al 2007; Mosse, 2004). Studies adopting this "top-down (policy) versus bottom-up (practice)" approach are limited in their capacity to deepen our understanding of how development rationalities and relations of power and authority are socially produced, maintained, and transformed; they instead often appear fixed, coherent, and cohesive (Grillo and Stirrat 1997). Such studies cannot appropriately map processes of transformation (Wright and Reinhold 2011), or analyze how development is constituted and thus "works" across levels of social scale (Mosse 2004).

Meeting ethnography can address two current gaps in development research: first, meeting observations can provide new and rich sources of data on the practices and relationships among funders, governments, and NGOs. Without observations of the interactions that link these organizations, we may create over-determined analyses of the power of global discourses to shape daily practices, which in turn hide opportunities for transformation (Gibson-Graham 1996). Meeting observations are almost uniquely positioned to provide this kind of insight into the relationships among development institutions that otherwise usually operate in differentiated socio-economic spheres.

Second, the "powerful institutions-as-discourse, powerless-recipients-as-practice" dichotomy generally leapfrogs the mid-level actors who constitute so much of the field of development in practice. These "skilled brokers (managers, consultants, fieldworkers, community leaders)" who, as Mosse (2004: 647) notes, "read the meaning of a project into the different institutional languages of its stakeholder supporters," fill the ranks of NGOs, ministries, and national offices of international funding organizations. Middle figures are essential to the translational work of these diverse organizations, much of which occurs in meetings held among the organizations.

Anthropologists of development have begun to explore the significance, meaning, and experiences of mid-level development agents—those contemporary actors who are responsible for transferring aid dollars ("development rent") from international funders to local populations (Bierschenk et al 2000; Olivier de Sardan 2005; Lewis and Mosse 2006). Careful study of international development middle figures can destabilize the simplistic dichotomy of funders/foreigners/powerful and "end recipients"/"locals"/powerless, and provide a generative starting point for studying through the development process and its constituent parts from the point of greatest mediation among these parts. Much of this research, however, has focused on middle figures within only one type of organization (e.g., NGO workers). Meeting ethnography offers a new vantage point from which to attend to these mid-level agents, as they engage one another across institutional types.

In sum, in order to better understand how power works in international development relations, we must critically examine the relationship between and mutual constitution of official policy, law, institutional mandate, discourses, and daily development practices. This requires a more consistent methodological starting point, in which discourse and practice are not disarticulated across levels of social organization. Meeting ethnography focused on development's middle figures offers a unique vantage point and methodological lever for accomplishing these goals.

Studying through Partner Meetings

A wide range of meeting types occurs within the international development arena. In this chapter, we focus on only one of these: the partner meeting. In most countries, there are a relatively small number of institutions that provide the majority of traditional development aid and project implementation.[2] Partner meetings are meetings called for a variety of official purposes related to aid *coordination*, at which this core group of organizations is expected to be present.

Partner meetings play a key role in development ideologies because the "participation" of all core organizational types (i.e., funders, recipient governments, NGOs) in partner meetings is expected to catalyze development aid "ownership," "harmonization," and "coordination." The international development community agreed in 2005 that these transformations in institutional relations toward greater equity were essential to improving development aid (Esser 2014). Meetings represent a central development technology because they are where and how the (equalizing) "democratic [participatory] moment" is supposed to be produced, as funding and recipient development institutions come together as partners on an "even playing field" to agree on what will occur. After partner meetings, coordination can be claimed, assumed, wielded, and abused. When the meetings are ostensibly hosted by the recipient government, this is also taken to imply government "ownership" of the meeting content and its outcomes, just as the presence of NGO "civil society representatives" supports claims of democratic engagement in development processes. Conceptually, then, partner meetings are essential sites at which to observe and map both the discursively desired and the practically realized relations of power among development institutions.

Partner Meetings in Malawi

Malawi, located in southeastern Africa, is an exceptional site through which to examine the constitution of international development relations in heavily indebted poor countries. As a UN-classified "least developed country" with a full 37 percent of its total annual budget provided by international funders (Dionne 2014), Malawi exemplifies the type of high-poverty, high-aid dependency context in which a flood of international development actors have come to "fix problems." With such scarce national resources to be shared across sectors, the Malawian context can throw into stark relief if, when, and how inequitable relations among development partners are established, maintained, and disputed. A longitudinal examination of partner meetings in Malawi can therefore provide fresh insights into the constitution of relations of power and authority in the international development education arena, and their consequences over time.[3]

In this chapter, we focus on partner meetings held in the education sector. In Malawi, there are four core groups involved in these meetings.[4] These include: (1) *funders*—the multilateral, bilateral, international non-governmental, and private-sector organizations, corporations, and foundations (e.g., the World Bank, USAID [United States Agency for International Development], DFID [Department for International Development], the MacArthur Foundation); (2) *government representatives*, typically from the sector under discussion (in this chapter, the Ministry of Education, Science, and Technology) and from the Ministry of Finance; (3) *"middle" organizations* that receive funding to implement development programming and are often, though not always, based in the funder country (for example, RTI, FHI360, Cambridge Education, Pearson, Save the Children US, CARE, World Vision) and often subcontract to national NGOs; and (4) *representatives from national (and sometimes regional, district, or community) nongovernmental organizations or their umbrella organizations*, (for example, in Malawi, the Creative Center for Community Mobilization; the Forum for African Women Educationalists, Malawi; the Civil Society Coalition for Quality Basic Education). Members of this latter category are expected to represent "civil society" and also, often, to receive international funding to implement projects or to serve as watchdogs for government budgeting and political processes.

These four groups compose the key institutional types in the partner meetings. They are the primary targets of efforts to coordinate development aid, and they represent the groups tasked, in various ways, with distributing the vast majority of development funds in Malawi.

In the remainder of this chapter, we root our questions of what can be learned about how inequitable relations among states, funders, NGOs, and development implementers "work," and what meeting ethnography as methodology offers for studies of globalized relations of power and authority, in three partner meeting vignettes: one held in 2000, one held in 2012, and one held in 2014. These three meetings provide a unique methodological space in which to "study diffused power in a concentrated way" (Buscher 2014: 133). In particular, they demonstrate the role of partner meetings in supporting the radical disempowerment of the Malawian state and the empowerment of funder and international NGO actors. They also show the rise of new forms of resistance to these processes on the part of Ministry and academic actors. Finally, the vignettes provide an opportunity to consider three different observational styles and analytic vantage points that can be taken in meeting ethnography.

Meeting observations were collected as part of longer ethnographic studies of international development education, conducted by Kendall from 1998 to the present, and by Silver in 2012. Kendall observed the first meeting while conducting research in 2000–2001 on how the introduction of free primary education, political democratization, and structural adjustment reforms in 1994 affected people's material and symbolic relations with schools and the state. Silver participated in the second meeting, a 2012 National Literacy Conference, as part of a three-month research fellowship on early-grade literacy interventions with the Malawi chapter of a prominent international NGO. Kendall attended the third meeting as the monitoring and evaluation staff member working for the international "middle" organization that convened the meeting.

Approaching Partner Meetings Ethnographically: Strategies and Data

Meeting ethnography requires that the researcher engage in meeting spaces. There are many different ways a researcher might do this. Each of the three vignettes presented below resulted from distinct observational methods, which were selected to address the study's goals, the meeting form, the researcher's role in each setting, and the researcher's style and observational strengths. Vignettes 1 and 3 represent closed meetings that were of relatively short duration (under three hours); observations were paired with interviews and a review of meeting agendas and minutes. Vignette 2 represents a more public meeting of much longer duration (full day); participant observation was paired with discussions with the meeting organizers and a review of the meeting agenda.

After each vignette, we discuss the observational approach adopted and describe its rationale, strengths, and weaknesses. We show how the three data collection techniques employed in the meetings yield different analytic foci, each of which works to deepen understandings of relations of power and authority in international development, but to different theoretical ends.

Meeting Vignette 1

An introduction to the field notes: In 2000, international funders provided about 91 percent of Malawi's non-recurrent education budget (Kendall 2004).[5] Funders convened numerous partner planning meetings to attempt to force Ministry of Education, Science, and Technology (hereafter, Ministry) officials to produce the kind of national education plan valued by funders. In 2000, funders were demanding a Policy and Investment Framework (PIF), which would serve as the government-approved blueprint for all government and funder decisions about how to "invest" in education. The PIF coordination meetings became a primary setting for official educational policymaking because representatives of the major funders, Ministries, and civil society organizations were all physically present and officially tasked with discussing what steps the government would take to assure continued funding for the cash-strapped education sector.

Despite the importance of these meetings as policymaking sites, they lay increasingly outside of the control of the Ministry in both practical and symbolic terms. For example, though PIF partner meetings were officially organized by the Ministry, over time, as we see below, funding representatives took over chairing and organizing them, and increasingly monopolized airtime in the meetings.

May 2000 (Expanded Field Notes)

I am sitting in the corner of one of the meeting rooms in the Ministry. The room is dominated by a large oval table, around which are seated nine people bathed in harsh fluorescent light. This meeting was organized by a consultant hired by [one of the major funding organizations] to sit (literally) in the Ministry and support them in developing a PIF that the funders will accept. The consultant was placed in the Ministry after the government's initial education plan was presented to and rejected by the funders.

*Funder representatives repeatedly say in the meeting that the PIF must be "aligned with the broader national poverty reduction plan"; it must focus on issues that the international funders refer to as "national" and "international" priorities (basic education, girls' education), and not on the Ministry's "pet projects" (special needs education); and it must be **prioritized and costed**—to date, the Ministry had refused to prioritize and cost out each line item because, they say in interviews, doing so would create unnecessary competition among education sub-sectors, and it would potentially discourage funders if the areas that were identified as "less of priority" in the PIF were the greatest priority to a particular funder.*

Relations between Ministry and some funder representatives have deteriorated significantly over the issue of costing the PIF. Though some funders are openly denigrating toward Ministry staff, staff continue to engage them. Government and civil society representatives consistently say in interviews and official documents that, since student enrollment rates nearly doubled after free primary education was introduced in 1994, the government can no longer fund education. So the Ministry must engage and secure support from funders to keep the education sector functional.

At the start of the meeting, no Ministry staff member is present. One staff member arrives late after being tracked down by the "civil society" representative, who leaves to find a Ministry representative when requested to do so by the meeting chair (the funder representative). The Ministry staff member comes in and sits in an empty seat halfway down the long end of the table. He is relatively young, and comes as close to slouching as I have ever seen in a meeting in Malawi. He has nothing in his hands—no paper or pens for notes, no agenda. He sits in near-absolute silence through the meeting. International funder representatives occupy each end chair.

The meeting agenda was created by the chair, and he uses the agenda to organize conversation throughout the meeting, pointing to its items if he feels that someone is moving "off topic." The meeting's conversation flows among funders, with occasional interjections by the NGO representative. The NGO representative's comments include questions posed to the chair, a brief description of work the NGO was doing that related to educational quality, and comments made in response to questions posed by the funders about what was happening "on the ground" in primary schools. NGOs were consistently and repeatedly referred to by the funders as the organizations that "understood what was happening on the ground." Ministry staff were not positioned in this way. The funders also asked the NGO representative's opinion on issues related to policy and programming (particularly how to assure successful implementation); they did not pose these questions to the Ministry official. The primary question posed to the Ministry representative was what progress had been made on redrafting the PIF since the last meeting: Had the promised meetings been held? Had the appropriate officials attended? Was there new agreement on a costing strategy? Was there consensus on priorities? The Ministry official either was not very sure of the answers to these questions (given his youth and low civil servant grade in the system, he likely did not attend these meetings if they were held), or he deliberately attempted to provide as little information as possible in his brief responses.

In this meeting observation, Kendall's broader interest was in understanding the political economy of free primary education. Her goal in the meeting observation was to document relations of inequality and their effects on the policy agendas that emerged from these meetings. Her observations therefore focused on the material and discursive inequities embodied in the meetings: the environments in which different organizations worked and met (e.g., meetings held in the Ministry versus funder embassies), how participating actors interacted—or failed to interact—with each other in these different settings, and if and how different government and NGO actors engaged—or refused to engage—the claims made by one another. Rather than capture exact conversation in her notes, she detailed: who was present and who was absent; who led the meeting and controlled the course of dialogue; how the seating arrangement offered a map of relative decision-making authority in the room; what participants' postures and modes of engagement revealed about empowerment and resistance in the process of policymaking; how the meeting's chair positioned actors in relation to one another; who controlled the norms of the meeting space; and if and how the meeting agenda reflected a broader funder push toward decentralization and support for primary schooling. Kendall noted that the funders controlled the vast majority of conversation in the meeting, and much of the funder-directed conversation revolved around what the Ministry needed to do to draft an education plan that would be acceptable to the funders, and how "decentralization" should be introduced in the education sector.

As with all meeting observations, this information cannot, on its own, generate a comprehensible analysis of power relations. The field notes and the conversation that occurred in the meeting are not legible without knowledge of who was at the meeting (for example, that the funders were mid-level or senior staff; the NGO representative was the president of the NGO umbrella group and a well-known activist; the Ministry official was a low-level bureaucrat); the patterns of engagement between international funders and the Malawian government that developed after the 1994 elections; and knowledge of the globalized development agenda being pushed by funders throughout Africa at this time.

For example, the push for a certain kind of education plan was not unique to Malawi; it was part of a broader global shift by funders toward "government-owned" development processes, which accompanied new funding mechanisms designed to strengthen the role of the state in development aid. At the same time, there was a strong, global funder push to decentralize governmental structures and funding. This followed more than a decade of structural adjustment policies that had deliberately weakened centralized governmental structures, and more than a decade of celebrating political democratization, which was increasingly imagined by funders as requiring decentralization.

With this broader framing, a political economic analysis of the meeting as part of a global set of development relations emerges. The national education plan and the question of if, when, and how to decentralize educational control would appear, on their surfaces, to be core aspects of state sovereignty; yet funders appeared to be controlling these policy decisions. How funders did this becomes analytically available through the meeting observation. The Ministry was denigrated, consistently positioned as out of touch and uncaring about "on the ground" school realities. When discussing the PIF process, the funders' constant push for costing and prioritizing ran up (and often over) a thoroughly different set of cultural and bureaucratic practices in the Ministry. Funders described this difference as a failure and perceived incompetence on the part of the Ministry.

NGOs, on the other hand, were held up by the funders as virtuous actors who knew and cared about the (decentralized) masses. The NGO representative went along with this dynamic, neither addressing nor attempting to include the Ministry official in his responses. The Ministry official stayed silent and visibly, actively disengaged throughout the meeting. Throughout, the NGO representative's talk was positioned by the funders as a participatory and democratic act, while the official could talk only from a (dysfunctional) bureaucratic perspective. This dynamic was repeated in interviews, in reviews of official documents, and in other partner meetings.

This first approach to meeting observation and ethnography allowed for an analysis of the forms of funder domination of the policymaking process through the meeting format, and the forms of resistance utilized by Ministry personnel in response. This meeting occurred at a point during funder/government/NGO relations in which Ministry personnel reported that they felt they had very little voice in sovereign processes; in which NGO/government relations deteriorated as NGOs and the Ministry increasingly competed for funding; and when funder demands for Ministry responsiveness (in large part through meeting attendance) reached a fevered pitch. This approach to meeting-based data collection provides glimpses of the different sociocultural norms and political economic calculations that dominated interactions among government, NGO, and funder actors, but the form and content of the observational approach favors an analysis of structural domination and resistance.

Meeting Vignette 2

An introduction to the field notes: Educational quality was codified as a key development priority in the 2000 Dakar Framework for Action and in the UN's Millennium Development Goals. While the original 1990 Education for All initiative targeted universal access to basic education, the Dakar Framework emphasized the need to look beyond access to quality, as measured primarily by test scores on standardized literacy assessment tools.

Malawi's 2012 National Literacy Conference was the first of what would become a series of high-level meetings held to position literacy as the core of Malawi's educational quality agenda. This emphasis on literacy-as-quality did not necessarily represent agreement among development actors about the core components of educational quality in Malawi; it represented a broad and multifaceted funder push toward a focus on early-grade reading, which came to full fruition in the 2010s, when USAID (and then other funders) pledged hundreds of millions of dollars in support for early-grade reading projects. The literacy convention's focus, therefore, marked synchronicity with a broader international agenda in the education sector.

Malawi's 2012 National Literacy Conference was held at an upscale hotel in the capital city. Officially hosted by Malawi's Ministry of Education, Science, and Technology (the Ministry) in coordination with two prominent international NGOs, the conference was, in actuality, planned, organized, and implemented by one of the NGOs, whose education sector staff traveled from a field site en masse to facilitate the meeting's logistics. (Very few of the NGO's staff actually stayed at the conference hotel, however, with most choosing to save their per diems and find more modest accommodations. Executive and international NGO staff did stay on site.) An international funder paid the NGO to run the event. I had witnessed extensive preparation for the meeting by NGO education sector staff in the weeks prior, and traveled with the caravan of facilitators from their offices several hours away.

The conference was discursively framed by the organizing NGO as a workshop designed to bring together the Ministry, funders, NGOs, teachers, and academics to strategize as a group how to combat illiteracy in Malawi, and then compile feedback for the Ministry to use in educational policymaking, broadly defined. With no specific mandate to create or revise literacy-related policy, the conference came across, instead, as a highly visible demonstration of harmonization in approaches to literacy on the part of international funders and international NGOs.

Aired live on a national radio station, the program's design featured welcome speeches by NGO executive directors and the Minister of Education herself, PowerPoint presentations on current literacy programming occurring "on the ground" by NGOs, panel discussions by literacy experts, and small group activities, all in a large and formal lecture hall. Events were punctuated by tea, lunch, and snack breaks for all attendees in a dining room with white tablecloths. The day was visibly well funded and, as such, designed to stand apart from more quotidian planning meetings.

The Minister of Education, who was thanked profusely by the hosting NGO for traveling several hours that morning to attend the day's events, gave a short speech signaling her office's commitment to literacy and basic education before leaving for unspecified reasons. Prior to her departure, all participants were asked to step outside for a photo opportunity with the Minister by the hotel's pool. This celebratory photograph took place after the conclusion of welcome speeches, interrupting the scheduled programming, and marking the meeting's success prior to its occurrence. The hosting NGO's executive director also stepped out when the Minister left.

In the guest of honor's absence, the rest of the morning unfolded as a high-budget forum for international NGOs and funders to take turns showcasing their programs. In one instance, a rural primary student and her mother who had been driven from their village to Lilongwe—the first trip out of their home district in their lives—were called upon to demonstrate the success of an NGO's recent village-based literacy activities with a cold read. No audience questions followed the presentations.

Discussion in the afternoon open forum, however, assumed a remarkably different tone than the morning's presentations, and featured poignant critique by academics and the few remaining government officials in the audience on the Ministry's disempowerment at the hands of international funders and NGOs. Specific comments addressed an earlier assertion made by a funder that rural parents were unaware of the extent to which Malawi's system of formal education failed their children, as well as the question of who "owns" literacy interventions in Malawi. On the latter point, one academic asked:

> *Given these interventions, who are the drivers of change in Malawi? Where are these coming from? I'm not very sure . . . But if you examine critically these interventions, you will see that they have foreign*

elements, many. And it brings issues of ownership, for example. It brings issues of sustainability of these interventions and when it comes to scaling up, it brings . . . problems of diffusion. How do you simply scale up interventions at a national scale when the local people simply do not understand what is happening?

This academic continued to call for the empowerment of local actors and the Ministry in particular. He continued: "I have wondered why should people come and tell us where we should go? Why should people come and force us or maybe convince us, simply because we do not have an argument better ourselves, we follow what they say . . . I'm asking for homegrown solutions to our local problems. Otherwise we'll be continuing to follow the bandwagon that is probably missing the target as far as our problems are concerned."

In response to these comments, one international funder suggested sharply that the Ministry go ahead and take the lead in driving change. (This, with the Minister herself now absent, and the remaining government officials remaining mostly silent as the debate between funders and academics ensued.) The irony of suggesting that the Ministry drive change when their presence at the meeting was so muted was hard to miss. And, when a Ministry representative did eventually speak, he both reiterated the need for local ownership while passing the onus of work onto local school districts themselves, echoing a decade-long policy of decentralization in the field of education. Yes, he argued, solutions should be homegrown—right down to the school level, bypassing the state almost entirely. In his words: "The issue of the ownership is quite critical and also, added to that, there is the question of who leads in these interventions, apart from the ownership. Because if the solutions are homegrown, as I said earlier on, currently we are looking at the schools to do their own improvement at the school level." His comment spoke in part to the fact that most funder support to the government for education was, by this time, being sent directly to districts for distribution to schools.

By this point in the day, the funders seated on the stage as part of a panel of experts were asserting again and again their wholesale agreement that indeed, local solutions were best. Yet according to one funder, Ministry-level ownership would need to assume a particular, legible form. She noted, "Right now the Ministry is developing ESIP Two [the newest version of the education sector policy and investment framework] and really, the Ministry owns this plan and if the Ministry sees this as important, then it needs to be articulated in the policy framework. If it's articulated in the policy framework, the [Terms of Reference] and the budget will follow . . . and the donors, etc. will wean off of it over time . . . Unless it's articulated in a policy framework, it won't happen, and that's up to Malawi."

The question of ownership continued to animate discussion for the remainder of the day. One audience member stood up during the *question-and-answer session to critique the negative presentation of government that he felt had characterized panel discussions, arguing, "We are busy fixing what is not broken and breaking things in the process." In the small group of which I was a part, a different academic called repeatedly to empower the Ministry, rather than allowing international NGOs to continue coming in and "bulldozing."*

The tension that characterized large swaths of the meeting, however, went unacknowledged at its close. As did the muted participation by government representatives themselves. Instead, the day was called a resounding success by its organizers, with general consensus reached by all participants that it should be held as an annual event.

The 2012 National Literacy Conference that Silver attended was intended to showcase harmonization among funders, NGOs, and the Malawian government around a shared commitment to the project of improved literacy. As such, Silver focused her note-taking on the more highly performative, even ritualistic, moments that characterized the conference, from welcome speeches by NGO executive directors (who then left the meeting), to the great import afforded the Minister's (brief) attendance. Her methodological focus on performance helps illustrate the symbolic weight placed on certain moments as the day unfolded. It allows us to consider why, for instance, the morning photo opportunity with the Minister was allowed to disrupt the day's official agenda (and radio broadcast). It helps us to consider why the conference occurred in such a formal physical space, with high-level representatives from participating institutions treated like dignitaries. And it calls us to ask critical questions about why the hosting NGO decided it was important to drive a young, rural schoolgirl and her mother hours from their home to do a cold read on stage. What kind of insights can be gleaned from highly ritualistic and performative moments such as these?

A rich body of literature addresses the nature of performance at large global summits in the field of sustainable development and the environment (Little 1995; Death 2011; Campbell et al. 2014). Campbell et al. (2014) call these public meetings spectacles and argue that paying attention to their "settings and staging" is essential to understanding their effects. Death (2011) argues that large environmental summits represent "theatrical techniques of environmental governmentality" (1). He draws upon Foucault to claim that these highly publicized events allow powerful players to perform their commitment to environmental protection, even if no meaningful change is achieved.

In Malawi, meetings like the National Literacy Conference allowed for this very same performance of commitment to a mass effort—in this case, early-grade reading—and of coordination, valorized in and of itself in the international aid arena. At these meetings, funders had very particular ideas about who needed to be present and what roles they were expected to play. Tremendous pressure was put on organizing NGOs to ensure that the Minister herself showed up to indicate full government support. Here, it was the institutional position of actors that mattered—not the individuals themselves, and not necessarily the actors' or institutions' long-term commitment to basic education. The photo with the Minister of Education marked the successful coordination of literacy activities in Malawi. It visually demonstrated the Ministry's ownership of educational interventions without requiring any actual ownership of the project or the cause; such ownership would probably actually have created friction and conflict, as the funders' vision of what constitutes appropriate early-grade learning is not particularly compatible with historical Malawian practices.

Attention to not only the "stages, scripts, casts, and audiences," of meetings (Death 2011: 1), but also to what counts as the "right" kind of meeting performance, including who must be present for such a performance, and who must direct the performance, offers a particularly fruitful approach to studying through power and authority in international development. This second meeting ethnography methodology is particularly useful for revealing the extent to which the claim of Ministry ownership of literacy and other educational interventions was symbolic; the conference, like literacy interventions themselves, was facilitated by an international NGO and sponsored by development funders. Ministry officials just had to show up and smile. Indeed, by 2012, the government of Malawi received very little development funding; the bulk of international aid flowed directly to implementing NGOs. At the same time that the performative analytic frame revealed the symbolic nature of "ownership," it uncovered new spaces and processes of resistance. Peripheral actors (academics) used a widely publicized event to critique the shallowness of the trope of ownership in Malawi, at the very height of its performance.

Meeting Vignette 3

An introduction to the field notes: The vignette below reflects on the first partner meeting convened for what in 2014 was the largest girls' education project in Malawi. The project was funded by a large bilateral development organization and disbursed more than $50 million dollars over the course of four years. Every single penny of the funding was disbursed to NGOs—the Ministry received no money. This near total withdrawal of international financing for the government was the end point of a very long process, which accelerated following the 2013 "Cashgate" scandal, in which it was revealed that tens of millions of development aid dollars were siphoned off for private use by government officials.

Despite receiving no funding, as we saw in the previous meeting vignettes, government officials were expected to participate in the girls' education project meetings. Here we see a significant shift from the 2000 meetings: the Ministry is not at the table in order to receive funding; they are at the table in the hope that in the future, they might receive funding.

Concerned that each goal of government "ownership," "coordination," and "harmonization" between governmental and non-governmental girls' education work was at risk because the government received no resources for these activities, the funder put out a bid for an NGO to place a consultant in the Ministry to assure that the project's policy goals were met. This was the same arrangement as in the 2000 meeting, but the consultant was not directly hired by the funder and had very limited financial resources to offer the government. A for-profit company based in the funder's country won the bid. Their team leader was previously a high-ranking Ministry official, now charged with convincing his former colleagues that he and the project should be taken seriously, even though he had no resources to offer them. In fact, thanks to the for-profit company's management, his first task was to beg for space for an office and office furniture from the Ministry. This process, not surprisingly, took months. As one Ministry interviewee noted, "If they are not going to provide funds to us but instead to NGOs, then let them be the responsible party."

Another of the team leader's key tasks was to create an effective communication structure among government officials and the various NGOs involved in the project. This was to be accomplished through partner coordination meetings, the first of which is described below.

The meeting is held inside the Embassy of the project's bilateral funder. In order to get to the meeting, we announce ourselves and show IDs, go through a metal detector, sign in a second time, and are escorted to the meeting room. The room is well-lit, with a range of electronic equipment against one wall and a large, white table around which everyone is gathered.

This is the first partner coordination committee meeting, and the primary goal, according to the agenda, is to have all actors agree on the committee's Terms of Reference. The meeting is chaired by the team leader. Though it took convincing, Ministry leaders are present at this first meeting. Of the 18 people in attendance, five are from the Ministry, and they include two directors and a deputy director. One person from each of the recipient NGOs is also present; they are generally top-ranking staff from each organization. The funder has two representatives present: their project officer and their monitoring and evaluation officer.

A Ministry Deputy Director opens the meeting by asking everyone to please commit themselves to the project so as to improve the life of the girl child and support many national and international goals, including Education for All, the Millennium Development Goals, and the National Education Sector Plan. Everyone introduces themselves: their name, their position, and a description of their organization. The chair then introduces the funder project officer. She asks everyone to examine the Terms of Reference, which are attached to the agenda. As people read them over, she says that although the project consists entirely of discrete funding, they realize that "girls' education is the government's." The idea of the committee is to deliberately bring together governmental and non-governmental "stakeholders;" this,

she says, is how key policy issues that NGOs identify can be fed into the
Ministry's overall girls' education programming.

She then moves to Agenda Item 2: a presentation of the project's governance structure. After one question about the project timeline (which is
already quite delayed), the conversation shifts to how the project is providing scholarships for secondary schoolgirls. NGO and Ministry staff note
that there are not enough scholarships for needy girls, that some seem to be
mistargeted or overlapping, and that there are no scholarships at all for girls
to attend university. Two of the Ministry staff then begin discussing tertiary
opportunities for girls, the need to rethink how vocational education and
employment for women is conceptualized, and the gender issues faced in
community day secondary schools (where most rural girls attend school).
One of the Ministry officials says:

> It would be important to begin thinking from the Ministry side on how
> do we manage the distance [to school that many girls face], and how
> do we support within the current system to make sure the girls are
> protected? How do we mobilize communities around those schools to
> make sure the girls are protected, because it is in the walking to and
> from schools and in renting [boarding] near the school that are the
> issues.

Immediately following this comment, one of the NGO representatives asks,
"Related to the M&E framework, how far are we in moving toward progress on the overall outcomes?" A second NGO representative adds, "Do
we have any targets that need to be finalized so that we have a framework
that we can move forward on and then others can move forward and join
this framework as the components are finalized?" The funder project officer
then responds to these two questions.

This pattern of the Ministry members calling for a deeper engagement
with both practical and theoretical barriers to girls' education issues, and
NGO representatives returning the discussion to project technicalities continues, with long stretches of time in between spent wordsmithing the Terms
of Reference (e.g., "We will deliberate instead of advise. Let's use action
language").

Each of the NGOs then presents a PowerPoint on their work to date.
The audience is attentive and provides extensive feedback to each pre-
senter, often on more technical aspects of their work (e.g., how did you
determine who would win the construction bids?). Interspersed with the
feedback are a series of Ministry-led critiques of various aspects of the
project. In a few cases, these are critiques of the NGOs and their work.
More often, the critiques are broader, and are presented to the committee
as case studies of particular schools (that is, these narratives highlight the
Ministry staff's familiarity with particular school-level events). The most
important and extended of these critiques concerns the potential backlash

that girls may face because this project ignores both gender relations and the realities of poverty, and provides resources only to girls and not poor boys. This critique, raised in detail by Ministry representatives initially, is seconded by NGOs. Despite over 30 minutes of critical conversation about this issue, and a careful analysis of how the current project could actually cause harm to the girls it is meant to serve, the funder project officer responds only by saying that the focus of the project cannot be changed, as this is a multi-country project. With this comment, the Malawian project officer reveals the extent of her own power, while at the same time silencing further discussion about the very real concerns raised by the other "partners" at the table.

In this meeting, Kendall took copious, word-for-word notes (which are largely excluded here because of space), allowing for a more focused discourse analysis, but providing less rich information about the overall flow of the meeting and physical interactions among participants. Drawing on Gee's (2014) approach to d/Discourse analysis, this conversation-focused approach to data collection revealed in detail the back-and-forth of conversational flow; the particular ways in which airtime was claimed, held, and directed by different actors; the sophisticated critiques leveled against the technocratic rationale promulgated by the funders and the meeting organizers; and the organization of speech-acts-to-directed-practice.

This third approach to meeting analysis reveals how projectized aid can create spaces (like partner meetings) in which government presence is demanded, even as presence is actively restricted to the symbolic. Nothing they said was taken seriously (it did not generate discussion, debate, or direct responses), nor did resources follow their goals or concerns. At the same time, this space also accomplished some of what "partner meetings" are intended to accomplish. Ministry officials did not sit comfortably—that is, silently—in the meetings. They pushed back on their positioning and talked to NGOs and funders. Unlike in 2000, the meeting thus became a space in which NGOs and Ministry staff were regularly communicating and in contact. These relationships were strained and they were difficult, but they were being negotiated, and over time, the Ministry took some discursive and organizational control of the space, if only to dismiss NGOs' suggestions.

At the same time that (and perhaps because) Ministry officials ruptured the roles they were expected to play in this space, a parallel "coordination meeting" was eventually constructed in which only funders and NGOs were present. This was, de facto, where decisions were made about money, data collection, and reporting. Knowledge of this second meeting space raises the question of whether the Ministry could act in any way to reclaim power in these "partner" meeting spaces. They cannot opt out of the meetings, but unless they play their prescribed (passive) role, opting in may lead to new forms of marginalization.

Concluding Reflections: On Meeting Ethnography Methods

Meeting ethnography provides unique insights into the complex, everyday processes through which relations of power and authority are (re)constituted in the international development arena in Malawi, and sheds light on some of the likely consequences of these relations. It allows us to address Bebbington et al.'s (2007: 599) charge that "more careful attention to organizational questions of power and difference is important for forms of critique that might contribute to any rethinking of empowerment strategies."

The three vignettes reveal how inequitable development relations are generated, deployed, resisted, and transformed through meeting discourse and practice: for example, we see over the course of the meetings how funders reorganize (through meeting discourse and financial distribution) the idea of who represents "the people" from government to NGO actors. We can trace from the first to the last meeting what happens when the Ministry and NGOs are placed in competition over shrinking pots of aid funding. We watch funders position NGOs as virtuous because of their knowledge of the "grassroots" (whether they actually have such knowledge or not) and the Ministry as incompetent, out of touch, and ineffective (whether they are or not). We see how discourses and assumptions about appropriate relations among funders, government, and NGOs are established through regular points of physical contact (or lack thereof) among the three types of institutions. We see where and how these claims gain traction—for example, when funders urge NGOs to claim certain forms of knowledge that put them in direct conflict with the Ministry.

The shift in concepts of who "really" represents "the people" allows funders to claim that money given to NGOs more directly benefits people and is more democratic in nature than money given to the government, creating ideological support for a new generation of de facto government structural adjustment as development aid is withdrawn from government coffers. These narratives are paralleled by a sharp shift from funders providing resources to the Ministry to funders providing resources to (foreign) middle organizations, and to the increasing dominance of globalized education policies in "Ministry-owned" education plans.

At the same time, we see a shift in the forms and actors involved in resisting these discourses and practices, as Ministry staff and academics actively and publicly question funders' knowledge and capacity to support development in Malawi, and critique the nature of funder power in the field of international development. And we see how funders and those they fund respond to these efforts by creating parallel meeting structures that are remarkably similar to the parallel forms of budgeting, hiring, and reporting that the Ministry (and international development meetings) have long decried as undermining the very "ownership," "coordination," "harmonization," and "mutual accountability" that partner meetings are supposed to accomplish.

Meeting observations thus demonstrate *how* international development in daily practice is transforming state sovereignty, international political economic relations, and the norms and institutions of "development" and "democracy" in Malawi, and in development organizations themselves.

We have offered three different analytic approaches to meeting ethnography (political economic, performance, and discourse), each of which relies on different data collection foci during meeting observations. Each approach yields important insights into how relations of power and authority are constructed in international development. Each also reveals the role, importance, and power of meetings as a technology of international development—a technology that is itself disputed, reconstituted, and celebrated by turns, just as are the ideals of participation, harmonization, and mutual accountability that meetings are supposed to embody. Each analytic lens provides important insight into the daily experiences and meaning-making of the mid-level actors who at once constitute and shape development as/in practice, but each also emphasizes different aspects of these relationships, of the shifts that occur in them, and of the consequences of these shifts. Political economic approaches may be less well-suited to elucidating the partial nature of the relations of power made visible in meetings. Performative approaches may make it more difficult to understand how those who participate in such performances make sense of their involvement. Discourse approaches may overly value what people say, as opposed to what they do. Meeting ethnographers must therefore scrutinize and map their own assumptions and goals, and recognize that different methodological starting points are likely to yield different insights into meeting spaces.

Meeting ethnography is particularly generative in the field of international development because of the role meetings are expected to play in officially producing participation and harmonization among unequal "partners." Nonetheless, even when meetings are a central technology in one's field of study, it clear that meetings are not sensible in and of themselves. A full analysis requires that bringing meeting observations into dialogue with other data collection methods: interviews, participant observations, document analyses, budget flow analyses, and other data gathered through institutional ethnographic methods. Moreover, as revealed in all three analytic approached adopted herein, a robust meeting ethnography methodology combines institutional and global ethnographic methods that situate and connect the meeting to the macro-political, economic, and social environments in which the meeting comes to make sense and, in the case of international development, to become a powerful tool for the practical constitution of sustained (but uneven, contested, and therefore changeable) relations of inequality.

We have offered three research approaches that utilize meeting ethnography to accomplish the goal of studying through relations of power and authority in international development. We have shown how these approaches all provide new and significant insights into how inequitable relations are generated, maintained, and transformed. We have suggested that in other global(izing) arenas in which meetings are a central technology, these approaches are likely to yield similarly important insights into the "how" of complex processes. In so doing, they can deepen our ability to understand, and thus transform, the processes and practices that fuel global inequities.

Notes

1 The term "donor" is often used to describe multilateral, bilateral, foundation, and non-governmental institutions that provide their own funds to so-called "developing" countries or communities. Given the extensive literature noting that many "donor" funds actually do not stay in the recipient country, the term donor is a misnomer. We therefore use the term "funder."

2 While we recognize that the last decade has seen a significant rise of "non-traditional" funders in most countries (see, e.g., Malawi Ministry of Finance 2011; Mawdsley et al 2014), partner meetings continue to represent and be peopled primarily by traditional funders.

3 This is made evident by examining which actors comprise the core "partners" in meetings over time. In 2000, for instance, foundations and for-profit international organizations were not regularly included in partner meetings.

4 Our data covers a period of time during which it became de rigeur to include "civil society actors" in top-level coordination meetings. Particularly over the last five years, there have been an increasing number of development programs that are not centralized nationally. We do not cover these newer forms in the paper. Other groups are visible in some of these meetings, including Malawian academics, consultants associated briefly with one or another of the four main groups of actors, "local" actors (such as master teachers), and so forth. These groups, who are peripheral to the regular structuring of the groups, often play important performative roles in the meetings themselves, but are not included as central actors here because their presence is not institutionalized in the same way as the other groups.

5 As Samoff (1999) has noted, the recurrent budget makes up the vast majority of the education budget. The non-recurrent budget must, however, support learning and innovation in the sector, such as creating and utilizing new curricular and teacher training materials. Thus, though the amount of money is small, international funders have an outsized influence on policy and reform matters, because it is their money that supports such efforts.

References

Angouri, Jo. " 'If we know about culture it will be easier to work with one another:' Developing skills for handling corporate meetings with multinational participation." *Language and Intercultural Communication* 10(2010): 206–224.

Bebbington, Anthony, David Lewis, Simon Batterbury, Elizabeth Olson and M. Shameem Siddiqi. "Of texts and practices: Empowerment and organisational cultures in World Bank-funded rural development programmes." *Journal of Development Studies* 43(2007): 597–621.

Bierschenk, Thomas, Jean-Pierre Chauveau and Jean-Pierre Olivier de Sardan, eds. *Courtiers en Development: Les Villages Africains en Quete de Projets*. Paris: Karthala, 2000.

Büscher, Bram. "Collaborative event ethnography: Between structural power and empirical nuance?" *Global Environmental Politics* 14(2014): 132–138.

Campbell, Lisa M., Catherine Corson, Noella L. Gray, Kenneth I. MacDonald and J. Peter Brosius. "Studying global environmental meetings to understand global environmental governance: Collaborative event ethnography at the tenth conference of the Parties to the Convention on Biological Diversity." *Global Environmental Politics* 14(2014): 1–20.

Chabbott, Colette. *Constructing Education for Development: International Organizations and Education for All.* London: Routledge, 2013.

Death, Carl. "Summit theatre: Exemplary governmentality and environmental diplomacy in Johannesburg and Copenhagen." *Environmental Politics* 20(2011): 1–19.

Dionne, Kim Yi. "Donor dependence, donor withdrawal: Implications of Malawi's Cashgate scandal." *AidData Beta: Open Data for International Development.* February 13, 2014. http://aiddata.org/blog/donor-dependence-donor-withdrawal-implications-of-malawis-cashgate-scandal.

Elyachar, Julia. *Markets of Dispossession: NGOs, Economic Development, and the State in Cairo.* Durham: Duke University Press, 2005.

Englund, Harri. *Prisoners of Freedom: Human Rights and the African Poor.* Berkeley: University of California Press, 2006.

Esser, Daniel. "Elusive accountabilities in the HIV scale-up: 'Ownership' as a functional tautology." *Global Public Health* 9(2014): 43–56.

Ferguson, James. *The Anti-Politics Machine: Development, Depoliticization, and Bureaucratic Power in Lesotho.* Minneapolis: University of Minnesota Press, 1994.

Gee, James Paul. *An Introduction to Discourse Analysis.* 4th Edition. London: Routledge, 2014.

Gibson-Graham, J. K. *The End of Capitalism (As We Knew It): A Feminist Critique of Political Economy.* Malden, MA: Blackwell Publishers, 1996.

Grillo, Ralph D. and Roderick L. Stirrat, eds. *Discourses of Development: Anthropological Perspectives.* Oxford: Berg, 1997.

Hunt, Nancy Rose. *A Colonial Lexicon of Birth Ritual, Medicalization, and Mobility in the Congo.* Durham: Duke University Press, 1999.

Katz, Cindi. *Growing Up Global: Economic Restructuring and Children's Everyday Lives.* Minneapolis: University of Minnesota Press, 2004.

Kendall, Nancy. "Education for all meets political democratization: Free primary education and the neoliberalization of the Malawian school and state." *Comparative Education Review* 51(2007): 281–305.

Kharas, Homi. "Trends and issues in development aid." Working Paper 1. Wolfensohn Center for Development at the Brookings Institution, November 2007.

Lewis, David and David Mosse, eds. *Development Brokers and Translators: The Ethnography of Aid and Agencies.* West Hartford, CT: Kumarian Press, 2006.

Li, Tania M. "Compromising power? Development, culture and rule in Indonesia." *Cultural Anthropology* 14(1999): 295–322.

Little, Paul E. "Ritual, power and ethnography at the Rio Earth Summit." *Critique of Anthropology* 15(1995): 265–288.

Malawi Ministry of Finance. *Malawi Aid Atlas 2010/2011.* Lilongwe, Malawi: Malawi Ministry of Finance, 2011.

Marcus, George E. "Ethnography in/of the world system: The emergence of multisited ethnography." *Annual Review of Anthropology* 24(1995): 95–117.

Mawdsley, Emma, Laura Savage and Sung-Mi Kim. "A 'post-aid world'? Paradigm shift in foreign aid and development cooperation at the 2011 Busan High Level Forum: A 'post-aid world'?" *The Geographical Journal* 180(2014): 27–38.

Mkandawire, Thandika. "Aid, accountability, and democracy in Africa." *Social Research* 77(2010): 1149–1182.

Mosse, David. "Is good policy unimplementable? Reflections on the ethnography of aid policy and practice." *Development and Change* 35(2004): 639–671.

Myers, Fred R. "Reflections on a meeting: Structure, language, and the polity in a small-scale society." *American Ethnologist* 13(1986): 430–447.

Nader, Laura. "Up the anthropologist – Perspectives gained from studying up." In *Reinventing Anthropology*, edited by Dell Hymes, 284–311. New York: Random House, 1972.

Odora Hoppers, Catherine A. "Poverty, power, and partnerships in educational development: A post-victimology perspective." *Compare* 31(2001): 21–38.

Olivier de Sardan, Jean-Pierre. *Anthropology and Development: Understanding Contemporary Social Change*. London: Zed Books, 2005.

Ortner, Sherry B. *Anthropology and Social Theory: Culture, Power, and the Acting Subject*. Durham: Duke University Press, 2006.

Samoff, Joel. "Education sector analysis in Africa: Limited national control and even less national ownership." *International Journal of Educational Development* 19(1999): 249–272.

Sutton, Margaret and Bradley A.U. Levinson, eds. *Policy as Practice: Toward a Comparative Sociocultural Analysis of Educational Policy*. Stamford, CT: Ablex Publishing, 2001.

Wright, Susan and Sue Reinhold. " 'Studying through:' A strategy for studying political transformation. Or sex, lies and British politics." In *Policy Worlds: Anthropology and the Analysis of Contemporary Power*, edited by Cris Shore, Susan Wright and Davide Pero, 86–104. New York: Berghahn Books, 2011.

2 Learning to Meet (or How to Talk to Chairs)

Simone Abram

Meeting Bureaucracy

Interest in the bureaucracy of politics has been intense since Weber's analysis of the separation of power, and Foucault's essay on the governance of governance (1978/1991). The work of Miller, Rose, and others (Rose 1991, 1994; Miller 1992) in identifying accounting as a governmental technology has been enormously influential in defining an approach to understanding government through a close examination of its technologies, both material and social. Yet the focus on numbers (Hacking 1990) overshadowed the importance of other bureaucratic practices in these analyses. In the context of this volume, it makes sense to consider bureaucratic meetings as a technology of government, which both enables and is, itself, government. Abrams's (1977) notes on the difficulty of studying the state are a useful reminder that concepts such as 'state' and 'government' are abstract and instrumental. In invoking the state and the governing of people and things, we simultaneously reinforce the impression that they exist. To paraphrase Abrams, the state is not the reality which stands behind the mask of council meetings; it is itself the mask which prevents our seeing meetings as they are[1] (Abrams 1977: 58). Schwartzman (1989) has made a convincing argument that organizations are constituted through the practices of their participants, building on wide-ranging arguments in anthropology about the effectiveness of rituals in transforming both persons and social arrangements. Latour and Woolgar can be read in the same vein, as arguing that science is made of the sum of activities of its adherents (1986). It is timely, then, to focus on the meeting as an exemplary form through which the ontology of politics can be explored. In particular, I address the intersection of ontology and temporality by asking how such practices are reproduced. How do participants become tuned into these practices? How do they begin to share in the repetitive practice of being the state, or, in other words, how do they/we learn to enact the universalizing technology of government that I suggest meetings to be?

What does it mean to talk of meetings as universalizing technologies of government? The phrase draws on histories of colonial practice and

DOI: 10.4324/9781315559407-3

international circuits of management. Just as signposts render a landscape legible to wayfarers (see Ween and Abram 2012), the standard form of meetings, with agendas, minutes, apologies, items, other business, etcetera, offers a navigable system that can be used and adapted around the globe. Once learned, these tools can be applied in many different contexts. The spread of a bureaucratic system, hastened by colonial control, and perpetuated by global multinational organizations, provides a veneer of legibility to governing systems around the world. Certainly there are anthropologists who have explored the variability that lies underneath the apparent uniformity of the system, but the form of the governmental meeting is unified enough to be recognizable despite local differences, offering the potential for a class of global political elites to enter into the system to some extent in many different locations. I do not underestimate the variation between implementations of the meeting form, but highlight its success both in its ubiquity and in its invisibility in plain sight. This invisibility, by which I mean the manner in which it is taken for granted, makes it an ideal ethnographic fact, about which to ask how different people in particular places come to learn the varied skills that are needed to master the art of managing meetings. The basic rules may appear simple, but they are further reaching than they may appear at first encounter, largely tacit, and their mastery is complex.

The complexity of governmental bureaucratic meeting rules is illustrated in the work of Walter Citrine, at one time General Secretary to the Trades Union Congress (UK), who published a guide in 1939 to the correct chairmanship of meetings. As such, it is a kind of normative ethnographic guide to current practice, committing to the form of a rulebook the kinds of practices that were then common and considered correct. Practices have since changed, but Citrine's *ABC of Chairmanship* (1939) is a remarkably rare entity. Although there are clearly common (and disputed) principles for the management of meetings in local state authorities, it is not at all common to see explicitly stated rules.

In fact, Sir Walter Citrine acknowledges in his guide that there are no legal rules of debate, but that associations tend to draw up their own rules or "standing orders." These orders tend to be rather similar, which is why Citrine was able to draw up a general guide in the first place, and he suggests a number of ways in which the practice of holding meetings can be considered to be a social fact worthy of ethnographic exploration. The similarity of meeting forms makes them a universalizing modern practice in which participants may engage in the disciplinary processes of the state; indeed, some participants enact the state through the kind of disciplinary processes and actions that I will describe in the chapter. In this context, the existence—or even the potential imagined existence—of a book of rules can be invoked to control situations of conflict or contest. If local politics can be defined as an arena where conflicting interests are pursued, then in this context, meetings are one of the primary mechanisms for managing an orderly progression through complex processes.

It is my contention, then, that the skills and knowledge needed to be effective at running municipal meetings are rarely contained in the written rules and regulations pertaining to municipal procedures. On the contrary, participants learn from each other in the meeting context, learning in the process how to interpret, manipulate, and bend whatever formal rules exist. There may be individuals who read Citrine (and his equivalents) and proceed according to his recommendations, and there is an industry of publishing about good meeting practices, but by and large in the situations where I have attended municipal meetings, practices are continually being taught and/or learned in meetings themselves. As noted above, I am largely referring to meetings of municipal councils, and, more specifically, meetings of planning-related committees in Norway and England,[2] although the cases discussed below are both from Norway. These include both official administrative meetings, meetings between political committees and their administrative support staff, and meetings between planning officials or elected representatives and members of what they call the public. The context is thus different forms of modern Western democracies and the ways that these democracies are pursued in practice through the form of the meeting.

Considering such meetings in isolation is plainly impossible, since they take place in a broader municipal context, in a time horizon either circular or linear, depending on perspective. As Schwartzman takes pains to demonstrate (1989), meetings can be thought of as punctuation in the progress of activities in complex organizations, functioning only with the support of the relations that are practiced around the actual moment of the meeting itself. However, taking the meeting as the focus of analysis can be considered as a classic ethnographic tactic, since the meeting becomes the lens through which municipal politics (in this instance) can be explored (see Peacock 2001). The form, that of the municipal meeting that appears to be so similar across national and social boundaries, offers a means of comparison, shedding light on the activities and relations that are practiced around and through the meeting, becoming a vehicle for the analysis of political process. These practices of governance are supported by all sorts of material tools, from documents to furnishings, to objects of prestige that lend authority and legitimacy to the meeting and the agreements reached—or announced—within them (see below, and Abram and Weszkalnys 2013). In other words, anthropological approaches to politics through the object of meetings have much to learn from studies of ritual in its broadest conceptualization. This includes the admission that starting with a universalizing term ("ritual," "marriage," "politics") is the contradiction at the heart of anthropological study that aims to avoid ethnocentrism, and yet starting with a familiar form is the means by which we embark on any comparative project, by assembling items that we believe to be somehow comparable, making what Marilyn Strathern calls "partial connections" where homology is impossible (1991).

If Citrine aimed to assemble a set of standards based on the broad range of common and accepted practices, formulating a doctrine from the variety of organizations and institutions he addressed, then his intention was implicitly to iron out differences. The trend continues, e.g., with Tropman (2014), broadening the context into the expansive definition of "decision-groups," making his modern-day Citrine into an even broader universalizing guide. There are many such guides to holding effective meetings, largely in the context of business or company management, where it is possible to see sometimes moralized, sometimes banal interpretations of what a meeting is and how it should (normatively) proceed. These guides tend to do the opposite of ethnography, placing little emphasis on the detail of current practice, and much on the functional or instrumental purpose of the meeting. In laying down normative principles, they further the notion that meetings are neutral as form, that they can be applied anywhere, and that they should follow rational rules and procedures. Considering meetings instead as an ethnographic object, it becomes possible to see the range of learning that is happening through meetings, both in terms of the stated aims to be achieved through meeting with others, and in terms of learning how to do meetings themselves.

Form and Function

Despite very different legal structures, political histories, and local practices, the everyday life of bureaucratic institutions in Western democracies is, as noted, remarkably recognizable from one to another. So remarkable, in fact, that it is relatively easy for us to locate the differences in manner, language, procedure, and documentation than it would be for systems that were entirely different. In one sense, it should not be surprising that European (and other) bureaucratic political systems are similar, given the history of European inter-colonization, such that governmental practice and procedure has been imported and imposed between various European countries over the centuries. As a former colony of Denmark, and with a former union with Sweden, we might expect that Norway would share bureaucratic systems with other Scandinavian countries (see Rian 2003), and through the Swedish connection, we might expect to see some similarities with French governance, since Sweden—and by default Norway—had a French king, "Karl Johan," alias Jean Bernadotte (1763–1844), former Minister of War to Napoleon. We might also note that "good practice" remains constantly in circulation between European countries, not least through the promotion of intra-European projects, and through the activities of international consultants seeking opportunities in the public sector. Governance practices are explicitly imposed or imported through international aid and collaborative partnerships as well. Whatever the cause, it can be said that the daily life of government—and governmentality—is substantially recognizable from one country to another.

Among of the most recognizable features are the practice and documentation of meetings, including those in local government of the kind I have participated in, primarily in England, Norway, and France, as part of various ethnographic projects. In each of these instances, a relative lack of formal training in meeting practice is common. While some civil servants do undergo training in writing agendas and minutes, few politicians who chair or participate in meetings are involved in any substantial formal training. Much bureaucratic time is spent on teaching and training in less formal ways, however. One model of learning that helps to understand these forms is that developed by Lave and Wenger (1991) and discussed by Gillian Evans in her 2006 book on situated learning. Evans emphasizes how learning is a social process in which the object of learning and the social context in which it occurs are inextricably linked. Elements of social prestige are tied to the ability to gain skills and knowledge in arenas of value, while value is attributed as a social process,[3] rather than as a fixed characteristic. While Evans is concerned with the way working-class children learn to be full social participants, her approach is important in exploring non-formal routes to learning and can be applied to the context of public political activities, as we will see below.

Lave and Wenger's theory of situated peripheral participation highlights the everyday learning that adults, as well as children undertake, as part of the performance of social personhood. In brief, the argument is that the learning we do as peripheral participants to a social process is akin to the learning of an apprentice. Gradually picking up insight into the situation through "proximal" and experiential learning, we slowly become more expert in our knowledge and skills, our ability to judge a situation, and the repertoire of responses on which we can draw to act effectively in a given context as we begin to take on a more significant role in the situation. This kind of experiential learning is, in fact, acknowledged by many professional organizations, who require suitably qualified people to demonstrate experience of practice before being eligible for full membership of chartered institutions (including, in the UK, medicine, engineering, and planning institutes, see Abram 2011: 136). For elected representatives, administrators, and others, learning to be an effective actor in municipal government usually requires such a process of gradual inclusion, first observing, trying, and gradually becoming more skilled in exploiting the opportunities that meetings offer to achieve desired outcomes.

If much learning is both social and informal, it is also often tacit, and the ethnographic project may include an attempt to draw out that learning, not to generate an explicit guide or manual to practices, but to explore the routes of learning, and to expose the inequalities it may generate, and to demonstrate the processes of exclusion and inclusion, empowerment and disempowerment that such tacit learning often entails. With this in mind, it is possible to ask where people actually learn how to "do" meetings collaborative.

Learning by Doing

In the small, functional community hall in the Stølsheimen community in western Norway, the district council is getting ready to hold its monthly meeting. Large thermos flasks of coffee stand on the melamine tables as people take their seats on the modern wooden chairs upholstered in office-burgundy. The table is soon littered with papers, files, and coffee cups and the buzz of chatter dies down as the mayor stands to call the meeting to order. His seat is at the head of the table, with the chief executive of the council at his side as secretary to the meeting and behind them a whiteboard on the wall. A few observers (myself included) sit away from the opposite end of the table, between the open room-dividers and partly in the adjoining function room, but most of the dozen chairs set out for observers are empty. The meeting is open to anyone who wants to attend, but a routine meeting does not attract very many citizens. Meeting papers are given to everyone, including observers, and they include a copy of the agenda, and a discussion paper. The mayor gets the meeting underway by welcoming the participants, particularly those who have not attended before. In the Norwegian system, each local elected representative has a deputy who attends meetings if the elected representative is unable to be present. Council members are elected on a list-system, and deputies are chosen from those candidates lower down on the list who were not actually elected, but who were presented to the electorate as part of the party list.[4] Unusually, in this district, the lists were not presented by political parties, but by groupings that roughly represent the two major settlements in the district.[5] In all, the population numbers only a few hundred residents, so the council is proportionally small, with only thirteen members. Disputes tend to arise where the interests of residents in the two different settlements conflict, or where a good is seen to benefit one settlement over the other.

Many of the council meetings I had attended elsewhere were quite lively, with intense debate and vehement speeches, and some degree of chatter in the background. In comparison, this meeting is remarkably quiet. Each person stands as they speak, the rest of the participants sitting silently with modest attention, so that the meeting has the air of a Quaker service, which is perhaps appropriate in this puritanical part of the country.[6] The mayor asks the attendees to confirm the minutes of the previous meeting, and goes through the matters arising from those minutes, informing the members of progress since that meeting, and listening to comments and questions about it. After a little while, one of the deputies begins to discuss an issue with another member across the table. The mayor interrupts her, politely, saying that as she is a new deputy who hasn't attended council meetings before, perhaps she hasn't understood the procedure. He explains that she must always address her comments to the chair of the meeting (himself), and not talk directly to other members. That is how council meetings are run. She apologizes, a little flustered, and tries to repeat her comments to the mayor, somewhat deflated. The other councilor replies to the mayor and the discussion peters out, the mayor moving on to the next point on the agenda.

I have observed a classic moment of explicit social pedagogy, with the mayor effectively communicating to the new participant, "This is how we behave in meetings here," in a manner both polite and firm. The new participants learn what is considered appropriate in this setting through a didactic intervention and explanation of 'rules' that are otherwise taken for granted. She might also have observed from the practice of the other participants that this was the norm for the control of speech at this municipal meeting, but it is interesting to note that these kinds of norms are often only made explicit when they are breached. In common with many social norms, as long as they are followed they are effectively invisible, but when breached they provoke disciplinary action among other participants. The categories of tacit, experiential, and situated learning do much to unpack the different ways that learning arises, but their formality simultaneously conceals the broad repertoire of chastisement, explicit pedagogy, and social normativity that can be brought into reproducing meeting practices. Certainly, this example shows someone learning through experience, situated in a very particular context, in which a failure in tacit learning gives rise to explicit pedagogical action on the part of the chairperson.

The mayor, in this instance, could be described, indeed, as a good chair of a meeting. Participants in other municipal meetings had clear, common criteria for a "good chair" that included a strong pedagogical element. The chair was skilled in keeping proceedings in order and ensuring that everyone present understood how things should be done. With this reminder still fresh, the meeting continued in a most formal manner, despite the informality of the surroundings and the relaxed dress and seating arrangements of the participants. Through his intervention, the rules of behavior were clarified for all the participants, and all those present were disciplined into a shared set of expectations for meeting practice, namely that at council meetings, speech is unidirectional, and this is not a setting either for general conversation or for arguments across the table. Procedure becomes explicit in such rare moments, where otherwise it remains implicit in the actual practices of the participants, from the banal to the crucial: members know that coffee will be served; they know already that they will stand when they have something to say and will avoid chatting while someone else is speaking, and they know they must address their comments to the mayor and address him by his title. There are very many such rules that they have already internalized and which they experience as the kind of self-discipline that, as Foucault long ago remarked, form the basis of governing mentalities (1978, 1979).

Some disciplining effects are produced by material conditions, such as the form of language and format of documents circulated, or the formalized settings of some council chambers. Others are learned and internalized, whether or not they are evident in the material context. For example, the Weberian separation of politics and administration in Norway requires bureaucrats to learn a particular kind of discipline that some are unable to maintain (Abram 2004). In Norwegian municipal political meetings, administrators are required to observe a subservient position, remaining, like the ideal Victorian child, seen and not heard, silent unless spoken to. They are the servants of the political process, and like servants they conduct much of the policy work behind the scenes, presenting it in codified documents for discussion at council committee meetings. These kinds of discipline are relatively explicitly encoded, and staff are trained to understand their role and position. In principle, communication between politicians and bureaucrats should be channeled via the person of the chief executive and the mayor (two corporate bodies, in effect), or via others delegated by them. In practice, strict adherence to this code would make everyday local government grind to a halt, so bureaucrats (and politicians too) have to learn how the rules apply and how flexible they are. For example, if a bureaucrat were to telephone a politician to discuss a policy, they would soon be chastised, and the story of their error would undoubtedly run the round of office gossip so that all other bureaucrats would be aware that this was unacceptable. A politician may request information or advice from a bureaucrat, but such a request should travel via the chair and secretary of the relevant committee, and any deviation from such a route would attract attention—the bureaucrat themselves would probably ask the question (i.e., "Is this request from the committee?"), to ensure that the politician was not seeking private or party political benefit from information provided by the public servant. On the other hand, were a politician and a bureaucrat to meet in the corridor, or chat in the coffee-and-pastry pause of a meeting, they might naturally (or, possibly, guardedly) discuss one or two issues of interest. It is therefore on such occasions that politicians might become aware of some useful fact that they had not known to ask about. All such nuances outside the meeting itself complement the meeting since all participants rapidly realize that knowledge of essential facts is a form of political power and helps to ensure that policies are well-founded and potentially effective.

In the different context of a large, wealthy municipality not far from the capital city in southern Norway, the discipline that governed administrators was particularly evident in everyday practice, such as through the physical layout of the council chamber, where full elected members sat at their specific places in the main hall, while administrators and other officers sat at the back with members of the public, waiting to be called if required. In the very formal council chamber, all public speech is amplified through single-speaker desk microphones, and councilors make their interventions from a podium. In this context, the control of speech by physical infrastructure is very evident, since an attempt to intervene from behind the councilors' benches would be both poorly audible and demonstrably unconventional.

For an administrator, sitting or standing (hanging around) at the back of the room, the walk to the chair's chair—or indeed to the podium in more formal council chambers—is a conspicuous act, and might be interpreted as assertive or intrusive, and indeed I never saw any administrator attempting this traverse without an invitation. Hence the physical layout of the room reinforced the idea that people without a seat were not part of the conversation, materializing the subservient position that bureaucrats learned to adopt. Many administrators preferred to be as inconspicuous as possible, while remaining available if called upon. They explained to me that last-minute interventions might be interpreted as an indication that the papers they had prepared for the meeting had not been adequate, an accusation they were keen to avoid. Physical layout and the use of papers thus reinforce the rules that administrators learn to avoid intervening in political debates.

The notion of 'order' is central to the council committee meeting, assuring the participants and observers that the world is proceeding according to recognized rules of engagement, and suggesting that work is being done, decisions made in a timely and just manner, and processes progressing. Elected council members know that they cannot just start to argue across the table, but they are also vehement about their right to disagree; indeed it is their duty to disagree where politicians are elected to represent different interests.

At the same time, elected representatives and administrators learn very quickly that the business of the full council—that which is conducted in the most formal meetings in the council chamber—is largely symbolic, with decisions having been made in advance either in party meetings or in the preparatory subcommittee meetings. In any council with an overall majority, even if that majority is a coalition, most cases on the council's agenda were up for ratification and publication, not for meaningful decisions. These full council meetings form part of the legitimizing ritual of state procedure (as described in Abram and Weszkalnys 2013, and Abram 2011). Such ritual has an important role in the democratic process, since the council meeting is the event on which the public gaze is focused, allowing an image of the council-at-work to be disseminated and giving participants an opportunity to demonstrate their rhetorical, political, and social skills.

Norwegian local government council meetings are open to the public (in some cases also regularly broadcast or webcast), so they become occasions on which politicians can also communicate with voters, demonstrating that their views are being communicated and considered, whether or not decisions go in their favor. In council meetings, a public case must be made to legitimize whatever decision is being proposed and to ensure that the procedure appears to be fair, but there are other gains to be made. Skilled opposition speakers can cast doubt on the wisdom of the decisions ostensibly to be voted on but actually already reached in subcommittees; they can use the opportunity to promote alternatives either by setting out options or by seeding a new idea that they can come back to at a later opportunity;

and politicians of all parties can mark themselves out as tactical and effective speakers, impressing their party colleagues in the hope of promotion within their own group. Politicians watch and learn from others whom they admire, and they learn to avoid the mistakes that others make, but such learning must also be reconciled with their expectations of moral and political norms. Hence, very strongly normative Norwegian ideals of transparency and openness in government mean that manipulative game-playing that may be admired in some contexts as skillful political maneuvering is more often interpreted negatively in the Norwegian context as dirty tricks. The kind of banal corruption taken for granted elsewhere (e.g., Gupta 1995) is considered inadmissible here—to the point where my tentative questions about corruption were considered out of place. In other words, the form of political discipline in the Norwegian council was particular, while still recognizably taking the form of the municipal meeting. Meeting procedures do not remove power play from the business of municipal government, far from it, but they offer an arena for such power play to be rehearsed, so a key skill for politicians lies in learning how to use this symbolic arena to advantage.

For politicians, part of the experience they gain in such meetings entails learning the knowledge of how to perform disagreement, both in the sense of putting on a performance for the audience (including members present, public attending, and those watching the debate on local television or online), and in the sense of acting on disagreement in an appropriate manner. This includes their ability to represent effectively the interests of their constituents and to have a properly political debate without personalizing the argument between representatives. Politicians whom I worked with in Norway often remarked that they got along with members of different parties perfectly well and had respect for their views, yet they would argue vociferously that they were wrong in the debating chamber. Indeed, the more formal the debate, the more vociferous the arguments. One might speculate that formality in meetings offered safety barriers against the personalization of arguments, since each politician taking their place at the speaker's podium in the council chamber for their five minutes of speech was evidently playing a clear role—Councilor Normann, and not everyday Ellie Normann, part-time estate agent and mother of three. The less formal the meeting, the more convivial and less aggressive the argument, even if the positions taken by the participants were, in fact, equally intransigent. Learning how to manage these boundaries was often reinforced through what we might call gossip—discussions in corridors or over coffee in which transgressions were criticized. The council meeting, with its rules and procedures and its material setting and props, offers some security in its separation of personal relations from political relations, so that politicians can adopt roles that need not interfere with their ability to work with people they disagree with in the future, and they are protected from personal attacks by their political position. Politicians soon learn these benefits of a system that can otherwise appear formal or arcane.

On the administrative side, learning how to participate in meetings also requires some skill. At the time of my fieldwork in the Norwegian municipal town hall, the chief executive was transforming the organization along neoliberal, or New Public Management lines. While not quite as extreme as the kind of new age business as that Salamon describes (2005), the idea that staff should "be positive" was clearly emphasized. Criticism was interpreted as "negativity" to be avoided, implying that bureaucrats were obliged to take great care in framing their professional opinion, and find subtle ways to resist the discipline that this management technique seemed to enforce. The ongoing managerial reorganization offered the chief executive the opportunity to force employees to apply for newly defined positions. In one administrative team meeting, the chair announced that he had applied for one of the new posts and had been told that he would not be appointed for that or any other post, since he had not been sufficiently supportive to the chief executive. He had openly voiced criticism of the chief executive's management decisions, and the result provided a lesson for all his colleagues (see also Abram 2004). It is possible to see that the playing out of this power struggle generated a particular kind of learning for his colleagues. For some, the lesson was to find a job elsewhere, while for others, it was to silence their critical thoughts. Later that day, one administrator met me for coffee in a nearby canteen and entered into a kind of extended self-criticism, particularly of her difficulty in restraining her enthusiasm and energy for the service she ran. Her excitability, the very qualities that made her an effective champion for her service, worked against her opportunities for progressing in the organization, since she found it difficult to adopt the passive persona expected in meetings. While this example has much to do with the particular management scenario in this organization, it also reflects the way that meeting talk can have consequences beyond the meeting, which participants have to learn from, since meeting protocol overrides the interests, personalities, or preferences of individual participants.

What is striking, even in the relatively simple municipal meetings described above, is quite how much meeting-related skill, knowledge, and practice has been internalized and is reproduced by the participants, and the extent to which meeting practice can be adapted to encompass such a wide range of issues and situations, a flexibility within boundaries that helps the formal meeting to endure as a political form across the world (see Richards and Kuper 1971). As Vike has described, debates held in committees and subcommittees draw on long-standing narratives and understandings about different party positions that can be manipulated by smart administrators or spokespersons (Vike 2002).

Amid all this disciplinary activity, politicians and bureaucrats find ways to work around the strictures of meeting speech. Breaks in meetings provide a moment for at least the partial relaxation of the rules of segregation and orderly speech of the meeting itself. As I noted at the time in my field notes:

> Breaks in meetings always seem to be the most interesting part. You sit through an hour of patronizing detail about how to distinguish goals from objectives (again) and everyone is terribly well behaved, and then in the break they reveal that they think it is rubbish or silly.

It was during one such meeting break that an opposition politician, Knut, reflected on his participation in a cabinet policymaking process as representative of a minor party in the district. He explained how difficult it was to be only one person representing real opposition, always being in the position of having to present alternatives or different models to those presented by the mayor or chair of committee. He described the process of policymaking as a cycle of meeting and dispersing, as he doodled for me a set of interlocking diamonds onto a scrap of paper. The diagram illustrated a creative process that moves away from a point, coming back together to make a choice, then moving away for more creative work, and so on, and also represents the gathering in a meeting and referring back to a broader constituency (such as his party group). Decisions that happen at meetings illustrate the point of punctuation in this process, as noted above.

The model could also describe the learning trajectory of politicians as they learn to make sense of political process over time. Experienced politicians tend to distill what they describe as the business from the performance, but they have learned that the performance has its own value, even if it does not change immediate decisions. The formality of naming the mayor while looking at him prior to launching into a speech becomes automatic, and yet it remains a crucial element of the meeting procedure. Each time it is said, the participants are reminded that the chair of the meeting is in the chair as an honorary role, aside from their role of representing a political position: they are there to keep order and to confirm the official authority of any discussions held in the meeting. At the same time, the mayor is reminded in this fashion that he or she holds the trust of the participants to retain order in proceedings, to give each a fair hearing according to the rules. Abuse of that trust is probably the most serious thing that a chair can do wrong, and in the political process it can have real consequences, including dismissal or other disciplinary action. Abuse of trust brings political procedure into the realms of the legal system, whereas on an ordinary basis, political decisions are rarely taken to the courts. Where it does happen, it is widely reported, and the attention given to cases where legal action ensues reflects how unusual this really is in practice. Repeated practices ensure that the lessons that have been learned about meeting personas and behavior are regularly reinforced.

Learning by Playing

While learning as an adult participant is part of the induction into political life and is an arena for the reproduction of political forms and practices, there have been various initiatives to try to initiate younger people into the ideas and practices of democracy through inviting them into council meetings in different ways, or by mimicking council meeting practices elsewhere.[7] Many schools in the UK and Norway have student councils and some hold mock general elections. Particularly in Norway, several political parties have youth wings, and in both countries universities often provide training grounds for aspiring politicians. The Oxford Union, for example, is one of the more notoriously elitist institutions that acts as a practice chamber for British parliamentarians, while more inclusive student unions in other universities provide opportunities for political engagement alongside the provision of various kinds of welfare services. The UN has long had a student council (in which my own mother participated as a medical student at Manchester University in the late 1940s). Pedagogical approaches to introducing young people into democratic practice are hardly new, but it is instructive to examine the forms they take today, and the kinds of lessons that participants learn in these preparatory contexts. Activities such as the youth council form part of a much wider approach to what is sometimes called civic engagement in Norway (or what Anderson refers to as "civil sociality" in Denmark, 2011). While participation in public life is sometimes measured through the proportion of the population who belong to associations (Tranvik and Selle 2005),[8] explicit pedagogical activities organized by municipalities via the schools under their administration[9] specifically aim to educate children about democracy through practice.

In this section, I recount one such program, which could be thought to collapse the notions of democracy, citizenship, and meeting practice into one arena. This example forms one of two models for educational experience of democratic practices. In the school environment, role play and learning through experience are implicit in activities such as mock elections, in which pupils take on the role of candidates representing different parties, urging their peers to vote for them. Such role-plays offer the opportunity to learn about the process of democracy, and its practicalities, since participants must adhere to a set of electoral rules that mimic national elections. Schools councils, on the other hand, are as much an experience of direct democracy as they are a pedagogical tool. In school councils (here I generalize for the sake of brevity), school students elect representatives who participate in school governance, sitting on committees at different levels. In Norway, since the 1990s at least, some municipalities have also established regular youth councils, of two key sorts. Both translate into English as "council," but one type could be termed a youth advisory board (ungdomsråd) while the other is a mirror to the municipal council (De Unges Kommunestyre, DUK). In the former, young people (not necessarily school representatives—recruitment and election strategies vary) are invited to join a board of young people who scrutinize the policies and decisions of the municipal council to ensure that they do not cause difficulties or disadvantages to young people in the municipality. They form an advisory and scrutiny committee who meet regularly to be consulted on policy and may be supported by a children's ombudsperson, for example. In both cases, participants are taught how to function through the medium of meetings, how to understand agendas and meeting papers, link one meeting to the next, and make arguments and interventions in public debates.

In this section, I show how students learn to behave in municipal meeting style, which provides not only training for future politicians, but a means to interpret municipal meetings that students may later encounter. The DUK is an arena in which school representatives may take their seats in the council chamber in a youth version of the full municipal council. While in some instances this is a purely symbolic activity, in others the youth council is offered a budget and the opportunity to make decisions on how that budget should be disbursed. In the municipality of Asker, which has since the 1970s become a wealthy commuter district for Oslo, the youth council has the power to manage a budget that is confirmed on an annual basis. The youth council meets annually, and in many respects mimics the full council. It includes the same number of representatives as the full council (forty-seven members in the year 2000, expanded to fifty-three in 2014), from primary and secondary schools, and is led by the mayor and meets in the council chamber. The stated aim is to promote the interests of children and young people in the district, to encourage the participation of students in their school and in the district, to give them some degree of influence in decisions that affect them, and encourage in them a sense of responsibility for their own neighborhoods, as well as offering a forum for dialogue between young people and the leadership of the council. As with council meetings, the youth council is held in public, with papers available freely from the council's website. Contemporary youth councils are broadcast live on the council's website, where videos of councils since 2007 remain available (https://www.asker.kommune.no/Lokalpolitikk/Video-fra-kommune styret/ accessed 27.2.15).

The description below is of a youth council held in 2000, although by all accounts it continues in a similar form today. In this case, schools in the district are invited by the municipal council to participate in the council. Schools agree to hold competitions in which groups of pupils propose projects with budgets that fall within the overall budget for the youth council. In each school, therefore, a competition was set up where students were invited to propose projects for the municipal youth council. School councils considered proposals and held elections, often holding rounds by school year and then between school years in the schools. Winning project groups then competed in each school sub-district to come forward to the youth council in the town hall. By all accounts, the competition in several schools was fierce. By the time the successful groups came together to present their ideas at the youth council in the town hall in late March, they were well prepared, each group bringing models or posters to illustrate the projects they hoped to get funded and having practised their presentations in previous rounds.

On a chilly day in late March 2000, children from the ages of around eleven to eighteen gathered in the town hall council chamber. The austere modernist 1960s concrete building, with its dark grey pebble-dashed walls decorated with a row of gold-framed formal classical oil portraits of former mayors, an abstract relief behind the chair's table at the front of the hall, and low-level lights glowing on dark-wooden benches arranged in ranks on three sides of the room. Despite the subdued surroundings, the excitement and nervousness of the participants were palpable in the livelier-than-usual atmosphere. All the students were accompanied, either by school staff or parents, who were invited to sit in the observers' chairs at the back of the hall. The mayor called the meeting to order from the front bench of the chamber with the council secretary at his side, welcoming the students, introducing the agenda, and explaining the basics of council meeting procedures. Every meeting begins with a register, he explained, to check who is there and that they are sitting in the right place, and so that everyone knows who everyone else is. The register was then called with names read out school by school, a process that took half an hour. One young boy was told by the council secretary that he could not sit at the table, since his school had only registered one representative, and could therefore only have one seat. His teacher asked if it would be all right for him to sit at the table during the meeting anyway, and was told that this would be acceptable, but that he would not have a vote and must sit back from the table, so that the secretary knew which was the authorized representative. The embarrassed boy sat timidly back from the table, while the teacher looked pained at the rather brusque dismissal of the boy's attempt to participate. It was clear to all that rules and regulations must be attended to, and that this was not an occasion on which "anything goes," or exceptions could be made merely to be nice to children.

The mayor continued, outlining the rules of participation: one should only speak to/through the mayor, addressing him as "Mr. Mayor," and not addressing other participants directly; they should keep to the point at hand and not start talking about other things; they should be concise and keep to the time limits allocated to each speaker. After this introduction, the mayor announced a break for all the participants to admire the models and posters that the groups had brought along, and the students tumbled into the adjoining foyer to see the projects and to try to convince each other to support their proposals. During the break, two girls who had participated in a two-day project called "Vi Bryr Oss," or "We Care" earlier in the month came over to talk to me. The project had been part of a government-sponsored programme that was sent out to districts nationally, intended to give general education on democracy and teach students how to be listened to. Students had been invited to participate, and to make short films about their views, to be shared later with others in the district through the council website and various film-showings. The project had been managed locally by Guri, an education officer from the council. Her work fell within the council's priority area of coordinating services for children and youth, and she was vehement about the importance of including young people in municipal activities, including the Youth Advisory Board, which, as mentioned above, was a committee made up of young people in the municipality who review all policy for its potential effects on young people in the district.

The girls had enjoyed the preparations for the youth council, they told me, having practiced giving speeches and prepared keywords that they might need. They had prepared a film during Vi Bryr Oss, but were disappointed not to be able to show it to the council, since the project organizers were still working on the editing. The slow turnaround was something that Guri was privately very critical of, since she felt that rapid response was essential. Young people need to see results quickly, she argued, for them to believe in them. Today, though, she was positive, enthusiastic, and encouraging. When the girls saw the mayor come into the room, they called out to him by his first name, "Morten, Morten!" and he came over to chat, asking them with genuine interest about the project, about their ideas for a youth disco and about the youth council. In fact, they had a long conversation about how they might organize a disco, and where it could be located, whether it should be in one of the smaller villages or central in the main town, which age group it should be for, whether the decoration in the existing youth café was too light for a disco, and so forth. He sat in the chair in front of them, leaning on the chair back to talk to them, and he received their ideas constructively and not patronizingly. In encouraging them to talk about their ideas, he demonstrated that he took them seriously, and also practiced political deliberation, showing that the town hall was a place for discussing ideas and proposals, giving them room to develop. At the same time, he gently brought in limitations and external concerns. When the girls started to talk to him about plans for a new swimming pool in the district, they said that they thought it shouldn't be a boring pool where people swim up and down, but should have slides and so on. He explained the costs of such a project, and said that although the council had tried to bring in a private developer, this had not happened, so their ideal pool would be too expensive.

After they went to get refreshments, the mayor asked for my opinion, and I acknowledged that I was impressed. "They are very confident," said the mayor, "so well prepared and smart." He would never have had the confidence to speak at the council at their age, he said, and he was impressed by them. The council had put up a real budget, of NOK 100 000 (around £10,000, or $13,000), and this had not been a difficult decision. However, the students' ideas were getting increasingly ambitious, so the total budget would have to be reviewed (in 2014 the budget had reached NOK 300 000).

In particular, the older students were bringing bigger projects forward each year, which he took as a sign of developing talent. The scale of projects had been a little controversial, though. Guri explained that in a previous project in Oslo, she had teachers calling to ask how they could get their projects through the youth council, and she had had to explain that the youth council was for young people to be heard, not for teachers and parents to get their projects approved. There had been some controversy around some of the projects put forward in this DUK, too, with accusations that some parents had been pushing their local projects forward as student projects. For the organizers of the DUK, this pressure on young people was interpreted as akin to exploitation, and against the spirit of self-determination that the youth council and DUK sought to establish. Guri also explained that the mayor was exceptionally good at the role, treating the students with respect, and being supportive and encouraging, and remaining genial throughout the process. This pedagogical approach was crucial to the success of the DUK, since the key element was that all the students should feel that their voices had been heard and their ideas taken seriously, whether or not they were eventually successful in the vote.

Returning to the chamber after the break, each group was invited in turn to walk to the speaker's podium and present their project, using overhead slides if they wished, and giving an argument for why it should be funded rather than other projects. Groups were given five minutes each to present, but most of the groups presented their ideas very briefly, with little detail, using only two or three of the minutes at their disposal, much the opposite of the methods used by adult politicians in the normal council meetings. The proposals were put forward very positively, that is, not using threats or warnings of dire consequences if their proposals were ignored, as adult politicians sometimes do. One boy waxed almost lyrical about the idyllic place where his group lived, close to a lake and with access through a canal to two more lakes where they could bathe. But bathing could be dull in the end, so they proposed putting in facilities, canoes, a jetty, beach volleyball, and a boat so that kids from all over the district could come and enjoy this lovely place. Another group presented their project using PowerPoint slides, but with no comment, and the mayor responded with complements for a very elegant presentation, but advised them that it would be more persuasive if they talked about it too. One group proposed buying video cameras to loan out for kids to record all the interesting things going on in the area, and another suggested sporting facilities and a music studio, which would be better than sitting at home watching TV (in 2000, this pre-dated the rapid expansion of digital home equipment). Once each group had presented their ideas, the debate adjourned for lunch.

Over lunch, negotiations started to get more serious. Two slightly older boys started to try to put together a joint proposal including projects from each zone of the district, to try to get something for everyone rather than all the money going to one big project, leaving other areas with nothing.

Theirs was one of the smaller projects, and they clearly were attempting to ensure their project was funded by gathering support from similarly sized projects. Another group of older students attempted to persuade younger participants to side with their projects, offering them small concessions in return for their support. Some of the younger participants were upset by this cattle trading, feeling pressured to give way to bigger students and bigger projects. Having imbibed the rhetoric of fair process, self-determination, even competition, and so on, the reality of corridor politics and deal making was an unpleasant jolt to some of them. While the older and more confident students operated in classic political mode, their clever operations made the others appear naïve and idealistic. Had they really thought that their proposals would just be put forward and then voted on without further comment?

Another session in the chamber offered all the students the opportunity to ask questions of the other groups and defend their own projects in response to questions or comments. In each case, a spokesperson for the group walked to the speaker's podium, bringing notes to refer to and speaking into the microphone on the podium for a limited number of minutes. They had been well prepared and understood the way they should present their ideas, and how to refer to proposals by reference number, for example. Some were nervous, hesitating, and breathless, while others were confident, even charismatic, testing out their chosen persona at the podium.

After this round of debate, at the end of the day, a vote was called, with each group presenting the number of transferable votes they were giving to each project. Once all the votes were tallied, the mayor announced that the youth council had decided to fund a centrally located music studio, and to contribute towards football equipment in one district and ice hockey equipment in another. The outcome of the vote was later reported in the local newspaper, which regularly reported on local council debates (debates that were also televised—and watched). As the newspaper reported, the aim of the whole process was obviously to teach the students to participate in a democratic process of prioritization. They could propose concrete, short-term policies for improvements in their neighborhoods, or to develop the district as a better place to live. The selected proposals would be implemented in the period April to June of the same year. In repeating the council's press release in this way, the local news media helped to secure the concept of the DUK as a pedagogical exercise with real intent and concrete outcomes, but it also helped to naturalize the council's broader political approach, in the context of what was then a coalition council between conservative and neo-liberal parties. Their overall philosophy entailed a rhetoric of transferring responsibility for the district from the council, as an administrative organism, to the citizens, or in their terms, away from dependency, and towards a balance between rights and responsibilities (see Abram 2007b).

While the rhetoric surrounding this event was about empowering young people to speak for themselves and to do so through the mechanisms and forms of local government, there were several kinds of learning going on. Students were learning the practices of municipal association—when to speak, how to address the chair, how to behave appropriately in the council chamber, and so on. This was the explicit aim of the exercise, from the municipality's point of view. At the same time, though, students were learning some harsh lessons about realpolitik, how deals are brokered, how pressure is exerted and experienced in the political process, and how stronger individuals can intimidate others. One could argue that for some of the students, much of the learning was about how to be a political actor, and how effective political actors operate. Some of the younger and less confident students were upset by the brash force with which older boys,[10] in particular, pushed their own agendas. Intimidating tactics were experienced as unpleasant, and some of the students turned to the teachers supporting the event for help. They were not given a great deal of sympathy, instead being left to understand that this was the tough world of politics. For some students, the experience of alienation led them to state that they would not get involved again, feeling that the whole system was unfair, but others were clearly getting a taste for the fray. Students were discovering their abilities or limitations as political actors, identifying the possibilities for democratic activity, and recognizing the way that some students could behave in powerful ways. It wasn't clear whether the nerve-wracking experience of speaking in public helped some of the students to gain in confidence, but it seemed apparent that the process affected them in different ways. Becoming disillusioned constituted an important experience for some of the participants.

The pedagogical framework itself can be understood as being mixed. It promised students a voice through a supportive democratic structure, yet enabled them to learn through experience how political deals are done in practice, how much back-room bargaining is entailed, and how far some participants were prepared to intimidate others for their own interests, sometimes explicitly, and sometimes with hidden agendas. The concrete outcomes of the democratic process were intrinsic, ensuring that participants would see real results for themselves in a timescale that was meaningful to school students (in contrast to much council business whose outcomes could be difficult to isolate from other influences, including national and international laws and regulations, and broader socio-economic contextual factors). These apparently conflicting messages suggested ambivalence about political processes, demonstrating that it requires participants to play by rules, but also to play with and around the rules if they were to be effective political actors.

Conclusions: Learning by/and Doing

The two examples discussed in this paper offer an insight into the varied registers of learning how to meet. In the youth council an expressly pedagogical intent was orchestrated by the local authority through the practice of political process in a controlled setting. The rules were clear and simplified, since only one budget was to be debated, and only one proposal per group was to be considered. There were no political party groupings in evidence, and consequences were relatively immediate. The exercise was set up to ensure that students should see the meeting of the council as the arena in which their voices could be heard and decisions could be made based on the hearing of information, and students were supposed to see how they could develop a political persona and imagine themselves as future politicians. Yet in practice, of course, the peripheral hard lessons of politics were also glimpsed; some participants felt that they had not done their proposals justice, and some felt pressured by more powerful groups, while others began to get a taste for doing deals and practicing realpolitik.

As a pedagogical project, its explicit intention was that the students should learn about democratic process, but there is little doubt that many adult politicians in the daily life of council politics are also learning through doing. Not only the deputies pictured at the start of the chapter, whose learning was again explicit, but also the long-standing elected representatives who continue to discipline and self-discipline from meeting to meeting (see Abram 2007a, 2004). Bureaucrats, too, gradually learn—both by experience and from colleagues—how to behave in meetings, how to prepare effectively, and how to cope with the discipline that the council meeting form imposes upon them. In their restrained behavior, bureaucrats practice bodily the separation of powers that defines the Norwegian political system. This provides particular challenges for those who play both roles—as elected representatives also employed by the municipality in bureaucratic roles. These individuals are constantly on guard against themselves, asking themselves whom they are speaking for in any meeting. If they cannot learn to master this discipline, they are obliged to stand down from one of the roles for the sake of political correctness (literally).

Participants in meetings learn to invoke the authority of the state through repeated practices of using role-names; referring to other meetings; choosing political rhetoric for symbolic effect; referring to statutes, regulations, shared knowledge, or norms. In invoking the state in this way, they reinforce the impression that it exists. Such practices must be done with skill that is learned largely through participation, observation, and experience. The skills learned are constantly tested, since meetings are not always predictable. They could therefore be understood as classic social skills; without delving into detailed debates about social practice, it is useful to invoke the idea that social action is a kind of improvisation or extemporization building on learned patterns and categories applied in new ways.

People learn how to accord with the practice of municipal meetings through direct pedagogy and social coercion, often observed through situated peripheral participation and what is sometimes called trial and error. These clearly demonstrate that local authority meeting practices can be explored as a form of learned, adapted, and complex behaviors that politicians and administrators are constantly feeling their way around, improving their skills, and testing in new circumstances. This involves the pushing and building of roles and their boundaries, self-scrutiny, and attempts to fit in with sometimes very restricted opportunities for self-expression. The particular practices described from Norwegian municipal contexts show how moral norms of political behavior—strict separation of politics and administration, avoidance of nepotism, bribery or other forms of corruption, emphasizing equalities and participatory democracy, and so on—are regularly enacted in performance of meetings. Just as the health workers described in Schwartzman's ethnography of the meeting were making their organization real through meeting in and about it, municipal actors are creating the state in the image of normative democratic ideals, tempered by their experience of everyday politics.

Identifying local authority meetings as an ethnographic object thus offers insight into political practice and the normalization of state presence, and the legitimizing effects of routine governance practices. As these actors produce the state through their practices, they are simultaneously discovering and negotiating the extent to which they share a vision of what the state could, and should be. One might argue that much of the political process consists of just this—the tussle over defining what the state is, where its limits are, and what its role in civic life should be. Recognizing the learning that practitioners engage in at each meeting highlights that the state consists of practices that are constantly in production, contributing to the current focus on ontological approaches in the social sciences, and showing how the legitimacy and authority of government is reproduced.

Acknowledgements

I thank all the participants identified in the text, especially Guri Sæther and Lise Lund, for welcoming me into the municipality. I am particularly grateful to the editors and contributors to this volume for their insightful and inspiring comments on earlier drafts.

Notes

1 "The state is not the reality which stands behind the mask of political practice. It is itself the mask which prevents our seeing political practice as it is" (Abrams 1988: 58).
2 Based on ethnographic fieldwork mostly between 1997 and 2005. Fieldwork in 2000 was made possible by a visiting fellowship from the Department of Anthropology of the University of Oslo.
3 In what Appadurai calls "regimes of value" (1986).
4 Norwegian elections use a system of direct proportional representation. According to official guidance: "The Norwegian electoral system is based on the principles of direct election and proportional representation in multi-member electoral

divisions. Direct election means that the electors vote directly for representatives of their constituency by giving their vote to an electoral list. Proportional representation means that the representatives are distributed according to the relationship to one another of the individual electoral lists in terms of the number of votes they have received. Both political parties and other groups can put up lists at elections." From the Ministry of Local Government and Modernization. https://www.regjeringen.no/en/portal/election-portal/the-norwegian-electoral-system/id456636/ (Accessed 10 Jan 2016)

5 The two small settlements differed mainly by location—one at the fjord's edge, the other high in the valley. The former had better communications (regular visiting boats, closer roads) and was the seat of the council; the latter had more employment as well as a larger farming community. Little else distinguished them. A football field was equidistant between the two settlements.

6 Religious adherence varies across the country, with some areas of particularly strong religious fervor referred to as "the bible belt," notably around the Southern coast and some way up the West coast. Norway has a Protestant state church, with strong Lutheran influence, as well as more puritanical sects (particularly around the southern and western coasts and in the far North).

7 Levinson (2011) outlines a history of education in "civics," pointing out how little anthropological attention it has attracted from educational anthropology.

8 In common with other European countries such as Finland and France: see Alapuro (2005).

9 Almost all schools in Norway are state-run, although recent educational reforms sought to establish a private school sector.

10 I have not focused specifically on gender in this article, but this does not imply that it is not a significant issue in this context.

References

Abram, Simone. "Personality and professionalism in a Norwegian district council." *Planning Theory* 3(2004): 21–40.

Abram, Simone. "Loyalty and politics: The discourses of liberalisation." In *Professional Identities: Policy and Practice in Business and Bureaucracy*, edited by Shirley Ardener and Fiona Moore, 87–107. Oxford: Berghahn, 2007a.

Abram, Simone. "Participatory depoliticisation: The bleeding heart of neo-liberalism." In *Cultures et Pratiques Participatives: Perspectives Comparatives*, edited by Catherine Neveu, 113–133. Paris: l'Harmattan, 2007b.

Abram, Simone. *Culture and Planning.* Aldershot: Ashgate, 2011.

Abram, Simone and Gisa Weszkalnys, eds. *Elusive Promises: Planning in the Contemporary world.* Oxford: Berghahn, 2013.

Abrams, Philip. "Notes on the difficulty of studying the state." *Journal of Historical Sociology* 1(1977/1988): 58–89.

Alapuro, Risto. "Associations and contention in France and Finland: Constructing the society and describing the society." *Scandinavian Political Studies* 28(4) (2005): 377–399.

Anderson, Sally. "Civil society and childhood education." In *A Companion to the Anthropology of Education*, edited by Bradley A. U. Levinson and Mica Pollock, 316–332. Malden, Oxford and Chichester: Wiley-Blackwell, 2011.

Appadurai, Arjun. "Commodities and the politics of value." In *The Social Life of Things*, edited by Arjun Appadurai, 3–63. Cambridge: Cambridge University Press, 1986.

Citrine, Walter (Sir). *ABC of Chairmanship: All about Meetings and Conferences*. London, Manchester and Newcastle: Cooperative Printing Society, 1939.

Evans, Gillian. *Educational Failure and Working Class White Children in Britain*. Basingstoke: Palgrave Macmillan, 2006.

Foucault, Michel. "Governmentality." In *The Foucault Effect: Studies in Governmentality*, edited by Graham Burchell, Colin Gordon and Peter Miller, 87–104. London: Harvester Wheatsheaf, [1978] 1991.

Foucault, Michel. *Discipline and Punish: The Birth of the Prison*. Harmondsworth: Penguin Books, 1979.

Gupta, Akhil. "Blurred boundaries: The discourse of corruption, the culture of politics, and the imagined state." *American Ethnologist* 22(1995): 375–402.

Hacking, Ian. *The Taming of Chance*. Cambridge: Cambridge University Press, 1990.

Latour, Bruno and Steve Woolgar. *Laboratory Life: The Construction of Scientific Facts*. Princeton, NJ: Princeton University Press, 1986.

Lave, Jean and Etienne Wenger. *Situated Learning: Legitimate Peripheral Participation*. Cambridge: Cambridge University Press, 1991.

Levinson, Bradley A. U. "Toward an anthropology of (democratic) citizenship education." In *A Companion to the Anthropology of Education*, edited by Bradley A. U. Levinson and Mica Pollock, 279–298. Malden, Oxford and Chichester: Wiley-Blackwell, 2011.

Miller, Peter. "Accounting and objectivity: The invention of calculating selves and calculable spaces." *Annals of Scholarship* 9(1992): 61–86.

Peacock, James L. *The Anthropological Lens: Harsh Light, Soft Focus*. Cambridge: Cambridge University Press, 2001.

Rian, Øystein. *Maktens historie i dansketiden*. Oslo: Makt- og demokratiutredningen 1998-2003. (2003).

Richards, Audrey and Adam Kuper, eds. *Councils in Action*. Cambridge: Cambridge University Press, 1971.

Rose, Nicholas. "Governing by numbers: Figuring out democracy in accounting." *Organisations and Society* 16(1991): 673–692.

Rose, Nicholas. "Expertise and the government of conduct." *Studies in Law, Politics and Society* 4(1994): 359–397.

Salamon, Karen Lisa Goldschmidt. "Possessed by enterprise. Values and value-creation in mandrake management." In *Magic, Culture and the New Economy*, edited by Orvar Löfgren and Robert Willim, 47–56. New York: Berg, 2005.

Schwartzman, Helen B. *The Meeting: Gatherings in Organizations and Communities*. New York: Springer, 1989.

Strathern, Marilyn. *Partial Connections*. Updated Edition. New York: Alta Mira Press, 1991/2004.

Tranvik, Tommy and Per Selle. "State and citizens in Norway: Organisational society and state – municipal relations." *West European Politics* 28(2005): 852–871.

Tropman, John E. *Effective Meetings: Improving Group Decision Making*. Third Edition. Beverley Hills, CA: Sage, 2014.

Vike, Halvard. "Culminations of complexity: Cultural dynamics in Norwegian local government." *Anthropological Theory* 2(2002): 57–75.

Ween, Gro B. and Simone Abram. "The Norwegian trekking association: Trekking as constituting the nation." *Journal of Landscape Research* 37(2012): 155–171.

3 Argentinean *Asamblea* Meetings as Assemblage

Presence in Emergence

Susann Baez Ullberg and Karin Skill

Introduction: *Asambleas* in Argentina

In the semi-desert landscape of the northwestern Argentinean province of Catamarca, by the foothills of the Andes Mountains, a group of people had gathered under an *algarrobo* tree for a meeting on a spring evening in 2013. They were the *asambleistas* of the Asamblea El Algarrobo, deliberating on actions to take against the mining company threatening the town's water supply with the extraction of precious metals by explosives, water, and chemicals in an open-pit mine project. Five kilometers away, in the town center of Andalgalá, the local office of the transnational mining corporation Agua Rica is located two blocks from the town's main square. As a means of communicating protest, the *asambleistas* had raised funds to build their own radio station by the meeting site with technical support from skilled alternative media activists from Buenos Aires. The antenna reached out to the evening sky, providing the *asambleistas* with both radio waves and an Internet connection. Just next to the *algarrobo* tree was the gravel road leading up to the mining site in the mountains. Large piles of stones and car tires on the side of the road reminded one of the roadblock that the *asambleistas* had been assembling since 2010 in order to stop the mining machines from entering "their" mountain. In the area there were rubber bullets dispersed from the violent encounter on February 15, 2010, when the provincial police Kuntur attempted to lift the roadblock to make way for the mining excavators. Numerous videos that depict this event were uploaded by the *asambleistas* to YouTube, resulting in thousands of views and comments among *asambleistas*. The *wiphala* flag, representing the indigenous peoples of the Andes, moved in the wind. On the side of the road was a banner with the colorful logo of the Asamblea, created by one of the artistically skilled *asambleistas*, depicting the *algarrobo* tree extending its roots deep into the soil, and with a slogan that connects this mining conflict to others taking place in Argentina and Latin America. At stake to the *asambleistas* in Andalgalá was the transformation of the landscape and their environment. At the *asamblea* meeting that night, a sense of urgency and even emergency prevailed—the catastrophe was lurking in the distance.

DOI: 10.4324/9781315559407-4

Seven hundred kilometers southeast of Andalgalá is Santa Fe City, located on the shores of the Paraná River and the Salado River in the La Plata Basin, a region characterized by humid weather and high temperatures. A few years before the Algarrobo *asamblea* meeting described above, on the evening of April 28, 2005, members from the many groups and individuals constituting the Asamblea Permanente de Afectados por la Inundación[1] had gathered in the city's main square. They were there to plan the actions and activities taking place the following day to commemorate the second anniversary of the flood that had struck the city two years earlier and to call for political accountability for the disaster. The social protests, consisting of street manifestations, public declarations, scientific investigations, and court cases, had been organized through regular *asamblea* meetings since 2004. That evening, members from the group the Black Tent had set up their tent in a military green color and put a black tarpaulin on the top of it. Between the lush trees in the square they had hung the large white banner, by now greyish and ragged, from the first year of protest, which read "Black Tent of Memory and Dignity." A large white stone, reminiscent of a gravestone by way of its form and inscription reading "Neither oblivion, nor pardon [of the government's omission]"[2] was placed next to the tent and facing the House of Government, symbolically facing the key site of political responsibility for the 2003 disaster. The previous year, more than a hundred wooden crosses had been stuck into the ground in the opposite corner of the square by another group in the Asamblea, the Torches March, to remember those who perished in the disaster and its aftermath. That evening in April 2005, activists in the Black Tent were planning to stand vigil in the tent overnight and start early the next morning with the street radio broadcasting directly from the square in which anybody would be allowed to participate. Upon being asked, they stated that they participated in the meeting as *inundados*, flood victims that the state had abandoned. Earlier that morning, a press conference meeting had been organized to present an independent technical inquiry into the causes of the 2003 flood disaster, commissioned by the plaintiffs in the lawsuit that some of the *asamblea* activists had pursued against the government. This meeting was introduced by Diana, one of the plaintiffs, sitting at a table covered with a white cloth next to an altar and in front of a large map of the city. On her left was an old lady dressed in the emblematic white head scarf, one of the local representatives of the well-known Argentinean human rights organization, the Mothers of Plaza de Mayo. On Diana's right were two young female lawyers representing the plaintiffs and, next to them, an older man, a professor of water engineering from the city's university and himself a disaster victim whom the Asamblea had commissioned as a technical expert. After Diana's introductory speech, the technical expert presented his report, which confirmed and even sharpened the conclusions of other expert inquiries that had been conducted. These reports contributed to the legal argument of the plaintiffs and to the moral argument of the *inundados* activists. By associating the claims of the *asamblea* with symbols of grief and violence, most notably that of the struggle of the human rights movement, the *asambleistas* achieved temporal and spatial resonance to other prior social protests (cf. Alonso et al 2007). The very presence of members/mothers from the Mothers of the Plaza de Mayo in the *asamblea* meetings in Santa Fe City (Ullberg 2013: 139, 146) or the Nobel Peace Laureate Adolfo Perez Esquivel in many different contemporary *asambleas* in Argentina (Salmenkari 2009; Ullberg 2013) empowered the claim in the public eye by appealing to this emblematic legacy.

These introductory vignettes of two different assembly meetings in Argentina aim at illustrating ethnographically the *asamblea* meeting as an assemblage constituted by heterogeneous elements like people, ideas, landscapes, knowledge, material and technologies, that is formed through a process of what Turnbull (2000) calls "social labor." This specific temporal-spatial conjuncture is what endows the *asamblea* meeting with its social and political capacity (DeLanda 2006). In twenty-first-century Argentina, the *asamblea* has emerged as a form of and for grassroots political mobilization. It is largely associated with the widespread dissatisfaction with representative democracy during the turmoil of 2001–2002, but has also been common in socio-environmental controversies (cf. Weinstock 2007: Skill and Grinberg 2011) and in post-disaster accountability protests (Salmenkari 2009: Ullberg 2013), in which the health and wellbeing of the locals is emphasized. Environmental disasters and risks transform people into activists/*asambleistas* who demand justice. They deal with technically and scientifically complex issues concerning anti-flood devices, open-pit mining, and climate change, that simultaneously connect global and local scales (Hastrup 2013). The Argentinean *asambleas* bear transnational traits of contemporary collective action, involving citizen participation, horizontal decision-making, deliberation, and consensus-seeking. Yet, they also feature particular discourses and practices related to the Argentinean political setting and to historical continuities in terms of collective action in Argentina and Latin America (Vara 2013), which also influence how contemporary *asambleas* are understood and organized. By *asamblea* we refer here both to a group of people constituting a collective actor and to the meetings in which the *asamblea* is constantly made. While assemblies as a meeting form are carried out in all kinds of formal and informal organizations, the *asamblea* referred to in this setting involves ideas and practices of direct democracy in which the assembly meetings are absolutely central. This chapter will examine the Argentinean *asamblea* as an assemblage, drawing on ethnographic research carried out in the last decade. The question that guides this chapter is thus, what is actually assembled during the meetings—that is, who and what is included and engaged, or omitted and excluded?

Assemblage Theory and Methodology: A Roadmap

Assemblage theory builds on a realist and materialist ontology (Deleuze and Guattari 2003: 15; DeLanda 2006) and forms part of what is currently labeled the post-humanist, ontological, or material turn (cf. Åsberg et al 2012). We propose this perspective as a productive approach to trace processes of collective action and the role of meetings in such processes. In the context of the work of Deleuze and Guattari, it has been noted that in French, to trace also means to draw, copy, and open a road (Deleuze and Guattari 2003: xvi). The term can thus be used metaphorically and methodologically as a strategy to "break away from the beaten paths" (Deleuze and Guattari 2003: xiii). As anthropologists we believe that using the assembly theory framework will enable us to inquire and to make a roadmap of what actually is assembled during the *asamblea* meetings, beyond discursive expressions and ideas. In this way we hope to make an analytical-methodological contribution to the present anthology of meeting ethnography.

Assemblages become in relation to other assemblages, like an *asamblea* meeting becomes in relation to the nation-state, social media, neoliberalism, transnational markets, the geography, and corporations, etc. This is the non-essentialist and exterior aspect of the assemblage—it is historically contingent (DeLanda 2006). Assemblages assemble heterogeneous elements that are both material and immaterial through processes of territorialization and deterritorialization (DeLanda 2006). The territorializing role maintains the elements and their relationships and thus, the durability of the assemblage. The deterritorializing role is made up of elements that recombine or replace elements in assemblage and can cause a reformation of the assemblage. Another aspect of this realist ontology is that an assemblage becomes larger the more elements that are assembled (DeLanda 2006). In this way "tools exist only in relation to the interminglings they make possible" (Deleuze and Guattari 2003: 90).

This text is an assemblage in itself (Deleuze and Guattari 2003). We have not only used a lot of "toxic ink and trees processed into paper" (Haraway 1988: 575) to make our points as researchers, but also our research experiences, field notes, computers, communication technology and wires. This chapter is the result of the collaboration in thinking and writing by two Swedish anthropologists who have both carried out fieldwork in Argentina in the twenty-first century, albeit in different projects. Our work comes together because it involves ethnography from different *asamblea* meetings that we have documented by way of our respective translocal and transtemporal fieldworks (cf. Ullberg 2013). Our scope is not comparative. We rather let our ethnographic cases mirror each other with the purpose of offering an analytical methodology to the anthropological study of meetings. Argentinean *asambleas* have a specific modus operandi (Rossi 2005) and there is a common protest mobilization pattern (Salmenkari 2009), which is influenced by a Latin American anti-imperialist discourse (Vara 2013).

DeLanda (2006: 28) argues that in order to avoid reification of the assemblages, researchers should focus on the historical processes that assemble elements. Assemblages do not just "appear," or "emerge," in the terminology of assemblage theory (DeLanda 2006: 28). To make (interdisciplinary) assemblage theory workable for anthropology, we suggest that Turnbull's (2000) concept of social labor can be used to analyze the very process of assembling. With this concept Turnbull refers to "the work of negotiation and judgement . . . put in to create the equivalences and connections that produce order and meaning" (2000: 13). We argue that it is important to focus also on the elements that have been discarded through social labor, in order to capture the contingency and non-linearity of assemblages. This is an argument for employing participant observation of the activities and the interaction that takes place at *asamblea* meetings.

Globalization and transnational neoliberalism of later decades seem to have spurred a renewed academic interest in how citizens organize (locally) to contest the effects of these politics (cf. Graeber 2009). Argentinean *asambleas* have proven attractive contemporary objects of academic study, just like the Zapatista movement in Mexico and the Brazilian Landless Workers' Movement (MST), perhaps because of their goal of reinventing the political and their desire for another possible world (Dinerstein 2003; Holdren and Souza 2005; Fernández et al 2008; Ouviña 2008). Argentineans have a long tradition of seeking political influence through gatherings in public places, plazas, and streets (Catela da Silva 2004; Salmenkari 2009), and later the anarchist movement has contributed with ideological influence (Rossi 2005). More recent examples in Argentina are the *piquetero* movement of unemployed workers, the popular *asambleas* that emerged in local neighborhoods to cope with the 2001–2002 economic crisis, and the closed-down factories taken over by the employees (Svampa and Pereyra 2003; Schuster and Pereyra 2001). Anthropologists have contributed to the understanding of these protests by analyzing how they are embedded in daily life (Manzano et al 2008). Inspired by recent anthropological work on social protest and grassroots mobilization (Graeber 2009; Juris 2012, Razsa 2015), we will analyze how the assembling process takes place at *asamblea* meetings.

Belonging and Becoming: Heterogeneous Configurations of People

It is generally claimed that everybody is welcome to participate in *asambleas*, where people meet because of common stakes and interests. Participants come from diverse backgrounds and have different experiences, knowledge, and cultural and symbolic resources (Svampa and Pereyra 2003). Sometimes however, they are made up of a core that is more homogenous in class or ideological terms (Rossi 2005). While the *asamblea* as an assemblage can be described as a contingent configuration of different material and nonmaterial elements, it is also a social community. As such, *asambleistas* not only identify with the cause at stake, but also have a strong sense of belonging to the *asamblea* community. One example of this sense is the activist in El Algarrobo who tattooed the *asamblea* logo on his upper arm. The non-essential aspect of assemblage theory emphasizes that different elements such as the *asambleistas* become in relation to other assemblages and through interaction (DeLanda 2006). As will be shown in the following, different bodies carrying different experiences and capacities are assembled at the *asamblea* meetings, which in turn "act back" on them. Hence, joining the *asamblea* meetings is belonging to the *asamblea*, but more importantly, it is becoming an *asambleista*.

Santa Fe City has close to 400,000 inhabitants. The Asamblea Permanente de Afectados por la Inundación started out as a social protest against the government's poor disaster preparedness and management of the disastrous flood in 2003 (Ullberg 2013). On April 29, 2003, 130,000 people living on a third of the city's territory were affected by the flood. People who participated in this *asamblea*, either as individuals or as members of a group, described themselves as *inundados*[3] regardless of whether or not they had actually been flooded and evacuated (Ullberg 2013: 112). The *asamblea* meetings turned victims into activists who claimed justice and compensation from the government by enacting protests in public. In the beginning, when the activists mounted an occupation of the city's main square in front of the House of Government, there were not enough available shifts for so many volunteers. These victims-turned-activists hurried to and fro between the square, their homes, and their jobs, keeping guard of the occupation day and night, and spending hours in the same square to deliberate in long *asamblea* meetings on how to pursue their goals. Their anger and determination to make the city remember the disaster and acknowledge the victims was what kept them going. The number of *inundados* occupying the square decreased during the six months that the protest lasted, however. The inconveniences were many, not least from the municipality that shut down electricity and threatened the *asamblea* with eviction. From hundreds of activists, only a dozen people remained at the end of the occupation of the square at the end of that year. In the years to come, this number would vary between a thousand participants in the yearly protest meetings on the anniversaries of the disaster, a hundred people in the assembly meetings preceding the protest meetings, and a dozen core individuals the rest of the year. The density and intensity of the *asamblea* is shifting during a year, and influences the meetings.

One of these *asambleistas* was Marta, a woman in her fifties who lived in one of the affected neighborhoods. She was the divorced mother of three teenage boys and had worked as a secretary most of her life. Prior to the 2003 disaster, she had never been affected by flooding despite living next to the flood-prone outskirts of the city. In the years following the disaster, she struggled to get back on her feet, both economically and psychologically. The engagement as a self-evacuee and *inundada*, Marta said, was painful because neither the government nor the judges had responded to any of their demands. Yet the protests she participated in were also rewarding because she had met so many other people with whom she shared the experience of being a flood victim. The assembly meetings were not only deliberations about strategies of protest, but also occasions of processing and making meaning of a traumatic experience and learn about citizen rights. Marta had never before been politically active or participated in a street protest. Even if several participants in the *asamblea* participated as representatives for different NGOs, and thus had prior experience of activism, a majority of the *inundados* activists were beginners in terms of social and political mobilization.

In the small town of Andalgalá the Asamblea El Algarrobo was founded on December 14, 2009, when several people, guided by a teacher, initiated a roadblock to stop the machines from entering the Agua Rica mining project. The inhabitants had prior experience of the establishment of the first Argentinean large-scale copper and gold mine, La Alumbrera, located in the same province. But in the mid-1990s, they just stood by watching and waiting for 'progress' to come to town (cf. Mastrangelo 2004). Progress didn't show up, and with time they felt betrayed and mobilized in protest against the new mining project Agua Rica.

The foundation of an *asamblea* is intimately connected to a public protest. With the foundation of the Asamblea El Algarrobo, which resisted the mining project by direct action and blocking the road, the local population became divided into pro-mining and anti-mining residents. The pro-mining residents accused the anti-mining ones of being "hippies," "against progress," and "outsiders" who cared more about the environment than progress in a region characterized by poverty and underdevelopment. A group of young people who had moved from the megalopolis Buenos Aires to rural Andalgalá in search of an "alternative" non-urban (or neo-rural) lifestyle indeed formed part of the core of the Asamblea El Algarrobo. Among the heterogeneous group of *asambleistas*—men and women, young and old people alike—there was a strong collective identification of resistance, based on the notion that they were the underdogs fighting against a stronger enemy, which was a transnational mining company and a corrupt state. There was also a strong territorial sense. Taken together, local and territorial, and transnational and cosmopolitan emotions and identities are elements that are mobilized in the *asamblea*.

In this section we have depicted how *asamblea* meetings are heterogeneous configurations, assembling different people and groups of people, regardless of whether they are affected directly or indirectly, or if they are 'authentic' victims of an event. The issue of 'authenticity' has been problematized in anthropological studies of ethnic and indigenous identities. Assemblage theory however focuses on the becoming and is hence non-essentialist (DeLanda 2006), yet based on embodied experience. In assemblage theory, the concept of affect and the capacity or ability to affect and be affected is central as a social force that makes becoming (Deleuze and Guattari 2003: xvi). That is, the sharing of experiences, places, and practices, and the embodying presence in time and place in the *asambleas*, can produce a strong sense of "feelingfulness" (cf. Feld 1982). Our ethnographic cases give account of this feature. Local residents and "alternative" urbanites join against the mining project in rural Andalgalá, and flood victims with no prior experience of political activism along with experienced NGO members in Santa Fe City unite in the claim for accountability. Different people become *asambleistas* through the affects, knowledges, and identities produced in *asamblea* meetings.

Practices and Participation: Ideas and Discourses in Tension

The notion of openness and inclusiveness in the *asamblea* ideology is enabled by organizing *asamblea* meetings in public (and symbolic) spaces in order to make them accessible like the city's main square or under a tree. This bears similarity to other contemporary public meetings in distinct places such as those in a public square of Quebec with the global justice movement (Graeber 2009), in New York City (Juris 2012) and Ljubljana (Razsa 2015) with the Occupy movement, and with those of the Hamar male herders in Ethiopia who gather under a shade tree (Strecker 2013). This openness and accessibility can have surprising connotations. At one Asamblea El Algarrobo meeting in December 2010, forty-something participants of all ages, gender, and, judging from the dialects, from different regions, had gathered around the *algarrobo* tree. Despite the strong local and territorial identity, the local *asambleistas* did not mind that people from other parts of the country, or other parts of the world, joined them and their struggle, even if it was for just one day. Increased connections enlarge the network. In the middle of this particular meeting, representatives from a national NGO suddenly showed up at the site of the meeting together with a famous Argentinean singer called Axel. The NGO had invited the singer to give a free concert the following day, as part of the *asamblea* anniversary festivities that would take place in the town center. Many *asambleistas* started to call friends and family members to take a picture with him. In the midst of this excitement, a middle-aged man remarked sourly, however, that to crash the meeting and engage famous artists instead of listening to the voice of ordinary citizens showed that the NGO had a different ideology than the *asamblea*.

Our ethnography shows how ideological and political heterogeneity sometimes turn into divisions within the *asambleas*, which are manifested in different ways. In the Asamblea El Algarrobo, tensions were mainly related to the fact that several *asambleistas* participated as political candidates in the local and provincial elections in 2011 and later accepted positions in the local government (Skill, field notes). In Santa Fe City, disaster victims were offered some economic aid by the provincial government as a means to facilitate recovery and reconstruction, on the condition that they would not bring any charges to the government (Ullberg 2013: 79–80). Many of the *inundados* activists accepted these terms, considering that the money would enable them a new start after the disaster. In both cases, the decisions of these activists were considered by their fellow *asambleista*s as acts of betrayal and moral corruption, which led to a decreased level of participation at large. In the case of Santa Fe, the "traitors" stopped attending the meetings because of the conflicts (Ullberg 2013: 146), while the *asambleistas* who turned into politicians and bureaucrats in Andalgalá were considered to have taken control of the Asamblea El Algarrobo and paid lip service to the expressed ideal of not engaging in party politics (cf. Ouviña 2008). These are examples of elements that can lead to dissipation and/or reformulation of the assemblage, which indicate that the notion of inclusiveness has limits.

The openness of *asambleas* implies that there is no requirement to sign up for the meeting beforehand. People just show up, and it is almost impossible to control the number and loyalty of participants. In February 2012, a tense moment arose in Andalgalá when pro-mining representatives adopted *asamblea* methods and blocked the main roads into town, to attempt to hinder people from other parts of the country from participating in the *Asamblea*'s commemorative activities of the repression in 2010. There were rumors about the special police force Kuntur coming to attempt to lift the roadblock again. These events made people gather in *asamblea* by the *algarrobo* tree. There were at least a hundred participants (compared to the ten to twenty during the rest of the year) who discussed how to prepare for a possible clash with the police, including illegal strategies. Several *asambleistas* had already been reported to the police for their participation in previous activities, turning their political participation into an illicit engagement. As the participants deliberated, a group of mainly young men left the meeting and walked some hundred meters away to actually get physically prepared. Interlocutors in the *asamblea* later revealed that these tactics stem from experiences during the clashes between demonstrators and police in the so-called Argentinazo in 2001.[4] It was in this context that a person was discovered recording the *asamblea* meeting, and was hurried away. Because it was a small community, someone had seen him enter the mining office earlier, and was suspicious of his intentions. The openness of *asambleas* thus implies unpredictability and constitutes a challenge to "security" and planning, yet it is a key aspect of the ideology of the asamblea and a central feature of the experimental nature of the assemblage. The ideology of openness has certain restrictions.

Organization and Objects: Communicating Experience and Experiment

Asamblea meetings are organized so that no particular member or group should take a leading role. The meetings are ". . . pure zones of social experiment, spaces in which activists can treat one another as they feel people ought to treat each other, and to begin to create something of the social world they wish to bring out" (Graeber 2009: 287). The *asamblea* of the *inundados* in Santa Fe City were organized by evacuees in evacuation centers located in schools and churches, and neighborhood associations. The calls for meetings were spread by word of mouth between neighbors as they were cleaning their flooded houses or queuing for the government's food boxes. As information about the government's negligence and mismanagement of the disaster was published, indignation also increased among citizens. Repeated assembly meetings among evacuees all over the city led to the establishment of one coordinating *asamblea*, in which representatives from all the *asambleas* participated. It was at these coordinating *asamblea* meetings that the occupation of the main square in July 2003, mentioned earlier, was proposed, discussed and planned. Despite conflicts and disagreements between the groups and activists that participated in the occupation, the *asamblea* was formally constituted a year after the disaster in order to better organize the activities of claim and protest enacted by different individuals and groups. Individuals were from then on supposed to join any of the groups and organizations that constituted the *asamblea*, but could also continue as individual participants.

Striving for horizontality and equality, tasks within a given *asamblea* often rotate among participants in order not to become permanent assignments. In the Unión de Asambleas Ciudadanas[5] (UAC) this means for example that different local *asambleas* around the country should arrange and host the meetings. Representatives of different Argentinean *asambleas* in different parts of the country meet three times a year in order to share experiences and support the strengthening of local mobilization and the power of claims (cf. Ouviña 2008). Due to the costs and time involved in travelling in this vast country, the majority of the meeting participants tend to come from the region where the particular UAC meeting is organized. The tenth UAC meeting was held in San Salvador de Jujuy in the northernmost province of Argentina in July 2009. Some *asambleistas* had spent days traveling by bus from other parts of the country. It was very cold in the big bunkhouse where the meeting was held. The bunkhouse belonged to one of the organizations that were in charge of hosting this meeting and it was so big that a microphone was needed for the speakers to be heard. Instead of sitting in a circle, which is more common at *asamblea* meetings, the meeting participants were seated on benches facing a stage at the end of the hall, where two facilitators were standing. The program mixed open discussions with organized educational activities. We argue, in line with Garsten and Sörbom in their chapter of this book, that meetings can be analyzed as sites where a sociality of experience and experiment is encouraged (cf. Rabinow 2003: 87). This turns *asambleas* into a kind of social laboratory. In the UAC meeting, one of the educational activities was to make a big map in which all the socio-environmental problems of the country were placed. Another task was to enact a role play. During the role play, approximately a third of the more than one hundred participants were told by the facilitators to act as if they were at a street demonstration. Four *asambleistas* were acting out at the middle of the backyard where the activity took place, while the other participants were instructed to intervene in different ways in order to enhance and empower the action. The facilitators explained that the purpose was to articulate and reinforce the links between deliberation, pedagogy, and direct action (Skill, field notes). This can be seen as an illustration of how the *asamblea* is assembled into a "body who thinks by doing" (Mattini 2002 in Dinerstein 2003: 197).

The *asamblea* is fundamentally a space of communication and, as such, a practice of social labor, both internally among *asamblea* members but also towards the surrounding community. *Asambleas* increasingly use social media such as Facebook to communicate internally and externally, and even create their own communication "hardware." In Andalgalá, the majority of the local radio stations broadcasted publicity for the mining companies, which speak about their "total care for the environment" and "sustainable" mining activities. The anti-mining stance of the Asamblea El Algarrobo hardly registered in local mass media, which was the reason they gathered funds to build their own radio station in 2011. This enabled the *asamblea* to be in control of the programs, what information is published and what publicity to allow, and thereby to make public a counter-discourse to that of the company. However, without *asambleistas* who work at the radio, it becomes a tool that doesn't enable any "interminglings" (Deleuze and Guattari 2003: 90).

Asamblea meetings strive to assure that all participants get to express their viewpoints (Fernández et al 2008). There is often a facilitator who sees to this and who moderates the discussions during the meetings. Participants nod to the facilitator or raise their hand to get signed up to speak. Some repeat more or less the same message as the previous speaker. Every now and then someone removes their name from the list by stating that their argument has already been voiced, but it is as likely that someone shares a lengthy opinion. In our respective fieldwork at UAC, in Andalgalá, and in Santa Fe City, we have observed that the ways that participants with no prior experience of this kind of public engagement deal with this varies, however. Some people, like Marta, seem like "natural talents" in speaking. She was so outspoken and charismatic that eventually she became one of the spokeswomen of the Asamblea Permanente, illustrating how a specific person *becomes* in relation to the assemblage. Other *asamblea* members do not feel "well spoken" and do not dare to share their viewpoints or ask for clarifications if they do not understand. They instead struggle to formulate their arguments about what action to take. This implies that there are heterogeneous ways to deal with expressing opinions in a crowded setting, given that "public discussions provide a forum where people can persuade others through skillful oratory" (Rosaldo 1973 in Brison 1989: 97). Meetings can thus have several functions, apart from taking and enforcing decisions (Brison 1989). Negotiations about what should actually be communicated to the public take place at *asambleas*. In post-disaster Santa Fe City, *asamblea* activists produced numerous statements and short reports issued as *documentos* (Ullberg 2013: 135–136). The *documentos* were presented at press conferences or read out loud during the demonstrations, and were then kept as written declarations, or artefacts of memory, of the Asamblea Permanente. In the years 2004–2005, at least fourteen such documents were produced and issued to the public. The *documentos* varied in length, ranging from one or two pages to seven or eight pages long. The writing of the *documentos* was a collective authorship that mostly took place during long *asamblea* meetings like the *asamblea* meeting in April 2005 described in the introductory vignette, which was to be read out loud during the ceremony. Many different authors had written different pieces of text that now had to be put together into one single statement. Emilio, one of the independent activists, read the draft out loud. A passage from a report issued by the House of Human Rights, which had been presented at the press conference that same morning, had been included in the statement. One particular phrase came to be heavily discussed in the *asamblea*. It was a rhetorical question of whether to continue voting for the same politicians in charge before and during the flood. Luis, who was the author of the phrase, argued that it was imperative to remind the people of Santa Fe that the power holders who were blamed for the disaster were still occupying posts in the government or the public administration. He wanted to remind people to think about whom they voted for in the forthcoming elections. Those who opposed this phrase argued that it focused exclusively on the act of voting, as if this was the only means of achieving justice. They argued that there were many other means to change things in the city, such as their own demonstrations. Hence, to them the phrase presented a too-narrow conception of how to contest power. After some arguing, voting took place. It was decided not to include the particular phrase in the statement. Luis grabbed his bag and left the square, upset with having his phrase removed, even if other parts of his authorship remained in the statement. The meeting continued and was concluded with a final *documento*. The next day, thousands of people in the Plaza de Mayo square listened in silence to the statement read out loud, which brought the disaster back to the present in their minds and bodies. As the final words resounded in the warm and crowded night, the people present in the square joined in the cries for justice:

> We can't, nor do we want to forget. Justice for our dead and sick! Trial and punishment to the flood maker! Confiscation of their property! Disqualification from holding public office! Total compensation for the people affected!

In this section we have highlighted how specific ideas about justice are assembled in different meetings through communicative practices such as talking, writing, and reading and how material objects such as documents and broadcast technology are technologies of the assemblage. In line with previous research that has shown that even if Argentinean *asambleas* value horizontal mobilization structures and often criticize governments, they are simultaneously using state redistributions and media attention, along with legal avenues and transnational norms, to make their case (Salmenkari 2009).

Symbols and Science: Mobilizing Support and Legitimacy

Contemporary social mobilizations draw on particular discourses to make their case. Contestation and criticism of the current global state of affairs is put forth in creative reformulation of problems as slogans like "Another world is possible," voiced at the World Social Forum organized in Porto Alegre in 2001. In the 2010s the Occupy movement stated that "We are the 99%" and the Spanish anti-austerity 15-M movement insisted, "We are not against the system, the system is against us." In response to the Argentinean financial crisis in 2001–2002, when pot-banging masses of people took to the streets, the phrase "they [the politicians] should all leave"[6] came to symbolize much of the protest against the political establishment. In contemporary Argentinean *asambleas* a number of discourses are assembled: a postcolonial, a human rights, and a non-political discourse, which articulate with past struggles (cf. Catela da Silva 2004) and existing symbols, making these discourses both meaningful and legitimate.

The book *They Come for the Gold, They Come for Everything: The Mining Invasions 500 Years Later*, published by the late Argentinean journalist and environmentalist activist Javier Rodríguez Pardo in 2009, is an example of material and expression (discourse) that is assembled. In this book, he describes the *asamblea* protests against mining exploitation in the cities of San Juan and Esquel. The book circulated widely among Argentinean environmental *asambleas* and operated as a source of knowledge and inspiration. On several occasions Rodríguez Pardo was invited to participate in meetings, and he was one of the founders of UAC (Unión de Asambleas Ciudadanas). In Asamblea El Algarrobo, the book was read by several members and discussed in a couple of *asamblea* meetings. The documentary of the same title, produced a couple of years later, has circulated on international film festivals.[7] This discursive logic articulates different environmental site controversies, such as contamination from open-pit mining, with the fumigations of soybean fields, claiming that the problem (of both) is the imperialist capitalism that has subjugated South American countries since the time of colonization. This discourse can also emerge in settings of collective action in which resource extraction was not the initial problem. In Santa Fe City, for example, the problem identified and discussed in the *asamblea* meetings of the *inundados* activists right after the disaster was the deficient government and the corrupt state that had not protected the city and its citizens from the risk of flooding. From 2008 and onwards however, environmental problems were suddenly raised as causal to the disaster. The province of Santa Fe is one of Argentina's historical "bread baskets" and it is currently one of the major producers of soybean. The fact that deforestation and the use of pesticides affect not only climate as well as soil and water qualities, but also the absorption capacity of the soil, which increase the risk for flooding, was raised at several *asamblea* meetings and soon mobilized in the public *asamblea* meetings through slogans and placards. This illustrates that assemblages transform over time, through social labor and interaction, not least in terms of the production of knowledge (Turnbull 2000). In this way assemblages are not like Russian dolls that fit neatly into each other, but rather overlapping in time and space (DeLanda 2006).

The choice of venue for some *asamblea* meetings is another example of how the postcolonial and/or anti-imperialist/anti-capitalist discourses are assembled symbolically with historical events, people, placards, and places. In Santa Fe City, the Asamblea Permanente mostly carried out their meetings and their actions at the Plaza de Mayo square. There are several Plaza de Mayo squares in Argentinean cities, and they are emblematic places, most notably because they carry the memory of the so-called May Revolution which led to national independence, but also because many social protests have taken place in these squares since then.[8] Another example is that of the *asamblea* meeting that was organized by the movement Paren de Fumigar[9] and UAC in September 2009. San Lorenzo was the scene for one of the more important and successful battles for emancipation from the Spanish colonial powers in 1813. It is located in the Province of Santa Fe on the shores of the Paraná River and currently hosts one of the largest private ports in Argentina, from where a large share of the country's soybean production is exported. In San Lorenzo, the train that transports the metals from the Alumbrera mine in the inland to the port for exportation also passes. One of the *asamblea* meetings transformed into a street demonstration. On one of the banners it said:

> From this port the wealth leaves the country and we are left with explosions, fumigations, poverty and illnesses.

The banner assembled ideas about the extraction-export model that involves mining, wood, and cereals, with the alleged health effects of the Argentinean population as a result. By choosing this venue for the meeting, a discursive articulation with past colonial oppression and contemporary capitalist exploitation was achieved. The postcolonial and anti-imperialist discourses that are assembled are also expressed through key symbols. It is common to find the *wiphala* flag that marks the territory of the Asamblea El Algarrobo, which symbolizes indigenous rights and territorial claims. The same goes for the *pachamama*, the Mother Earth in Andean cosmology, who is often "invited" to the *asamblea* meetings, along with images of Latin American revolutions and political struggles, such as the guerrilla soldier Ernesto "Che" Guevara, Chilean protest singers, and Argentinean folklore performers. Popular and emblematic Argentinean rock and pop songs, emically labeled *rock nacional*, are often used to create particular postcolonial soundscapes. The role play that was performed at the UAC meeting in 2009, mentioned earlier, was inspired by the so-called "Theatre of the Oppressed," an analysis used as means of promoting social and political change. It was developed in the 1960s by the Brazilian theater director, writer, and politician, Augusto Boal. He was influenced by the work of the Brazilian educator Paulo Freire, the founder of critical pedagogy. They largely shaped much of the political left militancy in Latin America.

In the wake of violent dictatorships and political, social, and institutional crises of recent decades, the notion of "the political" is highly sensitive in contemporary Argentina. The emic notion of *hacer política*, literally meaning to "make politics," refers to the deep politicization and clientelism that pervades Argentinean social life and has come to signify something of an invective to many people, in view of widespread corruption. The ideology of the *asamblea* is many times therefore non-political in the sense of being "non-partisan" and "anti-state," given that it is more often than not the Argentinean state that is the adversary of the *asamblea*. It goes perhaps without saying that if congregations like the *asamblea* emerge in the first place, it is because a group of people have claims regarding the failures of the formal institutions to address certain societal needs. Several examples show that this particular understandings of what "the political" (and the "non-political") is, governs the ideology of the Argentinean *asamblea*.

In the same way that *asambleas* strive to exert political pressure to achieve social change without being political, they walk the fine line between legality and legitimacy. While many of the actions organized and carried out by the *asambleas*, such as manifestations, demonstrations, marches, and *escraches*[10] are a feature of democracy, and hence legal, other activities are illegal, like the road blocking by the Asamblea El Algarrobo for example. Other activities, such as organizing manifestations, demonstration, marches, and *escraches* are legal, yet they can be controversial in local communities. Much time at the *asamblea* meetings is thus dedicated to discuss how to create legitimacy for illegal and legal actions alike. This is often done by appealing to supreme legal frameworks such the Argentinean Constitution and its Articles 41 and 43, which mention the right to a safe environment, in the case of the Asamblea El Algarrobo, or to the Universal Declaration of Human Rights, in the case of the Asamblea Permanente of the *inundados* in Santa Fe.

Legitimacy was also strived for by commissioning scientific reports, such as the one mentioned in the introductory vignette, and public knowledge about the reports was seen as important by the activists. They tried to get as much public attention as possible, generally by presenting the reports in *asamblea* meetings to which local journalists were invited. The inquiries and reports issued are examples of the elements of knowledge that are assembled through social labor. In other cases geologists have been invited to testify that the glaciers are threatened by the mining industry, or medical doctors and molecular biologists are brought in to inform about the health effects of pesticide use (Skill and Grinberg 2011). The *asamblea* strives to assemble evidence and legitimacy, which is part of the assemblage dynamics. The more support of the 'right' kind, the stronger the *asamblea*, since the capacity of the assemblage increases, not only with the number of elements, but more importantly, when legitimate and acceptable kinds of elements are assembled.

Conclusive Remarks: Presence in Emergence

Initially we posed the question about whom and what are being assembled at the *asamblea* meetings. Throughout the chapter we have shown, in line with the theory, that heterogeneous elements like books, ideas, skills, activists, experts, technologies, documents, the constitution, and the police force, places, historical events, discourses, and more are assembled through social labor at these particular meetings. The Argentinean *asamblea* meetings stem from contemporary transnational notions of collective action as much as local and historical practices of protest. As has become clear, the Argentinean *asamblea* is an emergent form of social mobilization that is characterized by heterogeneity and dynamics. Several of the *asambleas* we refer to, including the ones we have studied ethnographically ourselves, have been active for years, and continue to pursue their goals by assembling people, discourses, and objects mainly through the *asamblea* meetings. This is how this particular assemblage of collective action is put together, making the *asamblea* "a body who thinks by doing" in passing from one experiential state of the body to another and affecting that body's capacity to act. The meeting activities consist of deliberations to elaborate action strategies, often mixed with public demonstrations and *escrache* protests to mark presence and express claims, but also of *asamblea* education and socialization.

Presence matters a lot in Argentinean *asamblea* meetings, materially, emotionally, and ideologically, and is intimately connected to a recent (political) past marked by absences. Contemporary communication technologies are indeed one element in this particular assemblage, but physical presence of people is favored in order to carry out an *escrache* or to enact and socialize the *asamblea* critical pedagogy. The ideology of "being present" that permeates the *asamblea* and materializes through symbols like Che Guevara and the physical presence of the Mothers of Plaza de Mayo has connotations to the violent years of the last dictatorship, when forced disappearances of political activists were the order of the day. Physical and symbolic presence embodies becoming and the affective desire for a different future. These temporal dimensions of presence are related to the territorializing process of the assemblage.

As has become evident, the *asamblea* meetings are not only strategic and operative theaters of action, but are also moments of and for making meaning of traumatic experiences and social conflicts. Disregarding the origin of the *asamblea*, whether it is the result of the post-disaster accidental community as in Santa Fe City or as a mobilization against risky projects by transnational companies as in Andalgalá, the claim for justice is key. Here both mass media and science are crucial elements in this assemblage because they articulate and legitimate such claims. People with no prior knowledge about activism interact with established activists and learn *asamblea* meeting practices as well as practices of protest, the latter as the outcome and extension of the meetings. In sum, people become activists and the *asamblea* becomes collective action in and through the meetings.

Taken together, the Argentinean *asamblea* can be understood as emergent presence, assembled through historical experience, creative experimenting, and the interaction of multiple ideological and material elements through which people struggle in the twenty-first century to reinvent a (non)political future.

Notes

1 In English: Permanent Assembly of People Affected by the Flood.
2 In Spanish: *¡Ni olvido, ni perdón!*
3 In Spanish, *inundados* literally translates to "flooded people."
4 The so-called Argentinazo refers to the street protests and riots that occurred in several Argentinian cities on December 19 and 20, 2001. In total there were more than thirty fatalities after clashes with the police forces. The sitting president De la Rúa resigned two years before his mandate ended and fled the governmental palace by helicopter due to the furious crowds in front of the building in the Plaza de Mayo square in Buenos Aires.
5 In English: Coalition of Citizen Assemblies.
6 In Spanish: *¡Qué se vayan todos!*
7 *Vienen por el oro, vienen por todo* (2011) by Pablo D'alo Abba and Cristian Harbaruk.
8 The protest marches of the Mothers of the Plaza de Mayo initiated during the military dictatorship (1976–1983) are the demonstrations that are best known internationally.
9 In English: Stop Fumigating!
10 The *escrache* is a practice of protest that consists of a public demonstration that a group of activists carries out through sit-down protests, songs, or graffiti, usually in front of the home or workplace of somebody held accountable. The purpose is to unveil the accused and make public their alleged wrongdoings.

References

Alonso, Luciano, Araceli Boumerá and Julieta Citroni. "Confrontaciones en Torno del Espacio Urbano: Dictadura, Gobierno Constitucional y Movimiento de Derechos Humanos en Santa Fe (Argentina)." *Historia Regional* 25(2007): 11–32.

Åsberg, Cecilia, Martin Hultman and Lee Francis. *Posthumanistiska nyckeltexter.* Lund: Studentlitteratur, 2012.

Brison, Karen. "All talk and no action: Saying and doing in Kwanga meetings." *Ethnography* 28(1989): 97–115.

Catela Da Silva, Ludmila. "Nos vemos en el piquete . . .'. Protestas, violencia y memoria en el Noroeste Argentino." In *La cultura en las crisis latinoamericanas,* edited by Alejandro Grimson and Ana María Ochoa Gautier, 123–143. Buenos Aires: CLACSO, 2004.

D'alo Abba, Pablo and Cristian Harbaruk. 2011. Vienen por el oro, vienen por todo. https://youtu.be/qp0CIDPAOHk.

DeLanda, Manuel. *A New Philosophy of Society: Assemblage Theory and Social Complexity.* New York: Continuum, 2006.

Deleuze, Gilles and Felix Guattari. *A Thousand Plateaus: Capitalism and Schizophrenia.* New York: Continuum, 2003.

Dinerstein, Ana. "¡Que se Vayan Todos! Popular insurrection and the asambleas barriales in Argentina." *Bulletin of Latin American Research* 22(2003): 187–200.

Feld, Steven. *Sound and Sentiment: Birds, Weeping, Poetics, and Song in Kaluli Expression.* Philadelphia: University of Pennsylvania Press, 1982.

Fernández, Ana María, Mercedes López, Sandra Borakievich and Enrique Ojám. "Política y subjetividad: la tensión autogestión delegación en empresas y fábricas recuperadas." *Anuario de investigaciones* 15(2008): 195–203.

Graeber, David. *Direct Action: An Ethnography.* Oakland and Baltimore: AK Press, 2009.

Haraway, Donna. "Situated knowledges: The science question in feminism and the privilege of partial perspective." *Feminist Studies* 14(1988): 575–599.

Hastrup, Kirsten. "Scales of attention in fieldwork: Global connections and local concerns in the Arctic." *Ethnography* 14(2013): 145–164.

Holdren, Nate and Sebastian Souza. "Introduction to colectivo situaciones." *Ephemera* 5(2005): 595–601.

Juris, Jeffrey. "Reflections on #Occupy everywhere: Social media, public space, and emerging logics of aggregation." *American Ethnologist* 39(2012): 259–279.

Manzano, Virginia, María Inés Fernández Alvarez, Matías Triguboff and Juan José Gregoric. "Apuntes para la construcción de un enfoque antropológico sobre la protesta y los procesos de resistencia social en Argentina." In *Investigaciones en Antropología Social*, edited by Mabel Grimberg, Fernandez, María Josefina and María Inés Fernández Alvarez. Buenos Aires: Universidad de Buenos Aires and Antropofagia, 2008: 41–62.

Mastrangelo, Andrea. *Las niñas Gutiérrez y la Mina Alumbrera: La Articulación con la Economía Mundial de una Localidad del Noroeste Argentino.* Buenos Aires: Editorial Antropofagia, 2004.

Ouviña, Hernán. "Las asambleas barriales y la construcción de lo ´público no estatal´: La experiencia en la ciudad autónoma de Buenos Aires." In *La política en movimiento: identidades y experiencias de organización en América Latina*, edited by Bettina Levy and Natalia Gianatelli, 65–102. Buenos Aires: CLACSO, 2008.

Rabinow, Paul. *Anthropos Today: Reflections on Modern Equipment.* Princeton, NJ: Princeton University Press, 2003.

Razsa, Maple. *Bastards of Utopia: Living Radical Politics after Socialism.* Bloomington: Indiana University Press, 2015.

Rodríguez Pardo, Javier. *Vienen por el Oro, Vienen por Todo: Las Invasiones Mineras 500 años Después.* Buenos Aires: Ediciones Ciccus, 2009.

Rossi, Federico Matías. "Las asambleas vecinales y populares en la Argentina: Las particularidades organizativas de la acción colectiva contenciosa." *Sociológica* 19(2005): 113–145.

Salmenkari, Taru. "Political opportunities and protest mobilization in Argentina." *El Norte – Finnish Journal of Latin American Studies* 4(2009): 1–18.

Schuster, Federico and Sebastian Pereyra. "La protesta social en la Argentina democrática: Balance y perspectivas de una forma de acción política." In *La Protesta Social en la Argentina: Transformaciones Económicas y Crisis Social en el Interior*, edited by Norma Giarraca, 41–63. Buenos Aires: Alianza Editorial, 2001.

Skill, Karin and Ezequiel Grinberg. "Risk constructions in the controversy surrounding the use of glyphosate (RoundUp) in the production of GM soy in Argentina." *New Community Quarterly* 9(2011): 25–32.

Strecker, Ivo. "Political discourse in an egalitarian society." *African Yearbook of Rhetoric* 4(2013): 98–105.

Svampa, Maristella and Sebastian Pereyra. *Entre la Ruta y el Barrio: La Experiencia de las Organizaciones Piqueteras*. Buenos Aires: Editorial Biblos, 2003.

Turnbull, David. *Masons, Tricksters and Cartographers: Makers of Knowledge and Space*. Abigdon and Marsdon: Harwood Academics, 2000.

Ullberg, Susann. *Watermarks: Urban Flooding and Memoryscape in Argentina*. Stockholm: Acta Universitatis Stockholmiensis, 2013.

Vara, Ana María. "Un discurso latinoamericano y latinoamericanista sobre los recursos naturales en el 'caso papeleras.' " *Iberoamericana* XIII(52) (2013): 7–26.

Weinstock, Ana Mariel. "Imaginarios regionales y oro en Patagonia." Paper presented at the XXVI meeting of the Asociación Latinoamericana de Sociología, Guadalajara, Jalisco, 13–18 August 2007.

4 How to Avoid Getting Stuck in Meetings

On the Value of Recognizing the Limits of Meeting Ethnography for Community Studies[1]

*Japonica Brown-Saracino
and Meaghan Stiman*

Introduction: What Meetings Reveal for Community Ethnographers

Meeting ethnography is a crucial data source for many who study places or, more specifically, the processes or populations set in place, but how much focus on meeting ethnography as a data source is too much? We argue that ethnographic observation of meetings is a crucial staple of community studies. However, we also caution that meeting ethnography can become too much of a good thing, potentially preventing the ethnographer from generating a holistic portrait of and understanding of a place. That is, the very facets of meeting ethnography that make it a crucial tool in any community ethnographer's toolkit—accessibility, practicality, access to power holders, ease of translating into snowball sampling—may inadvertently narrow the ethnographer's focus.

To illustrate the benefits and risks of meeting ethnography for community studies, we draw on the first author's two four-community comparative ethnographies, a study of gentrifying urban neighborhoods and small towns and a study of lesbian, bisexual, and queer women's (hereafter "LBQ" for brevity) migration to four small U.S. cities.[2] We also draw on the second author's ethnography of second homeownership in a Maine tourist village. The meetings from our fieldwork took place, for the most part, in the public or parochial realm (Hunter 1985; Lofland 1998). That is, they are meetings that must be, legally speaking, open to the public (e.g., town meeting), that are fairly widely advertised, and ostensibly open to anyone belonging to a specific area or population group (e.g., block club meetings), or inclusive of those who share a common interest or concern (e.g., snowmobile club). While these meetings vary widely in scope, most were in some way, either formally or informally, connected to city hall.[3] We argue that these meetings instruct community ethnographers about the organized, premeditated life of a community and the stakeholders who constitute it.

DOI: 10.4324/9781315559407-5

We situate what meetings reveal for community ethnographers in Schwartzman's definition of meetings, which we adopt herein. She defines the meeting as "a social form that organizes interaction in distinctive ways" and "as a gathering of three or more people who agree to assemble for a purpose ostensibly related to the functioning of an organization or a group, e.g., to exchange ideas or opinions, to develop policy and procedures, to solve a problem, to make a decision, to formulate recommendations, etc. A meeting is characterized by multi-party talk that is episodic in nature and participants develop or use specific conventions to regulating this talk" (Schwartzman 1987: 274). Following Schwartzman, we define them as organized (and planned), purposeful, and guided by convention (Schwartzman 1987).

We propose that the meeting is an invaluable and nearly inevitable facet of community ethnography. Meetings are generally a practical point of entry for any ethnographer; many are accessible to an ethnographer (e.g., more likely to be open to the public than private sphere events), occur frequently, provide access to power brokers, and provide a point of entry as one seeks to develop a sense of the lay of the land and to cultivate an interview sample.[4] Meetings at city hall reveal crucial insights about the public facets of life in a place. Specifically, meetings provide ethnographers with the lay (and rules) of the land and provide a window into community hierarchy.

Despite the clear advantages of observing meetings, we find that relying on meetings as a primary or major data source in community studies is limiting in two important ways. First, ethnographers run the risk of neglecting the everyday, unscheduled life of the community or population they study as it occurs beyond city hall. Second, by over-attending to meetings ethnographers are not able to capture those who *do not* attend meetings. In our study sites these included some who were disenfranchised, alienated, or otherwise excluded—and whose perspective was crucial for understanding the dynamics we wished to study. We propose community ethnographers utilize meetings in a self-reflexive and somewhat cautious manner. Those who use meetings as a data source should be aware of how the meetings they attend serve as a data resource, and, potentially, as a limitation. Meetings, assuming that a researcher is observing a broad or representative sample of the heterogeneous meetings that take place in most locales, provide a crucial window into community life. However, this portrait is necessarily partial, both revealing and obscuring dimensions of the life of a place.

By specifying how meetings may obscure some facets of community life, the chapter advances an understanding of the precise role of meeting ethnography in community studies, arguing that observation of meetings best reveals the formal structure of local life, and in so doing provides access to power holders and publicly engaged individuals (Brown-Saracino 2009). Specifically, meetings reveal and help to constitute the stakes and stakeholders, distribution of power, facets of local culture and politics, local networks, and areas of agreement and discord. Meetings can also serve as a launching pad for interview research, as well as for other avenues of ethnographic inquiry.

The Drawbacks of Using Meetings as a Sole Method in Community Studies

The meeting is a crucial data source for ethnographers who wish to understand the interactions, decision-making processes, and community dynamics that take place within communities, urban organizations, and other place-based social forms. Scholars use meetings as ethnographic tools in a variety of ways. For example, Whyte (1943) uses meetings of political organizations and racketeers as a way to understand the larger social structure of the Italian neighborhood. To understand the rise and decline of local community participation, Small (2004) utilizes archival data of meeting minutes from a neighborhood community organization. In her study of four gentrifying neighborhoods, Brown-Saracino (2009) utilizes meetings to capture both longtime residents' and gentrifiers' orientations to gentrification. Finally, scholars not only observe meetings, but also sometimes participate in meetings. To understand the interests and actions of stakeholders in a predominately African-American gentrifying neighborhood, Pattillo (2007) acted as the secretary for her neighborhood's Conservation Community Council, taking meeting minutes (and field notes).

How community ethnographers approach and utilize organizations and meetings within their work varies by the research questions asked. Some scholars have paid specific attention to why organizations (and thus, the meetings within them) matter for community studies and ethnographers (Berry 2005; Marwell 2007; Small et al 2008; McQuarrie and Marwell 2009). For example, Marwell (2007) ask how local, formal organizations matter for the life chances of the urban poor. Small et al (2008) ask how organizational ties matter for neighborhood effects. Berry (2005) asks how different local organizations deploy "diversity" to pursue different political goals for Chicago's Rogers Park. As McQuarrie and Marwell (2009) argue, organizations both structure and are structured by their environments. For these reasons, attending to organizations is central to most community studies, for meetings can reflect and determine local dynamics that may be quite relevant to the researcher's inquiry.[5]

However, echoing our argument the literature points to three important ways that meetings can limit the scope of community ethnography. First, scholars note that meetings are a limited source of data simply because of who attends meetings and whose voices meetings elevate. In her study of small town local government meetings, Jane Mansbridge (1983) cautions against thinking of town meetings as a site of unitary democracy, or a democracy based on the consensus of the group. Her study serves as an important reminder for ethnographers of the limits of treating meetings as an unproblematic window into the community. In her case, those who attend meetings limit the extent to which the town government can be treated as representative. That is, even within a democratic setting, there are problems of representativeness. Some groups of people are more likely than others to attend and actively participate in meetings; participation varies by length of residence, age, gender, and class. For instance, despite the relatively equal attendance of women and men at the meetings she studies, men are more likely to participate, and run for and hold office. Similarly, although newcomers are less likely to attend the meetings, the ones who do attend tend to participate more actively than the longtime residents. Ultimately, Mansbridge argues that these four factors play a crucial role in not only who attends meetings, but also whose voices are heard during the meetings. Thus, she reminds that while town meetings play a crucial role in local life, they do not represent all residents or their perspectives.

Relatedly, in her study of participatory democracies in American social movements, Polletta (2002) finds that even within participatory democracies that are based on friendship, solidarity, and trust—like the women's liberation movement—inequalities within the meetings and organizational form still persist. Polletta cautions that friendship-based democracies may lead to hierarchies and exclusion because of the friendship cliques that form, which can inadvertently exclude newcomers from the organizations and preclude their participation. Here, Polletta reminds that even meetings that appear to be most democratic in their form and function can still be riddled with hierarchies, exclusion, and inequality. This is an important lesson for the community ethnographer.

Similarly, Deener (2012) notes the potential drawbacks of using meetings as the only data source. He also finds that some groups were more likely to attend meetings than others. In his study of Venice, California, Deener finds that Latinos in particular were regularly underrepresented at political meetings and less likely to attend. Specifically, some did not want to risk public participation because of their citizenship status, some were too busy working to attend meetings, and some women were hesitant to join without the support of their husbands. Thus, Mansbridge, Polletta, and Deener instruct that by relying on meetings as the only or even as primary data source community scholars run the risk of overlooking populations who simply do not attend meetings.

Second, ethnography of meetings should not be limited only to what happens within the boundaries of the meetings. Schwartzman (1989) argues that ethnography should not stop at the meeting itself because what happens *before* and *after* meetings is just as important as what happens within the meeting. After meetings, people "chat," "gossip," or "tell stories," which provides researchers a glimpse into important information regarding social status and social relationships (Schwartzman 1989: 83). We concur, but also advocate for looking beyond this to settings totally outside of the meeting (not just the before and after of the meeting). What happens in a place when others are in meetings? This information may be as crucial as knowledge of what happens inside the meeting sphere, especially if one's research questions are expansive and not primarily focused on the political sphere or organizational and institutional dynamics of city hall.

Third, and relatedly, by relying too heavily on meetings as a data source, researchers run the risk of missing out on the everyday life of the community or populations they study. Had Gans (1982) only relied on meetings as a data source, he would have missed how Boston's West-End Italian-Americans structured their social life via peer groups. Had Deener (2012) relied solely on meetings for his data sources, he would have missed the collective public life of Latinos in Venice, which tends to take place in churches or public parks, rather than in governmental settings. Had Whyte (1943) only attended to the formal life of the North End, he would have missed the degree to which social organization happens through everyday interaction, and literally on the street. Had Small (2004) stayed only in meetings, he would have missed the lives and perspectives of non-participants and crucial insights about how and why different social groups engage in distinct ways with their public housing project. Moreover, a great deal of collective public life takes place in the everyday facets of life (Bell 1994; Oldenburg 1999; Duneier 2001; Jerolmack 2013), and had any of the above authors stayed only in meetings we would not have portraits of the relationships formed, interactions, and other features of everyday social life.

The Benefits of Meetings for Community Studies

Despite the limits established by the literature, we believe that observation of meetings is nonetheless beneficial for community ethnographers—with the crucial caveat that ethnographers must be mindful of precisely how the meeting is a productive data source and of the ways in which it may not be such. We propose that for community ethnographers meetings are a valuable window into the work of city hall, the organized, premeditated life of a community, and those who compose it. Again, we emphasize that meetings in this case are prearranged gatherings of three or more people who assemble in relation to a group or organization (Schwartzman 1987). In this sense, we differentiate between meetings and other social occasions.

Within this context, we argue that meetings are important for two primary reasons. First, meetings reveal the lay (and rules) of the land. Meetings are a window into the structure of city or town politics, culture, and networks. Second, meetings reveal community hierarchy. Specifically, the conflict (or lack thereof) that takes place within meetings allows ethnographers to capture what some of the key stakes are within the community, how they are produced, as well as to identify stakeholders. This enables ethnographers to observe how power is distributed and how it operates within a given community. Of course, meetings do more than simply reveal dynamics of local life. Meetings themselves produce and reproduce power, hierarchies, and identities (Schwartzman 1989; Holmes 2000, 2008; Tracy and Dimock 2004). However, here we focus on what meetings can teach ethnographers about local place-based life; indeed, much of what ethnographers learn in meetings about local life are borne from the production of power, hierarchies, and identities within the meetings themselves. Thus, while we acknowledge the production processes inherent to meetings, we focus here on how meetings—and indeed, what is produced within meetings—are instructive for community ethnographers in large part because of what they unveil or otherwise render visible. Below we offer a few examples of how meetings enable ethnographers to capture both the lay of the land and community hierarchy, after which we offer suggestions of "good practices" for ethnographic observations conducted by community researchers. We encourage meeting ethnographers to sample multiple meetings, extend observations beyond the boundaries of the meeting itself, and take careful notes of who attends meetings and whose voices are heard within meetings.

Identifying the Lay (and Rules) of the Land

As an ethnographer studying gentrification in two Chicago neighborhoods and two New England towns, and, more recently, studying the migration of women to four small U.S. cities, the first author has spent countless hours in meetings. In fact, the very first scene that she observed for her dissertation was a meeting. This first meeting provided a crucial early lesson in the utility of meetings for identifying the lay of the land, including contentious local issues, and a map of local power holders, as well as for developing theory.

The meeting, a monthly gathering of a block club in a solidly middle-class island in the midst of Chicago's gentrifying Andersonville neighborhood was held in the apartment of a middle-class woman in her sixties.[6] Most in attendance were female, white, also in their fifties and sixties, and middle- or upper-middle class. The hostess served tea and cookies on china, and the women sat together on sofas and armchairs. Suffice it to say, this was not the scene she had in mind when she embarked on "urban ethnography." The minutiae of advancing gentrification—talk of gardens and public safety provisions—filled most of the meeting. However, an hour into the meeting the women began to discuss speed bumps for which the block club had lobbied their alderwoman, and suddenly the meeting became quite heated. The hostess expressed passionate concern about the disruptive noise that drivers generated scraping the undersides of their cars against the speed bumps. Another, with equal passion, insisted that they were a crucial safety mechanism. The women argued back and forth, their voices growing louder and louder. By the end of the meeting, women had cried. One had thrown a book in the direction of another.

This was an early indication that even seemingly "boring" or mundane meetings are settings in which, with time, an array of community dynamics and dramas reveal themselves. It was also a lesson in how important theoretical lessons rest even in the most mundane interactions and conflicts (after all, the relative import of speed bumps comes into question when, as an example, a few blocks away a whole building of residents—many with mental illness—were about to be displaced at the hands of advancing gentrification). Here, the meeting displayed how deeply residents care about their neighborhoods and how sense of self or pride can rest on local outcomes. The meeting also provided an early indicator of the fact that part of why each woman cared so deeply about her position was because she could be fairly confident that if she could persuade the rest of the block club to adopt her position—to keep the speed bumps or abandon them—the alderwoman would listen. As first- and second-wave gentrifiers, and as white, professional women, they had every reason to believe that the outcome of their disagreement would matter for local streetscape. Thus, for a student of neighborhood change, the meeting provided a crucial early window into how power is distributed and operates in gentrifying neighborhoods.

The block club struggle over speed bumps is but one minor example of meeting conflict and drama the first author has encountered. She observed police take to the stage to disband a heated conflict between pro- and anti-gentrification activists in Chicago's Uptown. She heard "urban pioneer" gentrifiers wish death upon African-American adolescents who cut the power source for streetlamps. She has been in the small council room of the Provincetown Town Hall when dozens of fishermen spontaneously pounded their boots against the floor to register their ire at the reconstruction of the town pier, the walls resounding with the sound of steel toes on wood floors. She has sat amongst neighborhood residents in the meeting room of a nursing home, also in Chicago's Andersonville, while members of a block club digested news that two blocks away a federal judge's family had been brutally murdered.

And, of course, the first author attended countless meetings devoid of obvious drama, such as an unexceptional meeting of a snowmobile club in Dresden, Maine's Old Town Hall, and a productive and cooperative meeting of Provincetown's Long Range Planning Committee. Yet, even these ordinary, unspectacular meetings provided vital windows into city politics, culture, and networks. One, the snowmobile club, revealed old-timer networks, while the Planning Committee revealed the influence of historic preservationists in Provincetown's town government. Taken together, these meetings, both the dramatic and ordinary, provided a collective portrait of local, organized life.

Best Practices for Meeting Ethnography

In what follows we offer three interlocking suggestions for meeting ethnographers in community studies that may be useful in other meeting ethnography settings. First, we encourage community ethnographers to sample a broad range of meetings to account for variation (or continuity) in how organizations orient themselves toward the community. That is, if the unit of analysis is a community—a neighborhood, town, city, or place-based population group—multiple meetings will become staples of the responsible ethnographer's routine. By sampling different types of meetings, ethnographers are able to chart the identity and practices of different organizations and in the second author's case, their varied orientations to town and community change. One winter evening the second author attended two meetings back-to-back. What at first seemed to be a long and arduous task soon became a night of rich ethnographic detail. The first meeting was held by the Chamber of Commerce at the Rangeley Inn, a quaint, historic inn located in the town center. The meeting was a meet-and-greet for town business owners and the general population to discuss the future of the Rangeley region. Organizers served hors d'oeuvres and provided a cash bar; most in attendance ordered wine. Near the entrance stood a table where people could write suggestions for the Chamber's new five-year plan. All of the suggestions focused on ways to draw in more tourists and to make Rangeley a more business-friendly destination. On the board, the president, who was wearing chinos and a button-up shirt, wrote in big, bold letters: "More people, more business, more promotion, more employees, more collaboration and more members = success!"

The second author left that meeting to attend her next meeting of the evening: a meeting of the Rangeley Region Guides and Sportsmen's Association. It was a potluck-style meeting in a cabin in the village of Oquossoc, five miles north of the town center. Everybody brought a dish, ranging from mashed potatoes to green bean casserole, and they also brought their own drinks. Most were drinking cans of Budweiser or PBR. The meeting focused on the recent increase in moose permits allocated by the State of Maine. Members of the association expressed concern that the state moose biologist overestimated the number of moose to be hunted, which, they feared would lead to an endangered moose population. The conversation then shifted to talking about possible new bear hunting regulations, which would prohibit the use of traps, bait, and dogs to hunt. They felt these regulations were too restrictive and would ultimately lead to a bear hunting ban. A man in his late fifties, sporting a camouflage hat and a fishing shirt, furiously raised his hand and declared, "The problem is, we don't want people coming in here who are not from Maine telling us how to run things." The room erupted with applause.

The value of these meetings, largely borne of the contrast between the two—wine and a call for tourism at one, casserole and disdain for outsiders at the other—was immediately evident. The second author was able to see the different practices and distinct norms and identities of two different organizations and their orientations to Rangeley and to changes related to expanding tourism: one group promoting change and encouraging tourists and visitors and the other group skeptical of change and cautioning against outsiders. Thus, a broad census of community meetings, and regular attendance of at least a substantial subset thereof, provides especially crucial insights into facets of local life.

Second, we argue that it is central for community ethnographers to extend observations beyond the meetings in city halls to interactions that take place before and after meetings to best capture community hierarchy and the lay of the land; ethnographers should keep eyes and ears open as one enters and exits meetings (Schwartzman 1989). The second author recalls one particularly heated board of selectmen meeting in which the board was set to vote on whether a local non-profit arts group would be granted a permit to use the town's park for their summer art festival. The board ultimately voted against the permit request because of a complicated deed, which restricted the park's use. While the second author saw heated exchanges by both groups—those for and those against the park permit request—within the meeting, what happened *after* the meeting also proved fruitful for her analysis. The heated discussion of the park permit did not end within the boundaries of the meeting, but continued into the parking lot. The second author watched a group gather who were furious over the politicians' "lack of foresight." She watched as one of her informants complained to his friends that the politicians were unable to see the true community benefit that the art show would generate, he argued, by bringing in more tourist dollars for everyone. Had the second author stopped observations at the close of the meeting, she would have missed the unfiltered, gut reactions of the locals to town policies and decisions, one that ultimately articulated some of the longtime residents' relationship to tourism. She furthermore would have missed seeing how different social groups formed outside of the meeting.

Third and finally, we urge community ethnographers to take careful notation of who attends meetings and whose voices are heard within the meetings themselves. This particularly helps researchers identify who the key stakeholders are and who wields the most power within the meeting and beyond. Within meetings, only certain groups and voices tend to be heard. During the second author's fieldwork, she attended Rangeley's annual town meeting. Throughout the meeting she observed moments of passion from the townspeople, usually in support of bills that were supporting tourism in a variety of ways. Throughout the meeting the second author counted the number of people in attendance and tallied the people who were vocal during the meeting. She counted roughly seventy people who attended the meeting. Of the seventy people who attended the meeting, only fifteen or so different people voiced their opinions. Of the fifteen people who voiced their opinions, only two of these people were women. Over half of those who voiced their opinions during the town meeting, usually in support of tourism, owned a local business or held a political position in the town. Here, the authors echo Mansbridge (1983) and Deener's (2012) arguments. Although meetings provide many crucial insights, they are limited in their representativeness and scope—especially when one's research questions pertain not to a single organization, but to an entire community. In the second author's case, it is impossible to say that the entirety of the community supports efforts to promote tourism. Rather, what the meeting does tell us is that certain groups, and in this case, male business owners, tend to be the leading voices promoting tourism in the town within the political sphere of city hall.

Meetings provide an obvious and (comparatively speaking) easy place to begin in the field, especially in municipal settings in which certain meetings must, by law, be open to the public. However, it is important to note that what observation of meetings will accomplish for ethnographers of course varies with a study's research question. For instance, for an ethnographer studying second homeowners (who rarely attend meetings) meetings might be most useful for identifying the lay of the land, or for providing context (i.e., for the second author, most meetings revealed an appreciation of and support for second homeowners and tourism, but limited contact with the second homeowners themselves). Knowing that there is much appreciation for second homeownership in Rangeley's public sphere is crucial but insufficient knowledge for understanding why second homeowners choose Rangeley and how they experience the town. However, generally speaking, meetings provide vital background or contextual information and reveal community hierarchy within a town, city, or neighborhood. Specifically, an ethnographer will find that meetings reveals access to formal ties, organizational dynamics, policy patterns, local attitudes, and even taste patterns (e.g., cookies and tea in Chicago's Andersonville, wine at one Rangeley meeting, and mashed potatoes and green beans at another). This is all good news for ethnographers. For these reasons—because of all of the exceptional and unexceptional facets of community life that meetings reveal—we argue that meetings must serve as a staple of the scenes community ethnographers observe. We encourage ethnographers to (1) sample a broad range of meetings, (2) observe interactions beyond the formal meeting itself including those that occur before and after meetings, and (3) take careful notation of who attends meetings and whose voices are heard (and not heard) within meetings. In practice, our suggestions for meeting ethnography aid community ethnographers in uncovering the lay of the land and revealing community hierarchies that operate in and through meetings.

However, in what follows, we offer caveats about the appropriate weight community ethnographers studying place-based population groups (e.g., LBQ women) or place dynamics (e.g., gentrification) ought to give to meetings. That is, we caution about the possible risks of treating meetings as the world; of letting meetings represent a place, population group, or community process. Below, we detail the reasons for our hesitation.

Risks of Meetings

First and foremost, we must be clear that our hesitation is not about observing meetings, but about the (very real) possibility that an ethnographer will get stuck in or simply spend too much of their ethnographic time and effort in meetings. We worry about this because we find that it is tempting to approach meetings as though they will do much of our work for us. Specifically, it is tempting to approach them not as providing one window into the context we wish to understand, but as the window.

Why might this happen? Why might we get stuck in or spend too much time in meetings? Not because we are lazy or blind to other possibilities for observation or other dimensions of local life, but for reasons that are quite valid. Namely, many meetings are, at least compared to the other dimensions of community life that one might wish to observe, convenient, accessible, and comfortable to attend. Strangers are (often) invited into them, and for this reason it may be easier to secure access to a meeting than other types of community events, especially those that are everyday or occur in the private sphere. Meetings are convenient; that is, they tend to be held at times and in locations that appeal to many residents. In our experience, many community meetings typically start after the end of the workday and end before most go to bed. Attending a Pride planning meeting does not require the same commitment from an ethnographer as staying up until 2 a.m. at a Pride Party, or observing interactions at a gay bar. At a meeting, you might have to duck when a book is thrown, or struggle to stay silent as offensive (to the ethnographer) ideas are expressed, but you nonetheless get to sit and take notes, not shuffle to the bathroom to scribble thoughts as you might during nights at a bar with your informants (Grazian 2005). Moreover, if interviews are part of an ethnographer's repertoire, it is relatively easy to translate observation of meetings into interview opportunities. After all, officials and others who run meetings may feel compelled to participate in interviews in order to be a part of official record, and meetings allow contact over time with actors that may increase prospective interviewees' comfort levels. This is all good news for ethnographers. But much of the work of ethnography is awkward, tiring, and uncomfortable, so while we advocate for starting in meetings, we urge community ethnographers to avoid stopping there.

What perspectives do we gain by leaving meetings? When we enter, ethnographically, community life that extends beyond meetings we encounter the everyday practices and attitudes of those who are excluded, ignored, or opposed in city and town halls, as well as those who avoid them for any number of reasons, from discomfort, to health issues to life stage. Below, building off of the extant literature we have reviewed we offer a few examples of dimensions of local life or perspectives we would not have encountered if we had remained in meetings.

The Everyday Outside City Hall

First and foremost, if we remain in city hall meetings—the organized and premeditated life of a community—we risk missing other facets of local life, particularly the unscheduled and everyday. This is not to suggest that meetings themselves cannot be relaxed or everyday in tone or feeling. Rather, meetings as we define them here (borrowing from Schwartzman) are organized and pre-scheduled, and therefore represent a partial portrait of local community life (1987).

If we had limited our attention to city hall meetings—i.e., those that take place in city hall or that are formally or informally sanctioned by local government actors—the first author might have missed how residents talk about affordable housing in their everyday interactions—at the grocery store, with neighbors—outside of the context of public policies or the watchful eyes and open ears of stakeholders. The second author might have missed the priest from the Catholic Church thanking seasonal residents during his sermon for their monetary contributions during the winter months, which helped pay the church's exorbitant winter heating bill. Because second homeowners rarely attend meetings that take place in the town halls, it would appear is if they had no interaction with local residents or local institutions. However, by observing interactions outside of that realm—at a church service, and in restaurants, for instance—a more complete story of the relationship between second homeowners and permanent residents can be told. Even interactions with officials take distinct form outside of city hall. The first author recalls the casual back-and-forth of longtime residents in a coffee shop discussing proposed changes to the local schools with the chair of the board of selectmen as she ordered coffee, their tone more openly contentious and partisan than at public meetings in town hall. She also recalls back and forth between officials before and after meetings began (which is not always about town business, e.g., the selectman who realized he hadn't been invited to a party hosted by another selectman, revealing much about local networks).

Beyond this, accessing interactions totally outside of the meeting context is as crucial as keeping eyes and ears open as one enters and exits meetings (Schwartzman 1989). The second author benefited from her time working two part-time jobs in Rangeley. At the ski mountain she listened to her co-workers argue in the break room over the benefits of tourism in Rangeley. She watched as local residents reacted to an emailed flyer for Rangeley's community "Visioning Meeting." The flyer posed questions for residents to think about before the meeting, one of which was how Rangeley could become less dependent on tourism. Together the residents debated and ultimately emphasized the importance of and support for tourism in Rangeley's new economy—an economy without logging or industry. The second author learned from this interaction some longtime residents' unfiltered reactions to the influx of tourism and part-time residents in Rangeley, completely outside of the organized meeting sphere. Moreover, the second author attended the meeting the next night, and the residents who were openly and passionately debating the merits of tourism, sparked by the meeting's flyer, never attended the meeting itself.

The second author also benefited from her time working as a waitress at a local restaurant where she was able to observe interactions between and among second homeowners and locals that were completely unrelated to meetings; her co-workers were all "locals" (i.e., longtime, year-round residents), most of whom have worked in the Rangeley restaurant industry for over ten years, and the patrons of the restaurant were primarily second homeowners and tourists. As peak summer season started, her co-workers began to excitedly anticipate the arrival of their "summer friends." Weekly, she would watch as second homeowners came into the restaurant giving hugs to and sometimes bearing gifts for the wait staff. This revealed that despite the transience of the second homeowners throughout the year, they were staples in some of the locals' lives, and vice versa. Had the second author let city hall meetings represent the community life of Rangeley, and even if she had devoted careful attention to parking lot interactions after a meeting, she would have overlooked the other kinds of ways second homeowners participate in the community (patronizing and participating in local businesses) and the social networks and ties forged through this participation.

As Francesca Polletta argues, democracy may be "an endless meeting" (2002), but a very limited, albeit important, subset of community interactions take place at city hall or even at block club meetings. To oversample meetings is to potentially misrepresent community life based on data that privileges speeches, votes, and other more public representations of local dynamics. Provincetown, for instance, is the town hall, but it is also a dark bar, a crowded beach, a club, a hidden fishing spot in the dunes favored by old-timers, busy sidewalks, and countless backyard and deck conversations. For these reasons, it is central to extend observations beyond the meeting.

Representativeness

Both authors have learned over time that only a modest proportion of local residents typically appear at meetings, whether the annual Town Meeting or events sponsored by community organizations, such as a block club's annual street party. Moreover, by focusing on meetings, we may miss not only a large segment of the local population, but also particular segments, such as those whose perspectives power holders oppose, ignore, or even deride.

In the first author's experience, it is not just the disenfranchised (literally and otherwise) who fail to appear at meetings. Certainly, Jamaican seasonal laborers who cannot vote in the United States—an increasing presence in Provincetown—did not appear at the town meeting, nor did the owners of Andersonville's Iranian and Lebanese shops and restaurants who had been priced out of the neighborhood attend local meetings. However, in some contexts even those who fit the profile of those who might attend, such as certain gentrifiers, are absent from most if not all meetings. Some of these gentrifiers, she came to recognize, were "social preservationists"

(Brown-Saracino 2004): gentrifiers who recognize their role in gentrification and work to prevent the physical, symbolic, and cultural displacement of certain longtime residents (Brown-Saracino 2004; see also Brown-Saracino 2009). Among this class of gentrifiers, some voted with their feet by staying home as part of an effort to maintain their "virtuous marginality" (Brown-Saracino 2007)—that is to avoid further disrupting the local context via their presence. If the first author had started and stopped with meetings she might have missed these community actors and their perspectives on their communities, as well as on gentrification.

In the second author's study of a tourist village, she found that second homeowners—a group of people who are hardly economically or politically disenfranchised in a larger sense—rarely attend meetings. However, it is not because of an effort to maintain "virtuous marginality" as Brown-Saracino (2007) found with some gentrifiers. The second author found that second homeowners do not attend meetings for two reasons. One, they do not attend because they do not have any voting power (they are not permanent residents), and two, they do not attend because, put simply, they are on vacation. Despite spending sometimes entire summers (June to October), entire winters (December-March), or every weekend out of their year in their second homes, the second author found over and over again that most second homeowners just want to be left alone; they *particularly* want to avoid the contexts that are public, organized, and planned. The second author recalls one second homeowner in particular who would travel extra distance to a grocery store outside of the town center just to avoid crowds of people—locals and tourists alike—and what she called the "hubbub." She never once attended a meeting in town. In fact, the notion of doing so seemed outside the realm of possibility. The second author asked if she participated in any organizations in the town and she laughed at the prospect. Instead, she preferred to stay in her home to cook, quilt, and enjoy the noiselessness of her beautiful second home on the lake. What the second author found was that much of the interactions between and among second homeowners and local residents take place in more everyday settings (if at all): in nature groups where people go on weekly hikes together, at the upscale restaurant in town primarily frequented by second homeowners and tourists, at the local ski lodge enjoying a beer after an afternoon of skiing, on boats or in streams fishing, or at dinner parties with select friends and family in the privacy of their own second homes.

Had the second author remained only in meetings, it would appear as if second homeowners had no real impact on or interaction with permanent residents, other second homeowners, or the community at large. However, attention to the everyday life of Rangeley proved otherwise. The second author found that although most second homeowners choose not to participate in the meetings that take place in city hall, they participate in other meaningful ways. For instance, a huge proportion of the ski school employees—over half of the hundred employees—at the local mountain are second homeowners or children of second homeowners (teenagers in high school). It was at the mountain that she observed, both in the ski lodge and on the slopes, the most interactions between second homeowners. She learned through her time working at the mountain alongside second home-owners that some forged friendships with each other that traversed both their first home and their second home. She met three families, all with high-school age children who work in the ski school, who would carpool from their first homes in southern Maine to their second home in Rangeley every weekend. This revealed that social networks of second homeowners do not neatly fit within the place-based boundaries of their first homes or their sec-ond homes, but rather extend beyond these boundaries. For a scholar asking questions about second homeownership, to overlook second homeowners would of course be problematic, but given that second homes constitute 57 percent of the total housing stock in Rangeley, to neglect them would pose a problem for any community ethnographer, regardless of the question (U.S. Census Bureau 2010).

For these reasons, meetings that take place at city hall allow ethnogra-phers to gauge public community engagement, which may be crucial data for many research questions. However, we argue that sole attention to meet-ings may lead ethnographers to overlook groups or populations who do not participate in meetings. Here, detailing *why* people do not attend meetings or whose voices are dominant within meetings is potentially just as impor-tant as observing the meeting itself.

Conclusion: What Meetings Do for Community Ethnographers

In short, we firmly believe in the value of meeting ethnography, but we also advocate for wariness or self-consciousness about the possibility of treat-ing meetings as a crutch or stand in for the myriad other scenes one must observe—especially in the context of a study that extends well beyond a sin-gle organization or group. A very low proportion of residents of the places we have studied serve on the committees or even attend the town meetings that direct the public life of a city neighborhood or small town. Likewise, very few of the LBQ women the first author encounters for her current study are involved in LBQ life in a public capacity (e.g., marriage equality advocates, Pride planners, etc.). To take the organizers of the Portland Dyke March or early marriage advocates in Ithaca, New York as representative of LBQ women writ-large would miss much of the collective social life and dynamics of LBQ individuals in the study cities. And yet, in moments when access was challenging it was tempting to rely heavily on meetings at the expense of other features of local life, especially in the frantic and anx-ious moments of early fieldwork when one often needs somewhere to begin. Meetings are a fine place to start, and will always remain a crucial tool in a community ethnographer's toolkit, but—with the exception of community studies that pose narrow questions about meetings—we cannot stay in them and they cannot be our only tool.

While our argument is, we hope, commonsensical, as readers we sometimes find ourselves wondering how far afield of meetings certain "community studies" or "neighborhood ethnographies" go. Along these lines, we encourage community ethnographers to be transparent about how much time they spend in meetings and how time devoted to public community life shapes their findings and conclusions. In other words, one ought to approach meetings as a resource and as a possible limitation when over-utilized. To do so necessitates a clear conceptualization of the role of meetings in community ethnographies. Precisely because of how we have conceptualized meetings in this chapter, we suggest that meetings instruct community ethnographers about the organized, premeditated side of community life and the stakeholders who tend to people it. With this in mind, we conclude with five ways that meetings can be useful for ethnographers who study communities.

First, we propose that by attending a heterogeneous selection of meetings, ethnographers are able to document different organizations' orientations to the town, neighborhood, or community they study. Here ethnographers are able to capture struggles over, among other things, identity and resources, and between and among different organizations. Second, meetings allow an ethnographer to capture which residents participate in the formal life of the community, and this should be carefully observed and recorded (such as by taking a census at meetings or securing copies of sign-in sheets). This enables ethnographers to verify or test hypotheses about which perspectives and groups meetings best represent. Third, city hall meetings also tell us who does *not* participate in public community life, and the absence of certain groups should be noted. Sometimes this will require active research, for some community members may be hiding in plain sight outside of the public realm. Fourth, by documenting and analyzing who attends and who does not attend meetings, ethnographers are able to capture how power is distributed and how it operates (Warner 1963). Finally, by attending meetings *in conjunction with* observing everyday life, community ethnographers are able to present a more holistic account of the processes or populations they seek to study, and to understand areas of disjuncture and overlap between the everyday and the meetings in city and town halls and between power holders and the disenfranchised.

Thus, by outlining some of the limits of meeting ethnography for community ethnographers we also provide a narrower and more precise outline of how meeting observation can benefit community ethnographers, primarily by serving as a nexus of the public and often defining facets of community life. For this reason, we would strongly caution against ignoring the public features of community life embodied in meetings. Yet, we also urge ethnographers to be self-reflexive and purposeful about what meetings can and cannot tell us about they places and people they study.

Notes

1 The authors thank Jen Sandler, Helen Schwartzman, and Renita Thedvall for their tremendously helpful suggestions. For productive feedback they also thank participants in the 2014 and 2015 Meeting Ethnography Mini-Conferences at UMass Amherst.
2 See Brown-Saracino (2009, 2011, 2014, 2015).
3 We use "city hall" and "town hall" here as an umbrella category for the meetings we observed and reference herein. These meetings often occur in city or town halls, or are sanctioned and/or recognized, either formally or informally, by such authorities. For instance, block club meetings are sometimes attended by aldermen, the Dresden snowmobile club used an old town hall for meetings (with town officials' permission), and in Rangeley, non-profits such as Rangeley Friends of the Arts and other community-based organizations, often have to seek approval from the town officials for their events. In other words, not all of the meetings we reference herein literally take place in town or city halls. Rather, we use the phrase to denote the class of meetings described above.
4 Of course, accessibility depends in part on the characteristics of the ethnographer and the group studied. In some instances, brokers may find ways to block an ethnographer's access—particularly if the ethnographer does not present as a member of the group(s) studied.
5 There are exceptions, of course. For instance, Richard Lloyd's (2010) study of gentrifiers in Chicago's Wicker Park primarily asks questions about the role of culture and local commerce in artist-led gentrification. Thus, his book primarily presents scenes from more everyday social occasions, such as at bars, galleries, and coffee shops. Had his research question been about interfacing between government officials and artists (see Zukin's Loft Living 1982), meetings may have been a more valuable resource.
6 A block club can be described as a neighborhood association of residents.

References

Bell, Michael. *Childerley: Nature and Morality in a Country Village*. Chicago: University of Chicago Press, 1994.

Berry, Ellen. "Divided over diversity: Political discourse in a Chicago neighborhood." *City & Community* 4(2005): 143–170.

Brown-Saracino, Japonica. "Social preservationists and the quest for authentic community." City and Community 3 (2004): 135–156.

Brown-Saracino, Japonica. "Virtuous marginality: Social preservationists and the selection of the old-timer." *Theory and Society* 36(2007): 437–468.

Brown-Saracino, Japonica. *A Neighborhood That Never Changes: Gentrification, Social Preservation, and the Search for Authenticity*. Chicago: University of Chicago Press, 2009.

Brown-Saracino, Japonica. "From the lesbian ghetto to ambient community: The perceived costs and benefits of integration for social ties." *Social Problems* 58(2011): 361–388.

Brown-Saracino, Japonica. "From methodological stumbles to substantive insights: Gaining ethnographic access in queer communities." *Qualitative Sociology* 37(2014): 43–68.

Brown-Saracino, Japonica. "How places shape identity: The origins of distinctive LBQ identities in four small U.S. cities." *American Journal of Sociology* 121(2015): 1–66.

Deener, Andrew. *Venice: A Contested Bohemia in Los Angeles*. Chicago: University of Chicago Press, 2012.

Duneier, Mitchell. *Sidewalk*. New York: Farrar Straus and Giroux, 2001.

Gans, Herbert J. *The Urban Villagers: Group and Class in the Life of Italian-Americans*. New York: Free Press, 1982.

Grazian, David. *Blue Chicago: The Search for Authenticity in Urban Blues Clubs*. Chicago: University of Chicago Press, 2005.

Holmes, Janet. "Politeness, power, and provocation: How humor functions." *Discourse Studies* 2(2000): 159–185.

Holmes, Janet. *Gendered Talk at Work: Constructing Gender Identity Through Workplace Discourse*. Malden, MA: Blackwell, 2008.

Hunter, Albert. "Private, parochial, and public social orders: The problem of crime and incivility in urban communities." In *The Challenge of Social Control*, edited by Gerald Suttles and Mayer Zald, 230–242. Norwood, NJ: Ablex, 1985.

Jerolmack, Colin. *The Global Pigeon*. Chicago: University of Chicago Press, 2013.

Lloyd, Richard. *Neo-Bohemia: Art and Commerce in the Postindustrial City*. 2nd Edition. New York: Routledge, 2010.

Lofland, Lyn H. *The Public Realm: Exploring the City's Quintessential Social Territory*. New Brunswick: Aldine Transaction, 1998.

Mansbridge, Jane J. *Beyond Adversary Democracy*. Chicago: University of Chicago Press, 1983.

Marwell, Nicole P. *Bargaining for Brooklyn: Community Organizations in the Entrepreneurial City*. Chicago: University of Chicago Press, 2007.

McQuarrie, Michael and Nicole P. Marwell. "The missing organizational dimension in urban sociology." *City & Community* 8(2009): 247–268.

Oldenburg, Ray. *The Great Good Place: Cafes, Coffee Shops, Bookstores, Bars, Hair Salons, and Other Hangouts at the Heart of a Community*. Boston: Da Capo Press, 1999.

Pattillo, Mary E. *Black on the Block: The Politics of Race and Class in the City*. Chicago: University of Chicago Press, 2007.

Polletta, Francesca. *Freedom Is an Endless Meeting: Democracy in American Social Movements*. Chicago: University of Chicago Press, 2002.

Schwartzman, Helen B. "The significance of meetings in an American mental health center." *American Ethnologist* 14(1987): 271–294.

Schwartzman, Helen B. *The Meeting: Gatherings in Organizations and Communities*. New York: Plenum Press, 1989.

Small, Mario Luis. *Villa Victoria: The Transformation of Social Capital in a Boston Barrio*. Chicago: University of Chicago Press, 2004.

Small, Mario Luis, Erin M. Jacobs and Rebekah P. Massengill. "Why organizational ties matter for neighborhood effects: Resource access through childcare centers." *Social Forces* 87(1) (2008): 387–414.

Tracy, Karen and Aaron Dimock. "Meetings: Discursive sites for building and fragmenting community." In *Communication Yearbook*, edited by Pamela J. Kalbfleisch, 127–166. Mahwah, NJ: Lawrence Erlbaum, 2004.

U.S. Census Bureau. DP-1. Profile of General Population and Housing Characteristics: 2010, 2010. http://www.census.gov.

Warner, Lloyd. *Yankee City*. New Haven: Yale University Press, 1963.

Whyte, William Foote. *Street Corner Society: The Social Structure of an Italian Slum*. Chicago: University of Chicago Press, 1943.

Zukin, Sharon. *Loft Living: Culture and Capital in Urban Change*. New Brunswick: Rutgers University Press, 1982.

5 Meetings All the Way Through

United States Broad-based Reform Coalitions and the Thickening of American Democracy

Jen Sandler

Introduction: The Ethnographer in a Land of Meetings

After the Team A staff meeting of the Coalition for Local Initiatives (a pseudonym, along with all individuals and places in this chapter), twenty-five supervisory and administrative staff members file out, most chatting. I made a split-second decision as to who to follow through the post-meeting meetings that would take place over the next half-hour. I would participate in one or two informal debrief meetings, and sometimes initiated debrief meetings of my own with key players. Then I hurried to the next meeting on my schedule. This was most often some form of a pre-meeting or project development meeting, wherein staff or leaders strategized interactions that would take place in an upcoming meeting. At early-stage pre-meetings, much of the discussion often had to do with the various 1-on-1 meetings that needed to take place before the larger project meeting could be considered. Big official meeting agendas were usually not produced during pre-meetings. Instead, agendas were post-hoc artifacts of late-stage pre-meetings. There were sometimes last-minute short meetings to discuss and amend agendas. The official meeting related to a pre-meeting may not take place for another few days, weeks, or even months, by which time everything may have changed based on 1–1 meetings and larger pre-meetings. After one pre-meeting, I followed up with a key informant to learn about some of the 1–1 meetings that followed a particularly important pre-meeting last week. All of this happened before 2 p.m.; I would not be done with fieldwork for the day until after 9 p.m., when the afternoon and evening phases of meetings in schools, community organizations, and leaders' homes concluded for the evening.

I came here to study a particular kind of activism: a broad-based social reform coalition which uses large-scale community organizing to affect urban educational and social policy change through elite projects. But I was in a world of meetings, and each of these meetings was itself an unknown world. This broad-based urban reform coalition located in metropolitan Middlestate, USA, called the Coalition for Local Initiatives (CLI), seemed to be meetings all the way through.

DOI: 10.4324/9781315559407-6

As I will describe, such multi-issue, elite-grassroots reform coalitions as CLI are inherently unstable. In order for a coalition to act as a collective body, it must constitute itself continually through collective projects and performative understanding. I argue that it is collective epistemic structure—spaces and moments of thinking together—that underlies the tenuous, good-enough, relationship-based solidarity necessary for powerful and diverse social reform coalition to hold. Moreover, it is the meeting, in many forms, that is the chief instrument and site of this production of coalitional knowing-doing.

In this chapter, meetings are used to understand exactly how such a reform coalition as CLI sutures elite power to local democratic processes. And, obversely, I explore the coalition as an interesting site through which to think about how meetings operate not only to circulate knowledge and structure work, but, ultimately, to make the core knowledge practices that underlie the coalition itself.

What Sort of Activism Is the U.S. Reform Coalition?

U.S. media is filled to the virtual brim with niche activism, specific causes attached to specific populations. Activism focused on the treatment and cure of specific diseases (breast cancer, diabetes, heart disease, Alzheimer's) perhaps best illustrate this form. These causes have narrow bases: people who have direct experience with the disease through themselves or a loved one. They also have narrow range within their bases; their activists are not working toward a better quality of life in general for all those who suffer from the disease, but simply toward relief from the disease itself. Breast cancer activists do not fight against police violence, even as many of their sufferers experience such violence. Indeed, it would seem absurd for them to do so. Similar logics and boundaries apply to issue- or cause-based activism beyond health, such as activist organizations dedicated to fair housing, educational reform, mental health services, drug addiction, gun control, etc. The effort against "mission drift" governs non-profit U.S. activism and advocacy. Such niche activism has a strong hold on the public consciousness and an edge in the market-driven media that privileges a simple story and the development of causes into clear and measurable products.

And yet, the United States has also long hosted forms of activism that do not "transcend" niches nor involve "collaboration" among niches, but that basically ignore the logic of niche activism altogether. Instead, they begin with a base—a population—and seek power to improve the conditions for the base. Some of these activist modes are essentially revolutionary; they seek to transform who holds power and how power is held. Recent examples are the Occupy movement and the broad black social movement toward which Black Lives Matter leaders' work gestures. But more common, and historically more long-lived, forms of base-centered activism in the United

States are broad-based civic reform coalitions. The elite-initiated settlement house movement of the early twentieth century (of which Jane Addams's Hull House is the most recognized) is one example. Addams's social reform activism famously combined a commitment to anti-ideological "intercultural exchange," social services, then-new forms of social research, broad political advocacy to improve the conditions of urban immigrant life, and a holistic form of education and cultural development (Addams 1990). She and her Hull House colleagues' advocacy were deeply rooted in their relationships with the people. Hull House served as a great part of her (as well as her first-wave feminist and global peace activist colleagues') ongoing education about the realities of urban life for the immigrant working classes, and the elite-poor relationships built through the activities of the settlement house movement were largely responsible for the successes of the Progressive Era's urban reform agenda. A mid-twentieth-century example of a U.S. broad-based reform coalition is the National Urban League, particularly as its reform-oriented broad-based agenda was developed during Whitney Young's tenure as president in the 1960s (Weiss 1989). Young's National Urban League, like Addams's Hull House, involved creating ongoing connections between the base (black communities) and both political and economic elites. Furthermore, like Hull House, the Urban League under Young reached both upward toward structural policy change and pragmatically toward the base of the organization. While Young's philosophy was more focused on using the base-building efforts of smaller black organizations, he also devoted significant Urban League resources to developing specific leadership aspects of the base, including alternative education toward college readiness and programs for black leaders to collaborate with one another on reform ideas.

Broad-based U.S. reform coalitions like the Progressive Era Hull House, the 1960s National Urban League, and the 2000s Coalition for Local Initiatives may be quite diverse in their specific aims and the political ideologies and identities of their leadership, but they share certain common characteristics. They bring together political and economic elites with an organic "base" of some sort; elites bring political and capital power, and the base brings political legitimacy, the direct knowledge of social problems, and community infrastructure for implementing programs and policies. Methodologically, social reform coalitions tend to mix some form of base organizing, innovations in educational and social services, and explicit efforts to influence public policy and the flow of public funding.

Such U.S. civic reform coalitions are thus broad in precisely the two senses that more publicly legible niche activism is narrow. First, they aim to improve the lives of a broad category of people, for example, poor people, African-Americans, or immigrants, often further specified as those living in a specific geographic area. Second, they aim to improve the lives of this broad category of people in their multiple dimensions of suffering or inequity, including health, education, housing, language, employment, child care and welfare, employment, civil rights, food access, and violence. The plethora of local base-focused organizations such as mutual aid, religious charities, and neighborhood improvement organizations, which may also have broad bases and address multiple dimensions of suffering among them, differ from reform coalitions because they focus on service provision for its own sake, and do not work toward structural and political reform. Reform coalitions, born of the left-pragmatic politics that stands in mild but bearable tension with American democratic capitalism, operate somewhere in between—or perhaps in a space that elides—the charitable and the revolutionary, aiming (though they would not necessarily embrace this rhetoric) for a form of participatory social justice that does not upend but instead tames the brutal potentialities of the elite power structure.

The challenge for contemporary broad-based reform coalitions is that they have to organize across two major forms of difference. The first is positional. U.S. coalitions require substantial involvement and investment from both political/economic elites and members of the base. Without the former, they have no consistent power to make change under U.S. capitalist democracy. Without the latter, they have no legitimacy or ability to function in their communities. Second, social reform coalitions that aim to have staying power can countenance no ideological or partisan litmus tests. Political winds shift, while broad-based social reform is a continual project. Strong coalitions are able to influence a wide range of political administrations to marshal elite power in many policy contexts. Furthermore, a strong coalition must be able to engage a base with a wide variety of challenges, diverse cultural practices, and a range of ideological perspectives. Jane Addams's settlement house movement, for example, engaged a wide variety of immigrant groups across religion, language, and politics. Young's Civil Rights–era Urban League aimed to maintain broad membership in a community whose ideologies ranged from Black Nationalism to community development through integration, holding diverse convictions that the core challenge for black people was civil rights or political autonomy or economic opportunity. A broad-based social reform organization's key challenge, then, is to hold itself and all of its diverse parties together, chiefly across positionality (power and proximity to the base) and ideology (belief about the cause of the base's suffering, and about a utopia where reform would not be necessary).

What sets reform coalition meetings apart is that meetings are the work of the reform coalition. Meetings are not the means to do the work, even ostensibly: they are unambiguously the coalition's core practices. Whatever else coalitions are doing, they are always meeting. The overwhelming majority of coalition meetings have nothing even outwardly to do with decision-making, and surprisingly little to do with information-sharing. This stands in sharp contrast with the majority of meetings in other types of organizations, from niche activist groups to corporate boards to university meetings, where decision-making and information-sharing are always explicitly central (even as many other implicit productive functions are certainly also taking place). Instead, coalition meetings are designed to develop an epistemic solidarity that enables the iteration of the coalition's power, and that undermines the otherwise potentially divisive differences of positionality, interest, and ideology.

Roots Without Boundaries and Meeting-saturated Fieldwork

This study presents a response to—and in some sense an opening for retrenchment from—the critique that underlies the increasingly popular multi-sited ethnography approach (Marcus 1995). This critique holds that there are limitations, given global flows of knowledge, people, and cultural artifacts and practices, to the traditional anthropological privileging of ethnographic situatedness. It posits that by following discourses and cultural objects across sites, through globalized "flows," ethnographers may be able to re-cast our project in a way that engages rather than evades the "awkward scale" of global systems. The aim of meeting ethnography is to grasp circulations of discourses in ways that engage and do not take for granted the core cultural practices of collective sense-making that often form the agentic context for such discursive circulation. That is, there are often—and especially in meeting-intensive settings—people designing the circulation of productive discourses, and these people often adapt and use such practices as key technological practices. Whether intensive meeting practices are local or global in scope, meeting ethnography orients the ethnographer toward the thickness of coalition actors' everyday technological practices of collective meaning-making, technologies of analytical and political cohesion.

Meeting ethnography offers an opening to consider the planned, intention-laden, discursive event of the meeting as something more significant—that is, as something that usually signifies more—than the discourses that comprise it, and a mandate to do so without either enacting structural reification or foreclosing the possibilities of discourse analysis. This move toward meeting ethnography is in part simply about keeping up with our research subjects, all of the diverse "para-ethnographers" of organizationally complex activist worlds who simply cannot stop talking about the meetings that structure, and through which they structure, their projects and in fact their sense-making. If coalitions are made through technologies of meeting, there is a need to take up and in some sense go beyond Holmes and Marcus's (2006) urging that anthropologists attend to our research informants as para-ethnographers, whose practices involve developing and using theory to analyze their own worlds. Tracing not only the sense-making processes of our informants but their infrastructural practices of sense making—meetings chief among these—suggests the possibility for developing a contemporary rootedness for ethnographic inquiries in settings like activist coalitions that include—and also transcend—the relatively clean boundaries of traditional organizations.

In this paper I will describe two kinds of meetings that build, make cohesive, and ultimately propel a major civic reform coalition, the Coalition for Local Initiatives (CLI, a pseudonym). Developed in the early 1990s, CLI focuses on improving the social, economic, and educational conditions for poor people in a racially and economically diverse major metropolitan area of a non-coastal, politically mixed-partisan U.S. state. I began studying this coalition in 2006, and collected field notes on over three hundred meetings—generally (if cursorily) planned, discursive events in which at least one party exerted intentional structure—in addition to examining archival records of many more.

To say that the coalition is meetings all the way through is to say that meetings form the structure, practices, and productive agency of the coalition. From 1–1 meetings to committee and team meetings to large ceremonial board and project meetings, it is meetings that form the *architecture* of the coalition (Sandler and Thedvall, Introduction to this volume). The reason meetings are so crucial to this particular coalition's work is that they are the *practices* (Sandler and Thedvall, Introduction to this volume) for circulating knowledge, the truths of how poor people experience social policy, up through staff and elites to those who implement and make policy. Moving particular truths toward power is the core of the coalition's work, and it happens through the complex meeting architecture of the coalition. Finally, it is meetings that produce, codify, and legitimize the knowledge of how social policies operate in the daily lives of people. Meetings are not simply circulators but also *makers* (Sandler and Thedvall, Introduction to this volume) of both the knowledge of policy effects and the epistemic orientations of the community and elite actors who, in turn (and through meetings), make this knowledge matter to professionals and policymakers.

Demonstration Meetings as the Way to Know Together What We Have Done Separately

In CLI, at any given time, there are at least half a dozen different major projects. These include policy-focused projects involving attempts to shape state and national welfare reform policies to have the least negative impact on CLI's communities. There are population-focused projects, such as a large project focused on all youth aging out of state custody. And there are several service reform projects that CLI administers, such as a before- and after-school program that serves thousands of children in over seventy schools for up to five hours each day (nearly as long as the school day itself). There are also training projects, such as a comprehensive and regular training and support program for the hundreds of non-professional, unlicensed home-based childcare providers who provide much of the early childhood education in poor communities. The array of CLI projects, reflecting the array of challenges that economically poor families face in the urban United States, is dizzying. And there is a complex meeting architecture that underlies each of these diverse projects.

Notwithstanding this range of coalition undertakings, the majority of coalition projects take place at the nexus of specific neighborhood needs, public policy opportunities, and funding circumstances. Such projects are built on a temporal structure of different kinds of meetings, through the circulation of knowledge and documents through this meeting structure. Such circulation practices ultimately serve to make fragile but productive coalitional forms of understanding, knowledge/power constellations that enable concrete policy and infrastructure changes. What follows is a public-event style meeting that serves as a capstone and testament to such a project.

It was 6 p.m. in a low-slung one-story wing of a large black evangelical church in an urban neighborhood of a major metropolitan area. The neighborhood was cut off from the bulk of the city by an eight-lane highway twelve years earlier. It was difficult to get in or out of this neighborhood, and most public and private services were located on the other side of the highway where gentrification was uneven but possible, where they could be assured of a more consistent base of customers. Several thousand houses were located on this side of the highway, but they had been largely separated from urban amenities from grocery stores to health and welfare institutions. There was one elementary school in the neighborhood. People began to arrive at the church building on this night to witness the successful agreement to develop a health clinic located in this school, a project that will bring medical, dental, and mental health services to the neighborhood for the first time since the highway, and that will make these services affordable for all neighborhood residents and nearly free for school children and their immediate families. This meeting was the culmination of several hundred smaller meetings over the course of two years of project organizing.

Three coalition staff members—dressed "business casual" in pressed khaki and button-down shirts—stood near the door. There were rectangular folding tables set up at the back of the room with food: boxes of pizza, a bowl of fruit salad, a plate of carrots, bags of Chips Ahoy cookies, cups and juice, styrofoam plates and napkins. Neighborhood families—mostly Latino/Latina and some black—were given programs by a CLI staffer who they knew. They were directed to nudge their children to the back to pile food on plates, after which the children were hushed and shuffled away to a childcare room. A white man and woman in upper-class clothing that suggested old money to me—both uber-wealthy CLI board members—came in and were immediately greeted by CLI professional staff, then handed programs and gently guided the other way, to seats at the front of the room facing a podium. The CLI deputy director, a middle-aged black woman, placed her coat next to them (functionally assuring they would not have unknown seat neighbors). Meanwhile, two executives of a private hospital, a white woman and man wearing drab business suits, had walked in, found the CLI managerial staff member one of them knew, shaken hands stiffly, and sat down as near to the door as possible. A woman in a gray skirt and cotton sweater, with a bulging briefcase, rushed in and smiled awkwardly at one of the coalition staffers, collapsed in a frazzled heap in a folding chair, and took out her laptop. She was the state program officer overseeing the large government grant for the clinic, and the only person who seemed to know no one. The site coordinator, a white male community organizer with the coalition who had been working with the parent leaders on this project for three years, beckoned two parent leaders (both black women) once they emerged from dropping off their children, quietly huddling with them as they expressed anxieties, went over prepared talks, and calmed one another's nerves with words of encouragement. Other parents made their way from the food in the back to the back rows of chairs and took seats, smoothing their dresses or pants and fiddling with the one-page programs. The church pastor and the school principal, both of them black men, came in separately and each seemed to make a show of greeting as many people as possible individually, walking through aisles to shake hands with all the people in suits, saying hello to a parent or two in each aisle, back-slapping the male coalition professionals and hugging the female deputy director. They each separately leaned in to talk conspiratorially with coalition staff, walked to the back to grab food, walked around, crouched down to speak with different neighborhood folks who were seated, and got back up again to get more food. When they and the khaki-clad coalition staff were the only people standing, all but one staffer took seats and the pastor strode to the podium, welcomed guests to this "special event for our community," and said a prayer for the food.

Before we even get to the meeting itself, it should be clear that the assertion of collective *identity* was impossible in this context. Any attempt to assert collective interest, to tell a collective story, to create a sense of forced solidarity, would have exposed fractures that were not under the surface but apparent to all in the faces, in the dress styles, and in the bodily comportments of the diverse actors. This health clinic was the result of years of organizing at many levels, from parents in the neighborhood to elite coalition leaders, mobilizing funds from three government programs for medical, mental health, and dental clinics, and developing a difficult contract with a major for-profit health corporation. Each of these contingencies was there for their own self-interest, and saw the clinic as part of their own vision or professional project. The parents had been organizing amongst themselves and pressuring their city council representative to help get the zoning changed. The elite board members had made their phone calls to encourage the unprecedented package of state grants to be approved. The hospital executives had been half-blackmailed with lawsuits and half-bribed with sweetened contracts to join the deal. Most of the contingencies had engaged solely in their own separate meetings to understand and fulfill their part of the project, and had never encountered one another directly. They each had different stakes, leveraged different forms of power, and had in some ways distinct visions of the project. When they came together, the disparate character of the coalition was instantly obvious: there was simply no center to hold.

It is worth asking a functional question here: *why meet?* Why bring all of these people into the room together at all? Everyone had consented to the project; all the buy-in had been procured, all the contracts had been signed. And, before the meeting began, it seemed as if everyone was coping with the awkwardness of uncomfortably different bodies and consciousnesses converging in time and space. What or who was this ritual for? What could it produce? Let us go back to the meeting to find out.

The program itself was short. There was a succession of quite brief, carefully crafted acknowledgements that without each contingency's work, this clinic would not be built. But the core of the meeting, for everyone, was the three neighborhood women leaders' speeches. They were extraordinarily well prepared, both in their language and delivery. The first presented a sort of testimonial-style account of what it had been like to live in a part of the city that was geographically and structurally cut off from all health services. She attested to her own children's absences from school for lack of dental services, her four bus rides to the hospital emergency room with her toddler suffering from repeated complications from ear infections, and how her own mother died of cervical cancer because no one in their neighborhood knew where undocumented people could go to get regular and affordable pelvic exams. The next speaker talked about the group of parents that came together to study different models of health clinics. She did not talk about the study itself, only the group: how much they learned, how capable they felt to come to understand the organizations in their neighborhood. The third talked about what her life is going to be like once the clinic goes in: that she may be able to keep a job for longer than from the end of one child's flu to the beginning of the next; that she won't have to make decisions between going to work and taking her kids to the dentist; that her asthmatic ten-year-old won't ever again nearly die because she can't keep an appointment a two-hour bus ride across town with the Medicaid-accepting doctor who will give them a new inhaler prescription.

These were carefully crafted statements, notable for what was absent. There was no discussion of ideology; no mention of personal obligation, of deservedness, of the role of the government, of rights or responsibilities; no blame or demand. And there was no paternalistic thanks, either, no cloying expressions of gratitude to the elites in the room. Just moving stories of what was reality before, how people have come together toward change, and, because of that coming together, what is now possible. After the women spoke, one of the coalition's elite board members got up, shook each of their hands, and said a few words about how the coalition—the organization—is about bringing people together around people's "wonderful, touching, strong" stories like these. And he thanked them for sharing and said he was glad to hear it and be a "part of this" with everyone in this room. The vague sentiment—the "part of this" hanging in the air, open to be interpreted differently by each attendee—contrasted sharply with the specificity of the women's stories. When he ended and the CLI staff began clapping to indicate conclusion, there was an almost palpable sense of relief in the room.

"We did it!" a CLI supervisor who was one of my closest informants said to me.

"What," I asked, "the health clinic, or this meeting?"

"Both! Ha—exactly!" he exclaimed, and winked at me as he sauntered off to slap the site organizer's back in camaraderie.

I think what he meant was: we all did something of substance together, and, for a moment here, we all knew together what it meant. For those who would continue with the coalition, including the elites, the organizers, and the base, both the doing and the knowing were essential components of the same endeavor. It was not simply that they went through the motions to meet and do what was necessary to design and develop the health clinic. It was that the making of the health clinic through these particular forms of circulation of knowledge produced the coalition itself, the means for future projects. So a capstone meeting was needed not to circulate knowledge for the clinic or to provide structure for the work of developing it, but to make the epistemic core of the coalition itself.

The coalition was constituted in and through being positioned differently and believing differently, but momentarily *knowing together* what it was that had been done and what that doing had produced. Such moments cannot always be thick, and they cannot generally be prolonged; difference runs deep, and everyone goes back to their own material and ideological home after the meeting. So demonstration meetings must be repeated, successfully (that is, without overt conflict) and with significant frequency, lest the coalition disintegrate into factions with ideologically distinct and materially oppositional interests. Such a meeting, the orchestrated demonstration of collective epistemic recognition that underlies policy and infrastructure reform, makes ongoing coalition work possible.

Meeting as the Infrastructure and Means of Coalition Relationship-Building

If the demonstration meeting is the coalition's ritualized space of epistemic recognition, where momentary common sense is demonstrated and shared through a collective project, then the perpetual small meetings that organize relationships are the coalition's chief mode of production. Most anthropologists are trained to seek out the nonformal in-between spaces of organizations and projects, spaces presumed to hold the prized stuff of the "everyday." In CLI, such nonformal, gritty, everyday interaction is inseparable from the organization's meeting-intensive culture. Unofficial but still usually planned, structured, intent-laden meetings take place in offices and cubicles, in the smoking room of the central offices and in cars, outside schools as children are picked up and on phone calls, over fancy lunches, and on the porches of trailer homes. These, too, are meetings, and are treated by core staff as technologies of coalition-building; as I will describe, their strategy and structure are even the subject of training. This section will bring focus to the micropolitics of nonformal meetings, the use of meetings as a technology for building the relationships that propel the coalition, both at the base and among elites. Through an endless series of planned, structured, informal meetings, CLI relationship-building processes go up channels of power, down into and through base communities, and across ideologies and identities. Relationships are the glue that holds the coalition together, and such relationships are developed through certain practices of nonformal meeting.

The building block of CLI's community infrastructure is the site council, a neighborhood (usually school)-based group of volunteers in charge of developing an understanding of community needs so that CLI staff and elites can leverage resources and policies toward addressing them. CLI uses many of the more radical community organizing strategies of school activist coalitions like the Alliance Schools and the community organizing groups in Chicago and Los Angeles to develop its reform infrastructure (e.g., Warren 2001; Lipman 2005). Indeed, the details of how CLI's site councils operate are not particularly unique to CLI; there are several national organizations that train people to organize low-income community residents in their churches, schools, and neighborhoods to build power and push for change. And while this methodology is not standardized in a strict sense, it is disseminated through national institutions and networks that provide assistance and codify strategies and trainings to help with each step. People Improving Communities through Organizing (www.piconetwork.org) and Communities in Schools (www.cis.org) are the most relevant national networks for CLI. But unlike these base-organizing groups, CLI uses community organizing strategies as an infrastructure for continual base-building and not as a method toward adversarial confrontation.

It is a truism among CLI leaders that relationships underlie all of the work of the coalition, at every level. The basic building block of CLI's organization-wide focus on ongoing relationship-building is the "1-on-1." A common community organizing tool, the 1-on-1 is even more crucial for a reform coalition whose goal is not to "win" in any final sense but to continually strengthen relationships among and between the base and elites. The 1-on-1 is basically a semi-structured conversation between two people. At first glance, a successful 1-on-1 looks deceptively like a good casual chat. Upon more focused investigation it is clear that these conversations are led with intention, resembling an artful ethnographic interview. In an organizing 1-on-1, however, the objective is to establish a rapport and to identify the self-interest of the other person in order to move toward some form of collective action.

The prototypical 1-on-1 at a CLI site looks something like this: a site coordinator (SC) will see a mother when she stops off at the CLI after-school program to pick up her child. The SC will greet the mother, introduce herself and establish who she is and, if appropriate, let the mother know who mentioned that the site coordinator should connect with her. The SC will then ask casual questions during which she will discover that the mother gets out of work half an hour before she picks up her child. The SC will then invite her to stop by before the day ends tomorrow to talk for 20 minutes—the talk which is to be the "real" 1-on-1. At this meeting, the SC will say something nice about the mother's child, will ask the mother about herself, and will put forth various questions that encourage the mother to talk about what is important to her. The SC will be very encouraging in this conversation, complimenting the mother in ways that are genuine and specific to her situation. She may then invite the mother to be on the site council, and will connect the work that the site council does to the interests the mother has expressed. These interests might include specific after-school activities that are offered, community organizations she is a part of, or health care issues she has faced. The SC will impress upon her how valuable her participation would be to the site council, and how the site council needs her enthusiasm and experience with this issue. She may ask the mother if she can have the site council chair (another parent) give her a call, or she may ask if they can talk again to check in before the site council meeting, depending on the situation. Often, the SC will ask the mother if there are any other mothers she knows who the SC might talk to about the site council. After an appropriate "action step" or follow-up plan is established, there will be more appreciation expressed and thanks given, and the two will part.

The objective of the 1-on-1 is not primarily to exchange information, but ultimately to establish a relationship and provide momentum for this relationship to develop the leadership—the action, which often consists of broadened relationship-building—of the person being organized. It is a methodical attempt to establish substantive relationships (social capital, by Robert Putnam's [1993] definition) based upon which the experiences of people can be shared, collected, and mobilized. The 1-on-1 is thus key to CLI's local knowledge production, and also, because of its ability to establish relationships, instrumental to the mobilization of this knowledge. That is, 1-on-1 meetings are the core methodological building block of CLI, underlying all other meetings and all action.

In addition to 1-on-1 skills, community organizing includes the effective orchestration of meetings in which knowledge is shared, rapport is built, decisions emerge, and action is planned. I say "orchestration" rather than "facilitation" because ideally site council meetings are facilitated by the head of the site council—a volunteer—and not by the site coordinator or an official CLI organizer. Most full site council meetings occur monthly. CLI's site council meetings are each preceded by one or more pre-meetings. Established site councils have an executive committee pre-meeting, including the site council chair or co-chairs, the secretary and treasurer, and any other core volunteers. But it does not begin there. Before the pre-meeting during which the meeting is planned, the site coordinator and site council chair often meet together individually, and each of them often meets with several parents, community members, and anyone who plans to present something at the meeting. Site councils that are early in their development may require meetings between the site coordinator and their CLI site supervisor and/or the CLI community organizing trainer. Often site coordinators will also meet with individual parents, school staff, or community members to help them to prepare a relevant agenda for the site council meetings. After each site council meeting there will usually be at least one debriefing meeting, and often more.

Site council meetings themselves are thus mostly orchestrated affairs—not so tightly as the demonstration meeting above, certainly, but enough that there are rarely surprises. Site coordinators and site council chairs (community leaders, not staff) usually know before the meeting what will be said and more or less how discussions will play out, because they will have spoken at some length with all of the key players. The meetings themselves are almost like plays in which all of the major actors have rehearsed with the director previously, but never in the same room until that moment. As the meeting unfolds, everyone begins to understand what the entire play— the state of the site and its work—is about. Everyone feels like their concerns have been included in the agenda if they are relevant to the site council. Almost everyone comes to the table with a positive rapport with the directors, already feeling a part of the main event. If there is an individual angry parent with a concern irrelevant to the entire council, that parent will have had their say numerous times before the actual meeting, so they will have had an outlet for resolving their individual conflict in advance. New participants in the site council observe a respectful meeting in which a lot of ground is covered, they learn many new things, and everyone seems to participate actively; they thus often want to return and to become part of this well-organized group of parents.

Besides making for enjoyable and productive spectacle, well-developed site council meetings serve another important purpose. The many pre-meetings and 1-on-1s that precede each site council meeting give site coordinators an early sense of when trouble is brewing. If a site coordinator is doing her job, she will never show up to a meeting and be shocked to find a mob of angry parents with a litany of complaints against the principal or against CLI. In fact, she will rarely find *one* angry community member who is able to derail the process. She will never find that the meeting becomes an unexpected venue for an argument between two factions of the community. This is certainly not because CLI neighborhoods are unusually unified or immune to power struggles and infighting. It is that when these issues come up, the site coordinator knows well in advance and is able to pull in the necessary resources to either neutralize the conflict (in the case of interpersonal issues) or turn the conflict to productive use for the site council. What follows is an example of CLI's main community organizing trainer's work on the skills of one site coordinator to begin to build this web of relationships.

CLI community organizer James and I were in the inner-city Glenwood neighborhood one evening, debriefing a large community meeting at a local bar. A young professional white couple sat down next to us, and James said hello. The couple told us that they had just bought a house around the block. They said that it's "great living in the city," the architecture is "historical" and the price of the real estate is "amazing." Of course, they noted, you do have to factor in another $15,000 a year for each child so you can send them to "a decent school." In a neighborhood that had become almost 50 percent white over the past decade, the local school was approximately 95 percent black, with more than 90 percent of the students eligible for free and reduced lunch. Gentrification was in full swing, and it certainly was not raising all boats.

I attended five site council meetings at this neighborhood elementary school, a run-down small building with trailers in the back serving as extra classrooms. The site coordinator, Jenny, was a young white woman with a bachelor's degree in child development and no experience working in the inner city or with adults in a black community. She was having trouble. Parent involvement in the site council was quite low, and Jenny had a conflicted relationship with one particular parent who had been a powerful leader on the site council before Jenny's arrival. She led the first site council meeting of the semester, an awkward non-meeting to which two parents showed up very late. After the conflict between her and the parent leader surfaced, James, a seasoned CLI community organizer, led the second meeting. This meeting was small and difficult for Jenny because the three parents in attendance were complaining about past problems at the school, dismissing Jenny's leadership, and seemed to have no interest in taking any leadership role themselves.

Jenny's site supervisor was Stacey, a white woman in her forties in charge of CLI's licensing and one of the least skilled community/meeting organizers on CLI's supervisory staff. James, a black man in his sixties and well-known local civil rights activist from the 1960s, was often called in to help site coordinators in such situations. The following meeting description represents the level of intensity and detail of the day-to-day work involved in training site coordinators for their community organizing meeting-focused work.

Jenny, James, Stacey, and I sat in the CLI administrative conference room for this meeting. James really ran the show. He began casually, a little scattered. Then he asked Jenny what the date of the next site council meeting was. She said the twenty-first. He started writing on the board, what at first looked like very simple steps: 1) List; 2) Call; 3) Meet. He asked her what kinds of people would be good to be on the list of people to contact for the pre-meeting officer's meeting. She listed people who came to the last meeting, people who she hoped would come. James suggested other people who might have leadership qualities, like people who seem to treat their kids in an admirable way; Stacey said what about people who relate well with other parents? James was very affirming with Jenny and Stacey, saying good things about their various suggestions. After we had about seven categories of people, he counted them up with Jenny: about seven people from the last meeting, maybe five more who she'd done 1-to-1s with, and maybe another seven or so from the last categories. James asked Jenny to list some specific people who fit into those categories. She listed about seven and he wrote them up on the board. He said we were now moving on to the second step: Call.

He explained that she was going to call each of these people and we were now going to talk about what she was going to say to them. He wrote on the board the four steps: communicate, edify, celebrate, communicate. He said that the details might be different with each person, so why don't we start with Mr. Crockett, a young man who was at the last site council meeting. He said that the important thing was for Jenny to also remember to "edify" each person, to engage with them based on what she has to communicate about specifically with them—their kids, usually. He went over specifically what Jenny would say to Mr. Crockett. Then they went on to Miss Jimenez, the parent with whom Jenny had problems. James said that what he would do first off if he were Jenny would be to tell Miss Jimenez how much she (Jenny) appreciated what Miss Jimenez said to her at the meeting. He said that he thinks that it's important to acknowledge and celebrate when someone puts themselves out there like that. Jenny looked a little skeptical, and she hedged—she did not believe Miss Jimenez had been sincere at the meeting.

James had been encouraging and even playful up to that point, like he was Jenny's buddy. But now he was looking her straight in the eye. He asked her very directly and seriously if she thinks she can call Miss Jimenez and say something like that. She said yes, she thought so, but sounded not quite sure. James said that he can't make the call for her, but that what he can do is to call Miss Jimenez before Jenny does, to talk to her and let her know that Jenny's going to be calling. Jenny said yeah, maybe that would be good. James moved on to the next person on the list, and we went through all the parents and exactly how Jenny would connect with them individually to invite them to the meeting. He noted that he doesn't know the other people she'd invite from the list part, but that it seemed that she had the idea. She confidently said that she did, that she could call them and invite them to the meeting. So James moved on to the third part: Meet.

James said that when they meet, they're going to have to have an agenda; he said, very kindly, that he knows that Jenny knows all about how to put together an agenda, but he's just going through everything anyway. So he went through the parts of the agenda that were important: *Introduction*; *Reflection*—the part where someone reflects on something to pull everyone into the meeting and away from whatever else they're thinking about; he made a comparison to church; *Focus*—he said that focus is a word that sounds like what it is (onomatopoeia)—and he said it slowly and crisply. When you write "focus" in the middle of an agenda with a list of things, he said, under it that's where everyone will immediately look. So he wrote below "focus" on the board, saying that this was the part where the parents would talk about what they were there to talk about. He said he was just guessing at some things they might talk about: leadership, finances, fundraisers. He said that the actual topics for the content part of the agenda would come from the conversations she has with the people on the *List* who she *Calls* (he pointed to the board with each step). James kept linking things back together, making it sound simple, and yet somehow this didn't sound condescending at all. He managed this tone easily and smoothly, in part by interjecting things like "I know you know this already, I'm just trying to remind myself" and "I don't know anything about this person, so you'll have to tell me" and "Exactly!" "Great!" and "Does this make sense? Is this okay?" Plus, he smiled big big big the whole time he was talking, except when he was making a particularly serious point.

At this point in the meeting Jenny's supervisor, Stacey, interjected with a question: Wasn't this "officers" meeting or whatever just going to happen all over again at the actual site council meeting? Why would the people Jenny calls want to come back three days later for the same meeting with the same people? James explained that Jenny wouldn't have to do this same process for every site council meeting; it was just her job to start it up, but that then once parents were involved in a positive manner that a process would be put into place so that *they* would do most of this—the lists, the calls, the pre-meetings, the agendas for meetings—and she would just support the process. Stacey didn't say anything. She looked skeptical.

Jenny said that all made sense, but would James please call Miss Jimenez like he'd said? She was worried too much time had passed for her to go back to what happened the last meeting, and she thought it would help if James said that he and Jenny had been working together. He said he'd call her right away after this meeting. Stacey said that Jenny should go back to those community people she had met with at some point before—the people from the library, local businesses, etc., and invite them to the meeting, too. James wrapped up the meeting by talking directly to Jenny, saying that up until now she's been going through Stacey to talk to him but that she needs to call him directly when she needs support, anytime. He said that he could call her but that's a little harder; he doesn't want to check up on her, just to be there for her if she needs help with anything over the next week or so with all these meetings and calls. She should still keep talking to Stacey, of course, but he's available whenever. He was adamant about it. He said very firmly but lightly that he sees how much she's growing in this process. She blushed, but did indeed look more confident.

Two weeks later, Jenny led a site council meeting with James as a backup facilitator. Seven parents attended, and after an awkwardly formal start they began talking about parents' ideas and experiences. The last two meetings of the semester (in each of the following months) were both led by parents. The first parent-led meeting, which neither James nor I attended, was a planning meeting that Jenny said to me afterward felt like the "tipping point."

At the last meeting of the semester, James, Stacey, Jenny, and I joined more than twenty people, all crowded into the small trailer where the CLI program was located. The meeting was obviously well planned. A parent facilitated, using an agenda she had put together with Jenny based on both of their 1-on-1 meetings with other parents. The meeting involved engaged and vibrant discussion about school programs offered and the need to build a better relationship with the principal moving into the next school year. The parents—about 80 percent of them black women, plus a few black men—shared concerns about the school, introduced themselves to one another and to the parent leader, and made plans for the next school year. Miss Jimenez made a point of noting how Jenny was doing an excellent job keeping their kids safe and listening to everyone.

Suddenly, there was a parent-led site council. After the meeting, James noted approvingly to Jenny that they would be ready the next year to "get to work." What he later told me that he meant by this was that they would be ready to identify local challenges and to engage (through more meetings) in bringing the resources of CLI staff and the power of CLI elites to bear on addressing them. Moving people's knowledge from 1–1 meetings to larger local meetings and, ultimately, to power is the circulation process that constructs the "base" of the coalition. Meetings provide the architecture for this knowledge production and movement, ultimately making the coalition itself. In this way, coalition meetings serve as architecture, practices of circulation, and makers.

Of course, it is not only the grassroots that requires 1–1 meetings as a component of the constellation of meetings that enacts the knowledge/power relations of the coalition. While the professionally facilitated grassroots of CLI is using 1-on-1 meetings to develop local leadership and a large and solid base, CLI's elites are engaging in a similarly perpetual series of relationship-building and strategy meetings. People who are far away from the experiences of the poor whose lives the coalition aims to improve—that is, elites—have to become capable of knowing welfare through the lived experience of someone who has been on welfare, state-sanctioned violence through people's experience of such violence, and public institutional power through the stories of people who must navigate public institutions to survive. Before any of this storytelling or coalitional understanding can be mobilized in the demonstration meetings, it must be practiced through smaller, often 1–1 meetings. Many such meetings take place between upper-crust elites and civic leaders who have the moral weight to represent "the people." Every CLI board member I spoke with cited cross-class, cross-race experiences in meetings as the core of their work and motivation for working with CLI. The very desire among coalition members for what CLI calls "bottom-up" reform must be constantly reproduced through intimate meetings between members of the base that experiences socio-economic challenges and the civic and corporate elites who leverage power to address these problems. During my time with CLI I witnessed such meetings between, for example, young parents aging out of state foster care and elites who know nothing of these worlds. Wealthy white community leaders and both wealthy and poor black community leaders met frequently. New CLI board members were initiated in part by listening to the stories of founding board members; nearly every such story focused on a memorable meeting.

In the realms of the non-meeting-based, everyday lives of elites and community people involved in CLI, there is simply no overlap, no norms of interaction that would permit the work of the coalition to unfold. Meetings within CLI's daily operations are ubiquitous and perpetual, an intentional production of the sort of knowing/doing that characterizes CLI's approach to social problems. Meetings serve to make relationships, circulate knowledge, and ultimately structure a will to action that is coherent and collective. The bringing-together of different types of social actors, particularly elites and the economically and racially marginalized, is the coalition itself, and meetings are almost always the context for that togetherness.

Conclusion: The Broad-based Reform Coalition and the Project of Meeting Ethnography

Ethnographers of social change activism, both reformist and revolutionary, often study critically how marginalities are produced and reinscribed through such political projects as I've described here. The pitfalls of liberal recognition politics is a common theme. Povinelli, to take one of the most creative examples of such a project, maps how various liberal recognition schemes are crafted, through the policing of boundaries, "bracketing," and "redlining" that produces categories of "others" who are left to live and die in the creases of late-liberal policy regimes (Povinelli 2011). She is particularly critical of liberal recognition schemes and intent on exposing unexpected spaces of possibility that elide them (2002). Her form of anthropological creativity, focusing as it does more recently on social formations not visible as either movement or organization, enacts a certain charismatic hubris: the ethnographer as exposing the radicalism not recognized, the liberatory events that go unnoticed, the social formations that do not confront governmentality but deftly and expertly elide its reach.

The meeting is, in a sense, the obverse of such uncoalesced activism: it declares itself important so often and so thoroughly in the daily lives of social change professionals that it has become beyond banal. Yet the actual contours of late-liberal projects cannot be seen without attention to the meetings that structure them and circulate knowledge and other resources. The broad-based U.S. reform coalition is a place where multiple and diverse actors spend the better part of their professional and personal lives pragmatically, non-ironically, and thoroughly engaging in performing late liberalism's most straightforward desires: universal progress, solidarity between owning and working classes, equality of opportunity, and (yes) multiculturalism. And the actual contours of this very project are, without ethnographic attention to meetings, illegible on the contemporary activist landscape.

The cost of ignoring the actual interactive performance of the desires of late liberalism is the production of ideological analytical critiques. Without seeing the coalition, the critical social commentator can only declare liberalism and its most fervent actors either idiots or victims, wrapped up in some form of bad faith. Critics of liberalism might cling to thin tropes as evidence: the liberal white do-gooder who locks her car doors when passing through a poor black neighborhood, or the philanthropist reformer of public schools who sends his own child to private academies. But tropes make poor ethnography. Meetings serve the same ontological function for ethnographers seeking to reveal the deep contours of contemporary late-liberal projects as Anna Tsing's matutsake mushroom serves in revealing the deep contours of late capitalism and its (simultaneous) aftermath (Tsing 2015). Meetings are what actually produce late-liberal projects, and paradoxically they are also the stuff of which the underlying structures of the projects themselves are made.

We need meeting ethnography that engages meeting participants at least significantly on their own terms. The meeting is not simply a lens, not methodologically akin to a fungus or nucleotide; at least in meeting-saturated forms of activism like the reform coalition, the meeting is always something more than an actant (Latour 1987). Reform coalition meetings both are and enact a method of "ordering knowledge" that is a viable alternative to the state-legitimized scientific knowledge that Jasanoff (2004) argues "orders society." Coalition meetings enact a methodology of drawing people from their disparate social and economic locations, ideologies, and interests to produce something together, and sometimes to produce the very notion of "together." Attending to meetings requires that ethnographers take seriously our informants' world-making projects, and that we take into account that we are always meaning-makers among meaning-makers. Meeting ethnography is, in part, a way of insisting on an expansive notion of what sort of social subject counts as a "keenly reflexive subject" of inquiry, and what sort of modes are appropriate for what Holmes and Marcus (2006) discuss as para-ethnography. Anyone who studies social activism and politics through layers of meetings such as those of CLI will be, in a certain respect, working alongside as many para-ethnographers as there are participants in each meeting.

In the broad-based U.S. reform coalition, I hope to have shown something of how diverse meeting forms engage people across radical differences of ideology and positionality to transform material and epistemic conditions in contexts of over-determined social suffering. Broad-based reform coalitions are basically "meetings all the way through," ongoing technical productions of knowledge/power that, at their best, aim toward no less—and no more—than the thickening of American capitalist democracy. For what it's worth, I would argue that they often hit their mark.

References

Addams, Jane. *Twenty years at Hull-House with autobiographical notes.* Urbana: University of Illinois Press, 1990.

Holmes, Douglas R. and George E. Marcus. "Fast capitalism: Para-ethnography and the rise of the symbolic analyst." In *Frontiers of Capital: Ethnographic Reflections on the New Economy*, edited by Melissa S. Fisher and Greg Downey, 33–57. Durham: Duke University Press, 2006.

Jasanoff, Sheila. "Ordering knowledge, ordering society." In *States of Knowledge: The Co-production of Science and Social Order*, edited by Sheila Jasanoff, 13–45. London: Routledge, 2004.

Latour, Bruno. *Science in Action: How to Follow Scientists and Engineers through Society.* Cambridge, MA: Harvard University Press, 1987.

Lipman, Pauline. "Metropolitan regions—new geographies of inequality in education. The Chicago metroregion case." *Globalisation, Societies and Education* 3(2005): 141–163.

Marcus, George. Ethnography in/of the world system: The emergence of multi-sited ethnography. *Annual Review in Anthropology* 24(1995): 95–117.

Povinelli, Elizabeth A. *The Cunning of Recognition: Indigenous Alterities and the Making of Australian Multiculturalism.* Durham: Duke University Press, 2002.

Povinelli, Elizabeth A. *Economies of Abandonment: Social Belonging and Endurance in Late Liberalism.* Durham: Duke University Press, 2011.

Putnam, Robert D. "The prosperous community: Social capital and public life." *The American Prospect* 13(1993): 35–42.

Tsing, Anna Lowenhaupt. *The Mushroom at the End of the World: On the Possibility of Life in Capitalist Ruins.* Princeton, NJ: Princeton University Press, 2015.

Warren, Mark R. *Dry Bones Rattling: Community Building to Revitalize American Democracy.* Princeton, NJ: Princeton University Press, 2001.

Weiss, Nancy J. *Whitney M. Young, Jr. and the Struggle for Civil Rights.* Princeton, NJ: Princeton University Press, 1989.

6 Small Places, Big Stakes

Meetings as Moments of Ethnographic Momentum

Christina Garsten and Adrienne Sörbom

High Stakes, High Fences

It is our first day in Davos, a Swiss alpine ski resort, and it's a cold, clear winter day in late January. Having just arrived in the village the night before in order to attend the World Economic Forum Annual Meeting 2011, we have ventured out to explore the meeting premises. The Davos summit captures the attention of world leaders and world media. Having failed at getting a formal invitation to attend the meeting, we decided to go anyway, and to see to what extent, if any, we could participate. As we approach the meeting ground, we spot the high-wired fence that has been erected for the meeting. No chance of climbing that one, we think, for a fraction of a second. Especially not since we are dressed for the occasion in boots, skirt, and coat. At the entrance gates for the meeting compound, a small shack has been erected for the occasion. Posted before it are four guards, in grey uniforms, and with automatic guns on their shoulders. Five more guards are posted on the inside of the gates. We observe guards from the Swiss special police forces standing on the roof of the Congress Centre, dressed in camouflage uniforms, wearing masks, and heavily equipped. CCTV cameras are posted around the entrance gates and stare at us from above. In the air, Swiss Army helicopters hover, and occasionally F/A 18 Hornets, a type of combat jet, intercept their trajectories, drawing white lines across the blue sky. The soundscape created by the air security embeds the small town with a constant pattering noise. After the summit, we learn that up to 5,000 Swiss soldiers took part in the security operation that was staged for the event.

Hesitatingly, we approach the gates. One of the guards asks us for our badges. We have no badges, we reply. Then you are not allowed inside, the guard responds. Unaware of the entry restrictions, we have arranged for a first meeting with a Scandinavian participant in the meeting area. Olafur Gunnlaugson, a top-level manager from one of the corporations funding the World Economic Forum (WEF) and thus an invited participant at the summit, has agreed to meet us in the pizzeria inside the gates. We have a meeting with someone at the Pizzeria Daiano in the meeting compound, we explain. It's important that we get inside. After a few minutes of arguing, pleading,

DOI: 10.4324/9781315559407-7

and looking desperate, the guard decides to let us in, but only so far as to the pizzeria, and never out of his sight. Thank you very much, we exclaim, sighing with relief. As we walk toward the pizzeria, the guard keeps a steady eye on us.

Over lunch, Mr. Gunnlaugson says that he is happy that we could meet inside the gates. As he explains, going in and out of the conference center is like passing into security areas of airports after September 11, 2001. He looks a bit troubled when he realizes that we are not invited to the meeting and will not receive badges, but during lunch he explains the reason why corporate leaders should be in Davos. If you are not here, at the meeting, you do not exist, he explains. By this he means that every actor or organization with some ambition to count as important in the global business arena is there, and should make sure to be there. The meeting is a melting pot of finance, politics, research—an institutional melting pot that works. What is also important is the political dimension, he contends. (Interview Davos 2011)

The interesting conversation with Mr. Gunnlaugson makes us more at ease; it is obviously possible to do interviews and learn about and understand the event even without a badge. After the meeting, we continue our tour around the meeting premises, following the wired fence all around the area. There are a couple more entrance gateways, but nowhere is there a place where the general public can enter. Having tried our luck with the guards all around, we venture disappointingly into the village center of Davos. Unable to sport a badge that would allow us to enter and participate, we are left with a feeling of shame, being excluded, unwanted and deprived. It is an uncomfortable position to be in.

As it turned out, researching the World Economic Forum is as methodologically and theoretical challenging as it is rewarding. While getting access to the WEF headquarters was fairly easy, accessing their events, such as the meeting in Davos, was more challenging. For three consecutive years we took the train up to Davos, without getting into the conference center. What, if anything, can we learn from doing ethnography in such a small, temporary meeting place, when we do not even have access to much of what seems to be going on, we asked ourselves? In this chapter we will discuss what may be learned from studying an organization such as the WEF, to which access is restricted and where the gates to meetings may be closed whenever it suits them. We will argue that in order to understand the practices constituting meetings we will have to broaden our perspective of the meeting as a social phenomenon. The meeting as research locus and focal point of interest should not be seen as a given entity, but rather as a contingent and continually constructed social arena. In the WEF case the meeting is both a continuing organizing effort, and an arena, temporarily bounded in time and space by both organizers and participants.

The chapter is organized so as to provide a theoretical discussion of what meeting ethnography can entail in an environment where access to meetings is severely restricted, and where meetings often transgress and challenge what appear to be the gates of the meeting. We first introduce the WEF as an organization, highlighting its interest in keeping their meetings closed. In this first section we also discuss how the WEF draws on meetings to leverage their visibility and authority as a global player. In the second section we present ethnographic vignettes from the meeting in Davos, but also from other WEF meetings in other parts of the world, in order to illustrate the role of meetings as part of a broader organizing effort. Finally, we conclude by discussing meetings in the context of the predicaments of contemporary anthropological fieldwork and ask in what sense meetings may be seen as *experiential and experimental sites*, in Rabinow's (2003) terms.

Meetings: Microcosms of a Larger Social Organization

The Davos summit is surrounded by air of seriousness and hype, but it is also something like a huge cocktail party. In essence, it is a kind of human beehive, attracting and organizing a multitude of actors around its core, each contributing to the existence of the beehive community, and each disseminating its ideas and perspectives to the world at large.

Being the showcase meeting of the WEF, it is also a microcosm of the organization, set up in a small place and speaking to bigger issues: market regulations, financial crises, environmental risks, armed conflicts, and the like. With the WEF's main mission being to "improve the state of the world," meetings are one of the fundamental tools used by the organization for reaching this end. The WEF is essentially a social world of meetings—staged, circumvented, formal, organized meetings—and meetings to which access is tightly restricted. The kinds of questions that arise out of fieldwork in organizations such as the WEF are to do with access, representation, validity, and the predicaments of doing ethnography in organized settings.

At a more general level, ethnographic fieldwork in organizations such as corporations, state agencies, and international organizations often entails that the ethnographer has to rely on meetings as the primary point of access. Oftentimes, this involves doing fieldwork in workshops, at ceremonies, and at other staged, formal events (Garsten and Nyqvist 2013). In addition, such fieldwork tends to be multi-local, mobile, and discontinuous. It may not provide as much of a flavor of the different local sites and a sense of "being there" as one would wish for. The tendency in anthropology to favor the informal, the "genuine" or "authentic," as well as the spontaneous, may leave one with a lingering feeling of having to make do with second-rate material, i.e., the formal, the superficial, and the organized. Fieldwork around staged meetings, to which one even may not get full access, may, from that angle, be frustrating at first, not least because much of an organization's identity may be built up around the meetings it arranges. But as we will show, a meeting is not merely that which goes on behind the walls designated by the organizers and participants as "the meeting." It is embedded and shaped in social processes, entailing both organizing and networking on behalf of individuals and organizations. Meeting ethnography therefore, even in the cases where one appears to have full access, also entails doing research outside the designated, labeled, meeting space. This makes the drawing of distinctions between the formal, or actual, meeting, and the informal non-meeting an ambiguous task.

With respect to the WEF, the official image, as cultivated by the organization, is not that of a bounded, inaccessible organization, but an open, transparent one. The WEF proposes an alternative form of organizing, more dynamic, inclusive, and open than that of the UN, for example, built on deliberation, participation, social development, and inclusion of "people from all walks of life." One would think that access to organizational practices in such an environment should not be that problematic. But reality is something else. This is an organization built on "meetings" and "communities" that nurtures the idea of "safe places" where sensitive political issues can be discussed without the prying eyes of the public and the press. Meetings surrounded by Chatham House rules and informality are meant to provide a sense of trust and to be conducive to honesty and free speech for those invited. This also entails that for outsiders, access is restricted.

Thinking that most of what is relevant was probably going on inside the meeting compound, in the inner circle of events, we tried to find ways of getting in. We talked to guards, trying to argue our way in, or direct their attention elsewhere. We sought media accreditation as freelancing reporters sent out to report by Sweden's largest daily newspaper, but failed to get it. We hopped onto buses chartered for the event, onto which only paying participants were allowed. A couple of times we managed to get into the meeting compound this way, to be driven past the guarded entrances and armed security checkpoints. But once there, we were chased off the grounds again by guards demanding to see our badges. At the onset then, we were caught up in the idea that we needed to "get inside" the formal meeting, "the meeting proper" as it were, to get access to the desired ethnographic data. This initial view was soon to be reconfigured.

Out on the periphery of the meeting staged by the WEF, there were other meetings going on. We talked to shop owners, who complained that the annual meeting did not make for good business. We chatted with drivers of meeting participants who were having dinner while waiting for the clients to call for them. These drivers told us interesting things about for example the security measurements for the meeting and the organization of these, simply by telling us what they could *not* tell us. Likewise, outside the compound, Occupy movement activists had raised tents and were preparing for a panel at the Open Forum, a session held for the larger public outside the security area, to which they had been invited by the WEF. Fighting to keep the cold out, they were gathering around the fireplaces, talking about how to best get their views across in the upcoming panel. At the peripheries of the staged meeting, thus, other meetings were taking place, partly defined by their outsidedness. This outsidedness itself had a lot to say about the organization, its boundaries, what kinds of interests it protects, and the kinds of hierarchies it nurtures.

In relation to the Davos meeting there is an obvious sense of inside and outside, created by the WEF. Those invited to step inside are given the status of "brilliant thought leaders" and may proudly put their involvement in the WEF on their CVs. They make up what WEF describes as their "community of communities" (interview September 2012). Analytically, we may say that it is through these communities that the WEF is able to construct authority (Coleman 1974) and influence other organizations in its environment. The creation and maintenance of these communities takes place through chains of meetings—varying in their degree of formality and informality, size, mission, and transparency—which together constitute the expanded and elastic community of the WEF. In order to understand its workings we need to deconstruct the boundaries they set up for these meetings and the creation of communities.

The Indistinct Beginning and End of a Meeting

The WEF organization rests to a large extent on the repetitious performance of the meeting as a cyclical event. Since the WEF itself is a relatively small organization, consisting of some 600 employed staff members, its manifestation as a large-scale transnational organization with a global reach depends on the continued assemblage of its members and partners into the social form of the meeting. The meeting is crucial for the construction of a sense of community. Meetings function as tools by which the organization may manifest itself as a whole for staff as well as for partners and to the outside world. Organized meetings are, so to speak, the lever that makes possible the articulation of the organizational sense of community and interest, which in turn is drawn upon to provide the organization with significance as a global actor. Lacking a mandate to influence global governance, such as that bestowed on for example the United Nations, it is partly through the meeting form that the WEF is able to have a say in matters relating to global business, governance structures, and investment opportunities.

When researching the WEF and similar organizations such as think tanks and independent research institutes, meetings thus appear as significant social phenomena. Internal meetings at the office or external meetings arranged for non-staff are integral parts of the field. In both cases there are, however, generally a number of meetings that have preceded each meeting, making them best understood as part of a process stretching over time. At times it may even be hard to find a start and end to the process. Sitting in at one staged meeting may provide a glimpse of the larger process, and sometimes that particular glimpse will catch something characteristic and significant. More often than not, however, one needs to attend more than the unique meeting (be that within four walls or not), to grasp what is going on at a larger scale. In our view, the singular meeting is to be understood as part of a continuous process of meetings, unfolding over time. This process may also stretch across geographical and diverse social borders. WEF meetings often link one geographical location to another, by moving its location from one occasion to the next, thus connecting spots on the map into an intricate network. Furthermore, new participants are added as new types of expertise and experiences are needed, and old ones are dropped along the way. Seen from this process perspective, the often taken-for-granted view of meetings as fixed entities in time and space is decentered and challenged. In practice, we may need to retain some focus on the unique meeting, as it is projected as a focal point of attention by the organizers and sometimes also by participants, in order to trace the larger process. Ontologically, however, "the meeting," as a research locus and focal point of interest, should not be seen as a given entity, but rather as a contingent and continually constructed social arena.

On the outside, WEF meetings are often hailed as unique events. Following the WEF in social media we see it as singling out one meeting after the other, for the media of the world to report and discuss. Moreover, many working hours are spent creating these meetings. They are significant tools for the WEF in its organizing efforts. Internally though, and in the broader context of operations, the significance of unique meetings is downplayed. Martin Lesoto, senior manager at WEF headquarters in Cologny, Geneva, says that meetings are of less importance, compared to the experience of being part of the WEF community.

> So, there's a lot of talk at the Forum, about building community. I believe that's fundamentally what the Forum does, and why we are able to engage. The projects, what we call the insight, even the events, those are all secondary. I mean, events are crucial to building community, but I've always said to my team, "Don't ever think a company becomes a partner or engages because of a project, because you know what, McKenzie, their own internal strategy team, we're not gonna be able to outthink an external . . . you know, a team of two people working on a project can't compete against a McKenzie or even a . . . ." So for me it's fundamentally about building community. And so the way we go about our business is essentially, in my view, we're appealing to the fact that people, business leaders in particular in our group, need to want to and get value from being part of a larger community, where they have a chance not only in a closed room setting to talk about the critical issues facing industry and talking about business and doing what a CEO should be doing in terms of a business, but actually as leaders they don't have many opportunities to interact with peers in a safe, quiet, confidential space. I believe that most, not all, but many CEOs, engage with the forum because we create that space where once a year in Davos, and increasingly with other executives and other activities, a chance to just convene as groups of leaders to talk about important

issues. At the same time they are doing business, making deals, perfect, but they're also learning and coming up with new insights. So, I fundamentally believe that that's been the key and a lot of what we do in my team is promote this by having rituals and symbols—you know, a chair; every year one of our communities will have a chair that's one of the CEOs . . . steering boards . . . . So we put in all the pieces that promote that this is also about creating a community, and then for me, once you've got the community that's very sticky and people don't . . . You know, people wanna be part of a group, of a community, and it also allows them to actually think outside the box and take risks as under the group. So for me, that's been the secret of the Forum is being able to create that community feeling. Not to get too philosophical but even Davos is like a community for every single person that goes, you know. I always use this analogy that, again, don't get too hung up on our content; I mean the content is important but nobody ever goes or doesn't go to Davos because of the theme—"Oh, I don't like the theme this year, I'm not gonna come."

(Interview with Martin Lesoto, September 2012)

Martin Lesoto describes the meetings of the Forum as parts of the larger process of constructing itself as an authoritative actor. The meetings are tools in these efforts and do not always carry significance in themselves. But in the larger organizing efforts they are essential in linking the diverse epistemic communities of policymaking into a larger whole (cf. Stone 2013). As Lesoto says, the CEOs he engages with in his team relate to Davos in many ways, and have many entries and exits for the same meeting. They will prepare for the meeting in various ways, by setting up meetings for doing business around the clock, as well as picking up on new opportunities during the actual week in Davos. In addition, they will draw upon the experiences after having returned back home, making plans for new projects. Thus, engaging merely with "the meeting proper" would blind us to large parts of their efforts since there is more than meets the eye to closed meetings in the conference hall. The organizing efforts of WEF may metaphorically be seen as a continued series of staged and circumscribed meetings, or as an assemblage of ongoing meetings. Meetings are in this perspective to be seen as communicative events that are embedded within a wider sociocultural setting (an organization, a community, a society) as a constitutive social form (Schwartzman 1993: 39). As Helen Schwartzman (1993: 39) puts it,

> . . . such an approach is motivated by an appreciation of the idea that the world does not appear to us as formalized concepts (such as structure of culture, or hierarchy and value), but only in particular routines and gatherings, composed of specific actors (or agents) attempting to press their claims on one another and trying to make sense of what is

happening to them. In this way it is possible to see how the process of meetings contributes to the production and reproduction of the structures of everyday life.

Meetings arranged by the WEF make up a series of meetings with no clear starting point or endpoint. The boundaries of a meeting do not really *contain*, but are more often interestingly crossed (cf. Hannerz 1997). It is through the processual reenactment of meetings and their interlinking that the WEF is able to get its priorities and interests, as well as its stakeholders and partners, coordinated and organized. In other words, the meeting form works as a lever for their mission to have an impact on world governance.

In Transit: Before, After, and Betwixt and Between Meetings

Even though meetings may be seen as indistinctly separated from each other, each new event still involves a degree of anticipation and expectation for organizers and participants. As participants arrive from across the world and begin to assemble at the event location, they eagerly attempt to identify one another, strike up conversations, and exchange business cards. On many occasions throughout our fieldwork, we have experienced this sense of growing anticipation, trying our best to merge into the WEF community already in the airport arrival area.

In June 2015 the WEF regional meeting on Africa was held in Cape Town. For this occasion we had contacted our main informant within the Forum asking for the possibility of hanging out at the conference site, or even better, to participate in some of the closed sessions. As expected, this request was turned down, although this time without any specific motivation. There simply was no answer to the request. As had become our routine, we went to Cape Town anyhow, with the intention of getting as close as possible to the meeting and the people attending it. In this interest we had booked ourselves into one of the conference hotels, at which some of the WEF activities would take place and where some of the participants would stay. As we anticipated closed gates at the meeting entrance, we saw the hotel as a place where we would be able to meet with participants, hop onto meeting shuttles, and participate in some of the meeting arrangements taking place at this particular hotel.

On the flight to Cape Town, with two government officials at her side on the plane from Johannesburg, Christina is drawn into a conversation regarding the WEF. The officials, a man and a woman, have never met before, but start a conversation when they understand that they are both attending the WEF meeting. The woman has additional plans for her stay, but the man intends to focus strictly on the meeting. They are both preparing their paperwork, exchanging views on the potential value of the trip. The man complains about the marginal return he expects from the meeting, while the woman appears to be more positive. "It's a waste of money," he exclaims. She laughs, but says smilingly, "It's a government commitment, so we should be positive." They both continue to discuss the potential value of the meeting and the expectations they have on their missions.

Arriving at the airport we meet a group of people less ambivalent about the meeting. We stop to take some pictures at the WEF banner that has been put up and are quickly approached by temporarily hired WEF staff, asking if we are there for the Forum. After a split second of mutual hesitance we nod, and our bags are then quickly tagged, and lifted on board one of the airport shuttles that will take arriving WEF conference participants, including us, to the hotels. Waiting for the bus to fill we are asked to fill in a return form. We do this, but with some hesitance. Will they be as eager to help us on the way back, when they understand that we are there as non-invited researchers? The shuttle is soon filled with young people, clapping their hands, singing and eager to make contact. This turned out to be the "Giza hub" of Young Global Shapers, as Abdul-Badi Issa, tells us when turning towards us. He promises that we will hear from this group throughout the meeting, as they will make sure that they are heard. Sitting just in front of us, Mr. Issa turns to us, telling that he is originally from Cairo but is now situated in Lebanon, where he works as the leader for an Internet-related project sponsored by Massachusetts Institute for Technology (MIT). The aim of the project is to spread knowledge regarding the Arab world and to improve the connections between this region and the rest of the world. This particular journey is paid by the WEF, although he must fund the stay at the rather expensive Southern Sun Waterfront hotel through his project. For him, the trip to Cape Town, as well as the other trips he is doing as part of the Global Shapers network, are completely worth the time, the effort, and the funding, since they make it possible for him to meet with all these interesting people and to have all these interesting conversations "such as I am having right now with you guys." Before every meeting, Mr. Issa tells us, he spends time going over the participant list, marking all the people he is interested in talking to. This time, though, he did not have the time to do this, since he just came from another WEF meeting in the Middle East. For him the WEF is "all about talk"; it is a platform for talk, which may involve travelling to other places and engaging other organizations and people. Asked about our own participation, we tell him that we have arrived to the meeting in Cape Town in our capacities as researchers, financed by the Swedish government. We are here to understand what the Forum is about, how it succeeds in doing what it is doing, we tell him. Mr. Issa laughs and says that he would like to understand that too! "Understanding what the WEF does, I mean . . . ." We laugh together at this perceived vagueness of the WEF. Approaching their hotel we exchange business cards and shake hands with the rest of the group, vouching to stay in contact. Staying on in the shuttle is Alexander Petrou, a Greek CEO who has taken some time off from the Greek crisis that is evolving at the time of the meeting. He enjoys coming to WEF events but is more critical than the Shapers. Just like them, though, he is interested in our understanding of what the WEF does, because this is unclear to him, too. Arriving at our hotel, the Southern Sun Cape Sun, the three of us get off. No vouching that we shall meet again this time. Having arrived for business contacts, we are not the main target group for Mr. Petrou.

As the above examples illustrate, the passage to a meeting, social interactions before a meeting has started, may be just as ripe with meaning as the meeting itself. In the spaces before and in-between the staged meetings social connections are made, manifested, and confirmed, or proved to be of less interest. Likewise, transfers within the scope of a larger meeting, between the plethora of meetings that make up a larger conference, are often highly informative. For example, using shuttle services has also been a productive way of making sense of the annual meetings in Davos. The annual meeting is stretched out over the village, the actual conference center is but one of a large number of places that are booked either by the Forum or by other organizations in some sense related to the event. Reuters news agency, for example, uses the Kirchner Museum Davos as their headquarters; Sneider Bäckerei was rented by one of the big partners to the WEF; and Hotel Cresta Sun is booked by the Forum itself for more private conversations. If you are a very important guest you will be offered a WEF car that will take you around these sites. If not, you will need to walk or use the shuttle system, consisting of three different lines, all intersecting at the conference center. Wearing a WEF badge of any sort (e.g., press, security, or participant) will give you the possibility of hopping onto the shuttle. From a gang of skiers, taking advantage of the fact that the slopes of Davos are practically empty during this week (since all hotels are pre-booked by WEF), we soon learned, however, that sporting a badge is not needed in order to use the shuttles. Uninterested in the meeting, the skiers used them as their collective taxi, free of charge. For us, on the other hand, they constituted an extended part of the annual meeting. Here we met participants, sharing a ten-minute ride, conversing about their and our experiences of the meetings so far. In time, through conversations such as these, we got a thicker picture of why participants would come to Davos, what they were aiming for, and what did not work out as they had planned.

One of the persons we met on our first ride was Mark Spencer, a British CEO who had been to Davos many times. Looking to be the typical Davos participant, he had grey hair, was in his early sixties, and wore a blue wool coat and his participant badge crossing his immaculate tie. It was late Friday afternoon, and Mr. Spencer told us about his coming evening in Davos. "I pretend to be working. But Hotel Belvedere is the political center of gravitation for all entertainment. There are lots of parties going on. I meet a lot of people I haven't seen in a long time. I've been coming here for many years, so it's a great opportunity to meet up with people. Tonight, I'll be working hard," he said with a gleam in his eyes, "four parties, but first a business meeting at the Belvedere." For Mr. Spencer and many others like him, the business meeting that constitutes the official reason for attending the Davos event is surrounded by other, less formal meetings. These may carry just as much significance as the business meeting, albeit from different points of view. Taken together, it is the continual process of meetings over and over again, in different forms, business and social, that endows the engagement in the WEF as a whole with meaning.

Being in transit, we have found, participants are not yet enrolled in their meeting roles, but open to share thoughts and aspirations. Airport transfers, shuttles, and other places of social interaction and communication before, after, and betwixt and between meetings, are key components in grasping the social world of the WEF as a whole. As much as the organization relies on the social form of the meeting, it also depends on the cultivation of community and aspiration that takes place in these interstitial zones. Paraphrasing Hannerz (1997: 2), we might say that the borderlands in-between the staged meetings are often "where the action is," where novel constellations of meanings emerge and new forms of community are created. Both participants and organizers acknowledge this borderland as a key aspect of the attraction of the WEF. When setting up an event such as those in Davos and Cape Town, the Forum will always designate a special area for "networking." This borderland is also a space in which participants reflect on their engagement and expectations, as well as on their understanding of the WEF, in a way that resembles a *para-ethnographic* stance towards the organization (cf. Holmes and Marcus 2006). Participants thus venture their own understandings and analyses of the meeting. For the ethnographer, such interstitial spaces are also valuable spaces for *polymorphous engagements* with participants (cf. Gusterson 1997), i.e., engagements that may vary in kind and topic depending on what opportunities for communication open up.

After Hours: Party Meetings

As Mr. Spencer—our acquaintance from the bus ride mentioned above—hints at, the WEF annual meeting in Davos also includes partying. Most of these are not arranged by the Forum, but are thrown by corporations and/or countries. One of the parties we went to was the Russian Night, in a heated tent opposite the Arabella Sheraton, set up by "Ekaterineburg expo 2020 Bid Committee" (the Russian failed attempt to host the 2020 world exhibition). The night was cold and snow was piling up around the entrance. Disco music was pumping and at the entrance two men in black coats greeted us welcome. Once inside it took a while adjusting ears and eyes to high volume and little light. A woman in exceptionally high heels offered us a gift bag to take home as memory of the Russian Night, containing among other things a small babushka magnet and a Russian scarf. The place was only half-full, and there was a somewhat odd mix of people hanging out in the bar and at the dance floor. Either they were men in suits, wearing badges, appearing to be well over their forties. Or there were very young, very slim girls with long hair, wearing high heels and short skirts.

In our sensible "walking-around-the-field-all-day-long-shoes" we felt at odds with what seemed to be expected of women to wear at the party.

Two days later, at another type of party, we felt more at home. This time we had been invited by one of our key informants, managing director Cassius Luck, to take part in the "media dinner" hosted by the WEF Saturday night during the Davos week. The dinner was held on the second floor at the Central Sports Hotel, and about one hundred people with media accreditation badges (journalists, camera men, editors, and others) filled the room. Spirits were high. Red wine in plain wine glasses was served and drunk at high speed. Soon they will serve the fondue, Beatrice Kallis, journalist from a major European news corporation, told us. She had been reporting from Davos many times and knew the routine. Mr. Luck, looking infinitely tired after this week, stepped coughing up to the microphone making a joke about how they will all have to report to him afterwards. Dinner guests were cheering and laughing at this. Luck ended the short speech by saying that they were happy to host the dinner for the media people, thanking them for their hard work during the week. More applause and cheering.

Kallis was, however, a bit skeptical about the whole arrangement. In her ordinary life at her newspaper back home, this was not the way journalists did things, clapping and cheering the guy from the organizing part. For her job as economic analyst it is important to be in Davos, she said, and she was really happy that she "inherited" the privilege of reporting from Davos from her predecessor. To her mind, the WEF is a valuable arena for business and politics. But it irritated her that the Forum tries to steer her and others' work as much as it does. "Journalists may only take part in a small part of the meeting," she explained, "giving us only minor access." Kallis also said that she knows that they are checking what she writes, and she would not dream of writing something that the Forum would not appreciate. She had already, several times, had to beg her way in. She would not risk being let out. During dinner, Forum staff walked around the room, greeting and conversing with people. Apparently, this was the night when the communication staff met with the media people, checking out how the meeting had evolved from their point of view. In between pieces of bread and meat someone from Forum also approached Kallis. They talked and laughed a bit. Afterwards, though, Kallis turned to us saying that this was an informal check-up of her reporting from Davos this year. "She had not planned, you know, to check me out. She merely took the chance while talking to me anyway," Kallis explained.

Parties are plentiful around Forum meetings. Participants see them as an integral part of the organizational experience. National identities, oftentimes turned into stereotypical representations, are showcased and marketed. Organizational community is celebrated and recognized, as well as contested and resisted. "Party meetings" are also occasions when participants may exchange stories about what actually went on during the meetings earlier the same day, what the message behind the speech given by the chairman of the WEF was, or exchange gossip about leadership changes in the organization (cf. Noon and Delbridge 1993). They are also instances when participants may practice making use of the narrative style of the organization, and contextualize the generic vocabulary of the meeting. As such, they often serve as meta-communicative events, at which participants are given an opportunity to reflect upon and comment on "the meeting proper."

In fact, without the "party meetings" and other less formal social events that take place in between the staged and official business meetings, the latter would lose much of their potentiality. The single business meetings may very well be the official and legitimate motive for attending events organized by the WEF and serve important communicative and organizational purposes. However, it is at the less strict and more party-like meetings that the participants may more freely discuss issues of interest, pursue their own agendas (that may not be part of their official agenda), get to know other participants and potential business partners, as well as let go of some tension and steam and just have fun. Such after-hours events are, while not part of the official agenda, interstitial spaces that are intimately entangled with "the meeting proper."

Concluding Reflections: Meetings as Experiential and Experimental Sites

Meetings, we suggest, as organized and ritualized communication events, may provide the ethnographer with a loupe, a magnifying glass, through which key tenets of larger social groups and organizations, and big issues, may be carefully observed. In meetings, political priorities, economic values, and social priorities are often condensed, played out, and negotiated, turning meetings into strategic sites from which to observe the organization at large. Meetings can turn out to be *experiential and experimental sites*, to borrow Rabinow's expression (2003: 87), where different versions of interpretations and claims are tested and tried out. Even when access is denied or restricted, or when people do not want to talk, that in itself is indicative of what the organization is about and what is at stake in meetings. A small place like the Davos meeting ground is, in our view, one spot in the larger infrastructure of the social world of the WEF organization, and speaks to much bigger stakes, concerning participation, voice, and power in global governance matters, issues that may have large-scale implications. Thus, to return to the question raised in this chapter regarding what we may learn by doing ethnography in temporary meeting places, such as the ones constructed by WEF, without even having access to the formal meeting compounds. As we have shown, it is both worthwhile and rewarding, but in order to understand the practices constituting meetings of this nature we will have to broaden our perspective of the meeting as a social phenomenon. The conventional view of meetings as entities fixed in time and space needs to be challenged in favor of a processual view of meetings as communicative events, continuously staged and instantiated, that are constitutive of a larger organization. As suggested above, we see meetings as part of a social process of organizing that transcends the boundaries of the meeting set by organizers for what constitutes "the meeting proper." As for our "participation," it has, from one angle, often been limited to being outside of the conference rooms or meeting participants after hours or in betwixt meetings. On the other hand, our presence as researchers in large, semi-public events represents the same level of participation as experienced by most of the audience. We would thus agree with Aull Davies (1999: 73–74), in contending: "This tendency of both ethnographers and readers of ethnography to evaluate the quality, and validity, of ethnographic findings on the degree of participation which an ethnographer is able to achieve is unfortunate. A more useful guide is the way in which ethnographers ground their observations in critical reflection on the nature of their participation and suitability to the particular research circumstances, and the relationship between researcher and subjects." And these relationships are often established in conjunction with meetings—before, during, and after meetings.

With reflections on the nature of anthropological fields, concerns have been raised that anthropology may be turning away from the study of the everyday and from thick description to "quick description," and from prolonged stays in the field to a series of flying visits, or *jet-plane ethnography* (Bate 1997: 1150). Organizational anthropologists, Bate exclaims (Bate 1997: 1150), "rarely take a toothbrush with them these days." So, is ethnography turning towards a speculative exercise, justifying the thinnest of accounts, the most fleeting engagements and the most unsystematic of observations? We believe worries of this kind, however legitimate, to be reflective of the changing nature of our empirical fields and the kinds of engagements we are able to establish with them. Much of ethnographic fieldwork in formal organizations is conducted in meetings of various kinds, and often in less formal meetings before the formal meeting, or after the staged meeting. As the ethnographer works on getting access to the perceived core of meetings, to get "inside" of the organization, as it were, he or she often has to make do with what appears to be the peripheries of the desired field site. It is often with a sense of frustration that one engages in the "borderlands" of the field, imagining that the more valuable insights are to be gained only inside the "meeting proper." Our experiences of doing fieldwork at the WEF, as well as in and among other organizations, have taught us that while persistence in getting full access remains worthwhile, there are as important insights to be gained from circulating the field at large. Engaging with meeting participants before or between meetings may confer a sense of what is actually at stake, what their hopes and fears amount to, and what kind of "value" is placed on different kinds of connections (cf. Mahmud 2013). Even *not* being granted access tells one a story of the organization that may be just as interesting as the one told from the inside, as it were (cf. Schwegler 2013).

In the case of the WEF this is a story of high stakes, security, and aspirations ranging from the individual interests to global governance.

Grounded ethnography in complex and organizational fields may ask more of us as ethnographers in terms of defining what actually makes up the field, what is really at stake in the field, where boundaries of formality and informality are being drawn, and what the connections between sites are. It may involve meeting the informants where they are, going "where the action is," to meetings—whether in Brussels, Stockholm, Washington, DC, or some other locality. It means understanding the perspectives and problematizing the accounts of organizational actors, spatial and temporal, and exploring their local and translocal contexts (Garsten 2009).

In much the same vein, and in response to the anxieties related to a perceived loss of depth in ethnographic research, Marcus argues that "the standard of depth in ethnography must be understood with reference to a differently identified community of scholars in relation to subjects . . . The old question of *depth* in the creation of functionalist ethnographies is now mediated by questions of *identity*—the anthropologist's preexisting extent of relationship and connection—to the object of study" (Marcus 1998: 246). Oftentimes, researchers doing fieldwork in and around meetings may been given the role of the responsive interlocutor, and sometimes even the role of informed interlocutor. By conversing with someone from the outside the organizational boundaries, so to speak, members of the field may also receive news from "the other side," test out their own tentative viewpoints and talk more freely about the huge challenges ahead in working towards corporate social responsibility. Often, we have accepted these roles as best we could, wary of the preciousness of each engagement. For our informants, these encounters may well have opened an opportunity to step out of the role of "organization man" (or woman) for a moment, to be released from formal meeting format.

The WEF and other organizations like them, such as think tanks, research institutes, NGOs, and PR consultancies, are inhabited by people constantly on the move, alternating between organizations, depending to a large extent on both formal and informal meetings for their continued existence. Meetings may provide points of reference in otherwise unpredictable work practices and environments; they provide spaces of condensed meanings and dynamic tensions, zones of priorities and aspirations. Not least, meetings provide legitimate spaces for the temporary stitching together of social practices involving representatives of different interests, groups, and organizations. The policy relevance of the knowledge gained from studies conducted by think tank experts, for example, is negotiated, contested, and made legitimate "at the interface" of different types of organizations—the state administration, multilaterals, NGOs, and funding organizations (Garsten 2009), i.e., in meetings arranged and orchestrated to attract and engage participants from different organizations. In the case of the WEF, staged and formal meetings provide the lever through which the organization may expand and gain authority and legitimacy as a global player on issues relating to global governance. At the interface, in conferences and similarly staged events, we may find that interactions and relations in the field may be quite dense around the topics at heart, that differing interests are intertwined in quite complex ways, and that ethnography in translocal fields may very well be "grounded" in its own particular way, in reference to the character of the field. Zooming in on meetings as part of a larger effort of organizing social practice allows us to see how the process of meetings contributes to the production and reproduction of the structures of everyday organizational life. Potentially then, meetings are spaces where we might gain some ethnographic momentum.

References

Aull Davies, Charlotte. *Reflexive Ethnography*. London: Routledge, 1999.

Bate, S. Paul. "Whatever happened to organizational anthropology? A review of the field of organizational ethnography and anthropological studies." *Human Relations* 50(1997): 1148–1175.

Coleman, James S. *Power and the Structure of Society*. New York: W.W. Norton & Co, 1974.

Garsten, Christina. "Ethnography at the interface: 'Corporate social responsibility' as an anthropological field of enquiry." In *Ethnographic Practice in the Present*, edited by Marit Melhuus, Jon P. Mitchell and Helena Wulff, 56–68. Oxford: Berghahn, 2009.

Garsten, Christina and Anette Nyqvist. *Organisational Anthropology: Doing Ethnography in and among Complex Organisations*. London: Pluto Press, 2013.

Gusterson, Hugh. "Studying up revisited." *Political and Legal Anthropology Review* 20(1997): 114–119.

Hannerz, Ulf. *Flows, Boundaries and Hybrids: Keywords in Transnational Anthropology*. Stockholm: Stockholm University, Department of Social Anthropology, 1997.

Holmes, Douglas R. and George E. Marcus. "Para-ethnography and the rise of the symbolic analyst." In *Frontiers of Capital: Ethnographic Reflections on the New Economy*, edited by Melissa S. Fisher and Greg Downey, 33–57. Durham: Duke University Press, 2006.

Mahmud, Lilith. "The profane ethnographer: Fieldwork with a secretive organisation." In *Organisational Anthropology: Doing Ethnography In and Among Complex Organisations*, edited by Christina Garsten and Anette Nyqvist, 189–207. London: Pluto Press, 2013.

Marcus, George E. *Ethnography through Thick and Thin*. Princeton, NJ: Princeton University Press, 1998.

Noon, Mike and Rick Delbridge. "News from behind my hand: Gossip in organizations." *Organization Studies* 14(1993): 23–36.

Rabinow, Paul. *Anthropos Today: Reflections on Modern Equipment*. Princeton, NJ: Princeton University Press, 2003.

Schwartzman, Helen B. *Ethnography in Organizations*. Newbury Park, CA: Sage, 1993.

Schwegler, Tara A. "Not being there: The power of strategic absence in organisational anthropology." In *Organisational Anthropology: Doing Ethnography in and among Complex Organisations*, edited by Christina Garsten and Anette Nyqvist, 224–240. London: Pluto Press, 2013.

Stone, Diane. "Shades of grey: The World Bank, knowledge networks and linked ecologies of academic engagement." *Global Networks* 13(2013): 241–260.

7 Meeting to Improve

Lean[ing] Swedish Public Preschools

Renita Thedvall

Introduction: Studying Preschools through Meetings

The six of us are spread around the table looking at the long piece of brown paper offhandedly taped along the wall. We are taking part in a Lean "improvement group" meeting in a Swedish public preschool. The three preschool teachers around the table are guided by two Lean Coaches having particular expertise in the management model Lean. On the brown paper there are different color post-its—green, yellow, and pink (although the pink post-its are referred to as red): the three colors of Lean modeled on the traffic light. The preschool teachers are set to identify a "flow" of the morning activities at the preschool from 7 a.m. until 9 a.m. This is the time when parents drop off their children and before the actual pedagogical activities start at 9 a.m. They are attempting to make the "flow" of morning more efficient with the help of the Lean model so that they are able to create a more unhurried atmosphere around the drop-offs. Each yellow post-it symbolizes a "flow unit" in a work process. The color green indicates if there are solutions to the "bottlenecks" in the flow of the work process, and red (pink) post-its indicate that there is a need for making an "action plan" to get rid of the bottleneck.

The purpose of this chapter is to explore the role of meetings when implementing and operating the Lean management model. The study reveals the significance of meetings when operating management models such as Lean. Specifically, it shows how the Lean model is played out in Swedish public preschools through meetings. What ideas and practices circulate in the Lean meetings? What kind of knowledge is particular to the model? What kind of employees and work practices do the Lean meetings make? Furthermore, it brings to light what kinds of knowledge may be produced through fieldwork in Lean meetings.

It is easy to find management literature that celebrates the meeting as a way of improving business, such as having "improvement group" or "board [whiteboard] meetings" suggested by the management model Lean (Womack et al 1990), "quality improvement team" or "problem solving teams" in Total Quality Management (Deming 1988), or "team learning" in the

DOI: 10.4324/9781315559407-8

Learning Organization (Sense 1994). A critical analysis of the role of meetings in management models is, however, hard to find.[1] There is a specific strand of research highlighting the role and power of language regarding management reforms (Miller and Rose 1995; Shore and Wright 1997; Urla 2012; Tamm Hallström and Thedvall 2015). Shore and Wright (1997) discuss the role and power of language in policy in terms of *semantic clusters*. This research points to the fact that management models and policy ideas carry certain clusters of words such as "effective," "quality," "benchmarking," "empowerment," "continuous improvements," and so forth, that together form a particular language. Although the main power of management model semantic clusters lies in the fact that they are able to harbor many different interpretations, they do guide the direction towards what is perceived to be relevant problems and also appropriate solutions to these (cf. Rose and Miller 1992). Language thereby becomes a vehicle for mobilizing and signaling new patterns of governance (Bourdieu 1991; Islamoglu 2009), but also for influencing the minds and subjective perceptions of employees (Foucault 1988, 1991; Martin 1997; Oakes et al 1998).

While language functions as a framework in management models to influence what can be discussed and what is possible to "improve," meetings do so in more material ways. Lean meetings in preschools are *architectural*, in the sense of determining, structuring, configuring, and affecting discussions, practices, and decision-making processes (Sandler and Thedvall, this volume). The meeting form determined by the Lean tools contributes to what kinds of work practices may be "improved" by Lean. But as proposed in the Introduction (Sandler and Thedvall, this volume), meetings are not only containers through which things move but they are also *practices of circulation* whereby ideas, documents, discussion, power, resistance/acceptance, decision-making, etc. circulate, perform, and transform. In the case of Lean, the model is built on meetings as practices of circulation, both for Lean as an idea and as a tool. Furthermore, the Lean meetings also operate as *makers* (Oakes et al 1998) of improvement-oriented workers and flow-focused bureaucrats, as will be shown in this chapter.

In this chapter, Swedish public preschool becomes an example of a study on meetings in the Lean management model. Ben-Ari (2002) emphasizes that there are few attempts to study preschools from an organizational perspective with the aim of understanding the relationship between childcare and the type of policy that governs the organizations through which such care is provided. The specific policy that governs preschool in Sweden is the *Curriculum for the Preschool Lpfö 98, revised 2010*. The way to achieve the goals of the Curriculum is, however, left to the preschools, and this is where a management model such as Lean can be one tool used. To give some context for the ideology of Swedish preschools, there is a basic idea backed by the Swedish state that all parents should be able to afford to put their child in a preschool if they want to. Parents pay a fee every month, but it is heavily subsidized by taxes.[2] Almost all preschools in Sweden are public, since they are financed by taxes. However, some are run by private companies and others by municipalities. This is a study of preschools run by a municipality. There is no recognized qualitative difference between privately run and municipality-run preschools. Instead, parents' choices are based on such things as the preschool's reputation as a good school or not, the impression parents get when they visit the preschool, or where it is located. Each child holds a voucher, which can be used at the preschool of the parents' choice. This is a preschool market created for free choice, but still with some of the recognizable features of the Swedish model where the state subsidizes preschool fees so that most, if not all, can afford to put their children in preschool. In other words, the preschool system exemplifies a Swedish version of neoliberalism (cf. Garsten et al 2015). In practice, there are few parents that have an actual free choice, a recognizable feature in so-called open markets, since the priority of most is to have a preschool near home (or perhaps near the workplace). Furthermore, in many places in Sweden there are not enough preschools, so it is more a matter of getting a placement in any preschool reasonably close to home.

In the next section, I present the Lean management model, beginning with the car industry from which it originates, to explain the context of Lean's development and how the different tools Lean brings are intended to lead to improvement in contexts such as preschools. In the following section, I reflect on my fieldwork, my empirical material, and what it means to make *punctuated entries* (Thedvall 2013) into the field via Lean meetings as well as what kinds of knowledge may be generated. I then turn to the main part of the chapter, where I show how the Lean model is played out through Lean meetings and how meetings contribute to which kinds of work practices may be "improved" by Lean. In the conclusion, I explain what ideas, problems, solutions, and practices are possible to circulate in Lean meetings and what work practices and employees Lean meetings make.

Lean[ing] through Meetings

The Lean management model was introduced in 1990 by Jim Womack, Daniel Jones, and Daniel Roos in the international best-selling book, *The Machine That Changed the World*. It was based on the Toyota Production System (TPS) developed by Taiichi Ohno, Shigeo Shingo, and Eiji Toyoda at Toyota between 1948 and 1975. In the car industry, Lean production is about creating efficient "flows" in the production processes and eliminating wastes that do not add to customer value (Womack et al 1990). The assembly line is understood as a flow where the car should go through and move between different stations as efficiently as possible, eliminating elements in the work process that do not add value from a customer perspective. In Lean language, each station on the assembly line is a "flow unit" and the time between stations, all the way to the customer, is "cycle time." To ensure that "wastes" are eliminated, the Lean model requires different types of meetings where staff meet to make "continuous improvements."

The Lean method of making sure that staff members are constantly involved in "continuous improvements" is to have "board meetings," which are stand-up meetings usually in front of a whiteboard. In the car industry this is done by setting targets for how many cars should be produced. These targets are made visual and their "status" is tracked by green, red, and yellow symbols, where green signifies that the target is met, red indicates that the production of cars is failing the target, and yellow is a warning that the production is starting to fall behind. The green, red, and yellow dot for status is generally put on the board (whiteboard) where the organization and its production processes are visualized. The board is often centrally placed on the factory floor and it is not unusual that staff meet in front of the board before every shift starts to go through what has been working and what has not. If the status is yellow or red, it indicates that there is need for improvement and staff are encouraged to come with suggestions or volunteer to take part in an "improvement group" meeting to come up with solutions.

At "improvement group" meetings there are a number of Lean tools that can be used depending on the issue at hand. If there is an understood problem with flow efficiency the staff may use a "value-stream-mapping" to clarify what is "stealing time" on the assembly line. A group of employees meet in an "improvement group" meeting and do a "value-stream-mapping" by identifying "flow units" and "cycle time" in the production processes to be able to detect and get rid of so-called bottlenecks (Modig and Åhlström 2012). The flow unit and cycle time should be as effective as possible and the staff in the "improvement group" meeting should identify the bottlenecks and come up with solutions for rectifying them. If there is an understood mismatch between how the car is produced and what the customer finds valuable, the tool "moment of truth" can be used to identify in what instances in a flow that the organization meets the customer, and then determine if that meeting creates value for the customer—that is, if the customer's opinion about the organization or the process is left positive, negative, or neutral. The goal is to come up with solutions to rectify the "moments" where the customers are left negative or neutral.

These "board meetings" and "improvement group" meetings along with the Lean tools have to be adapted to the work environment of Swedish public preschools. Lean has recently spread like wildfire in the public sector in Sweden and abroad (Chalice 2007; Prounlove et al 2008; Arlbjørn 2011; Pedersen and Huniche 2011; Modig and Åhlström 2012; Radnor 2012), and the model has changed when moved into new contexts. Sahlin-Andersson (1996) suggests the notion of editing to explain how various management models are translated and interpreted in script and discourse in manuals specific to the organizational context. At the core, however, Lean is recognizable and similar to the "original," and staff need to find ways to fit their work activities into the labels and tools of the model.

Punctuated Entries into Lean Meetings

This chapter is part of a larger project based on ethnographic fieldwork between February 2012 and March 2014 in different meetings pertaining to Lean in a municipality in Sweden, as well as participant observation as part of the full-time staff in two different preschools for six weeks during the fall of 2013.[3] This fieldwork—what I have elsewhere called *punctuate entries* (Thedvall 2013)—into different meetings in the municipality consisted of a Lean Coach training course held by a consultancy (three days) where I became a Lean Coach together with employees within the municipality, six Lean Forum meetings including all Lean Coaches in the municipality, and one Lean Network meeting where the Lean Directors within the municipality met. I have also participated in two "board meetings" and four "improvement group" meetings. Apart from these meetings I have also attended several meetings, both Lean and other meetings, as part of the staff in the two different preschools. Even during my fieldwork while conducting participant observation as part of the staff, most of my field notes are from different meetings. The participant observation as part of the staff gave me a deeper understanding of the work practices, the jargon, and the organization of the preschool, but it was in the Lean meetings as well as other types of meetings, such as the "weekly meetings" and the monthly "workplace meetings," that the organization of work in the preschool was discussed and negotiated.

The prevalence of meetings gave the fieldwork a particular quality that was characterized by punctuated entries that corresponded to the meetings. My fieldwork was also punctuated in the sense that I had to negotiate entering the meetings, even as part of the staff. Punctuated fieldwork can be challenging, and there are particular challenges when such fieldwork takes place primarily in meetings since meetings are such particular data collection contexts. When I took part in the meetings I sat among the group as a participant, but I mostly observed and took notes of what was said. It was always very hectic, since I tried to write down everything that was said. Of course it was not possible to write everything, but at least I captured a pretty good sense of what was said. A problem with the constant and intense note-taking was that I did not have much time to see people's facial expressions or bodily movements as they talked. Their tone of voice, however, often revealed their state of mind. I also got a feel for the atmosphere in the group and in the room that I would not have had if I were not actually there. There were some difficulties, however. Sometimes I did not fully understand the discussion, since they were using a terminology with which I was not familiar and I would have disturbed the flow of the meeting by asking. At other times, I was unable to follow the discussion because I was too busy writing what had been said before, and thus I missed some of what was said.

The fact that I followed the work with Lean in preschools for about two years and that I had a child of preschool age was important for my understanding of the organization and the terminology of Swedish public pre-schools. During the course of the two years, as well as my earlier experience as a parent of a child in preschool, I did come to gain a fuller understanding of the organization, the jargon, the discussions and their implications. And if I was interested in how preschool teachers work to improve their routines in the morning with the help of, for example, "improvement group" meet-ings, then the meeting was where I needed to be.

Meeting to Improve Flows: Pedagogical Documentation

One important notion that circulated in Lean meetings was the importance of efficient flows. The Lean model was based on the idea of a flow that needs to be made more effective, and it became important to constantly improve the flow. In the preschool environment, the flow must be translated from car industry assembly line flow to another flow. One translation of the assem-bly line flow in the world of preschools was the work organization of the morning discussed in the Lean "improvement group" meeting in the begin-ning of the chapter (also see Thedvall 2015). Another translation of the flow was the continuous flow of the preschool teachers, called "pedagogical documentation."

One recurring problem, and something that teachers hoped would be resolved by Lean, was the problem of continuously keeping up with the pedagogical documentation. Preschools were governed by the Curriculum for the Preschool 2010. It states that the fundamental values that should govern preschools are "human rights," "democratic values," "respect for our shared environment," and "the intrinsic value of each person." The curriculum was then divided into a number of goals and guidelines under the headings of "norms and values," "development and learning," "the influence of the child," "preschool and home," "co-operation between the preschool class, the school and the leisure-time centre," and "follow-up, evaluation and development" (Curriculum 2010: 8–16). One of the guide-lines in the last heading stated that each child's learning and development should be systematically documented, as should how the child's learning changed over time (Curriculum 2010: 14–15). The preschools where I did fieldwork, like many of the public preschools, had chosen to account for the children's progress by this form of "pedagogical documentation."

Thus, "pedagogical documentation" was the most important tool for organizing the pedagogical work at the preschools. Many public preschools in Sweden were "Reggio Emilia–inspired" preschools and, in the Reggio Emilia pedagogical philosophy, pedagogical documentation was a cen-tral educational tool. To do pedagogical documentation the teachers first observed and documented, much like an ethnographer takes field notes, how the children reacted and interacted around a specific theme, for exam-ple, sand, water, stones, or a book they liked. For example, my son, at the age of two, brought his favorite book to the preschool and showed it in the assembly. The preschool teachers documented, among other things, how my son showed the other children how they should knock on the doors portrayed on the pages before turning to the next page of the book.

The teachers then translated their field notes into a presentation, focusing on particular instances that represented the agreed-upon theme. The presentation, in the form of pictures and/or text, was then shown to the children during the assembly, for example a picture of my son showing the other children how to knock on the page. The children commented, through words or gestures, on what they saw in the pictures and/or texts. During this reflection, the preschool teachers also documented how the children reacted and interacted, in this case with the presentation itself. Afterward, at a reflection meeting, the teachers reflected on, analyzed, and interpreted the original observation and the children's reflection in relation to a particular theme related to the curriculum, such as the children's influence, gender, social interaction, mathematics, pedagogical environment, or language and communication. According to Reggio Emilia, it was "pedagogical documentation" only after it had been reflected, analyzed, and interpreted by children and teachers (and, if possible, parents).

It was often the case that teachers did not have time to complete the documentations when they sat down during their "planning time" (also known as the child-free time) and then they had to start over when they had the time to sit down again. Or someone else had to finish it.

The management at one of the preschools also found that some did too much documenting, while others did too little. The solution was to ask a group of preschool teachers to meet in an "improvement group" meeting to find a way to have pedagogical documentation continuously and regularly appear on the documentation wall [at the preschool] for children and parents to take part in—not doing too little or too much, but having a regular flow in all four divisions of the preschool. The chosen Lean tool was "moment of truth." There was an assumption made that if children and parents took part in the pedagogical work at the preschool by the documentation continuously and regularly appearing on the documentation wall, the children would have a better pedagogical education and the parents would recognize that their children were being educated. In Lean language, children and parents—both represented by parents because they fill in the user surveys—would feel like value had been created for them in the "moment" where the customer meets the organization.

The preschool teachers, consisting of Lina, Carla, Sigrid, and Ingrid,[4] were asked to fill in the "moment of truth" document, formatted with one circle in the center and bubbles around the circle symbolizing the moments when the customer met in the organization. The group put pedagogical documentation at the center circle and attempted to identify the moments when the children and parents—actually parents—interacted with the pedagogical documentations. The group quite quickly agreed that it was the pedagogical reflections and the documentation appearing on the wall that formed the "moments of truth." The question was how to make the pedagogical documentation appear on the documentation wall to begin with. The Lean Coaches, Margaret and Jennifer, changed strategy and instead wanted the group to think in terms of flows and make a value-stream-mapping of the pedagogical documentation identifying the "flow units." The group went through the different steps in the pedagogical documentation and identified the "flow units." After a break, Carla pointed out that it is not flow of the pedagogical documentation that is the problem but actually doing it, finishing it. The problem was to make employees focus on the pedagogical documentation during their planning time, Carla emphasized. The group refocused.

Margaret asked the group to remember that the goal also must be measurable. It must be possible to evaluate whether the solution the "improvement group" had agreed on actually worked. There were certain practices circulating in the meeting that were determined by the model, such as evaluability. There was an idea that changes must be made measurable in numbers, so that it would be possible to show results. And the results should be made comparable in the form of graphs and diagrams. As many other management models, the Lean model was based on performance management (Miller and Rose 1995). These models shared an ethics of evaluation where work processes needed to be constantly evaluated to make "continuous improvements," and where objectives and results needed to be presented to evaluate and compare (cf. Thedvall 2015). This was not unique to management models such as Lean used in preschools. Public preschools were already teeming with various assessments and user surveys, and the preschool teachers were used to thinking in the evaluative form.

One way to make it measurable and possible to evaluate was to measure the number of pedagogical documentations made. After some discussion, however, Lina, Sigrid, and Ingrid agreed that the number of hours teachers spent on pedagogical documentation was a better measure. Lina suggested that they use 50 percent of their planning time for pedagogical documentation. Sigrid said that if it's half of their planning time they can use eight hours per month for pedagogical documentation, four hours for meetings and four hours on the educational environment at preschool. She agreed with Lina that this was a good idea. Ingrid pointed out that some need more time to make pedagogical documentation than others. "If it takes four hours for someone and one hour for someone else, then it's important that they are not identified as being slow and unproductive. Even if someone only finishes two and someone else finishes five pedagogical documentations, during the same time, it should not be compared in that way." Lina re-thought and reminded them that the important thing was what was in the pedagogical documentation, not the number of hours put on them. Ingrid clarified and said that if we needed to measure we should measure the number of hours and not the number of documentations. In the end, they decided to measure the number of hours spent on the documentation since they already had an established form where the teachers wrote how much of their "planning time" had been used for each month.

In this way, there are certain practices circulating in the room which are brought by the ideas and tools of the Lean model and how the Lean model is performed. The Lean model points to particular problems that have to do with the flow, where the flow of the pedagogical documentation becomes the problem that needs to be solved rather than the substance. The content of the documentation, "the important thing" mentioned by Lina, is harder to get ahold of using Lean, although it is the substance in the pedagogical documentation that is key according to the curriculum (*Curriculum for the preschool* 2010: 14–15). Ultimately, substance was not something the Lean tools were well suited to achieving, even though there was an effort to expand the model to solve this problem. Lean also points to the measurable, which makes the solution quantitative rather than substantive. In this case, the Lean "improvement group" meetings make mechanisms for identifying flow-focused problems and measurable solutions.

Meeting to Evaluate the Mood: Lean Board Meetings in Preschools

Another important notion that circulated in Lean meetings through the Lean management model was the idea of "continuous improvements." This was a notion that businesses can and should be continuously improved and that each employee should be involved in this work. There was an assumed correlation between an active employee constantly improving the organization and a satisfied employee feeling "joy at work." The Lean method of making sure that staff was constantly involved in continuous improvements was to have "board meetings." Lean "board meetings" had particular aesthetics. It was important to stand up in front of the board, often a whiteboard. Susan, a Lean Strategist in the municipality, said in the Lean Coach training course: "In the 'board meetings' you stand up. They are effective meeting. We won't talk about having car trouble or if we like the workplace head or not. It should be complete professional focus." There was an underlying notion that seated meetings had a tendency to drag on because then you were too comfortable and started talking about other things. Also, the preschool teachers spoke of themselves as a group that liked to think, analyze, and reflect with a cup of coffee in front of them, lingering at length. However, the teachers' analysis of the efficiency of stand-up meetings contradicted many of my observations of how such sit-down coffee-and-talking meetings actually functioned. Their analysis spoke less to the actual efficiency of board meetings than to the ways that Lean "philosophy" permeated the preschool.

One day, in a management meeting at the preschool, consisting of the Head of Unit, the so-called pedagogist[5] responsible for the pedagogical work in the unit, and the four workplace heads of the four preschools of the Unit, we were discussing the weekly meetings in relation to Lean "board meetings." In the meeting was also the municipality's Lean Strategist Gudrun, employed to make sure that the municipality became a Lean organization. Gudrun asked if all employees took part in the weekly meetings. One of the workplace heads, Sigrid, responded that it was one from each division in the preschool. Gudrun continued and asked if it was possible to have everyone join. Sigrid said with a bit of irony in her voice that someone needed to take care of the children. Angelica, another workplace head, asked, "But how important is it that everyone is in the meeting? We have a structure that works well and I don't have to be involved in everything." Gudrun said that it's difficult to get everyone to feel included if they're not in the meeting. She said, "If I don't see my name on the board [whiteboard], if I'm not able to give my viewpoint in the meeting I don't feel the same responsibility. Then the 'board meetings' are only for a selected few." Sigrid disagreed. All the names were on the whiteboard at her preschool. She continued and said that she thought the weekly meetings were important. Nina, another workplace head, agreed. Gudrun answered with an irritated voice:

> You mustn't think so much of how it works for you. If I know that there's a group in front of the board and I'm not part of it then I don't feel the same responsibility. If I see my suggestions from the "workplace meeting"[6] on the board and then am allowed to participate and discuss in front of the board then I become more involved. The Lean board is a board for visual management. And the point of visualizing is to see what's going on in my company and what my responsibility is. And if I'm not at the Lean Board meetings I will not be motivated.

The Lean philosophy arrived with the idea that employees would feel responsible for the work organization if s/he saw her/his name on the Lean "board" or discussed the issue in front of all employees in the meeting. Implicitly, it was understood that some employees were not taking responsibility and this was a way to gently, or not so gently, force them to be responsible for "continuous improvements" and make them accountable when they were set to "improve" a particular task by having their name put on the board.

Nina wondered pensively how it would work. Gudrun, the Lean Strategist, suggested that they would go inside a group at a time. The Head of Unit, Kristina, launched the idea of having fifteen-minute sessions divided into four groups. Sigrid said in a grumpy voice that it would mean fifteen minutes for everything that needed to be discussed. "Where will we discuss the things that we don't have time for?" Kristina wondered what was taking such a long time. Sigrid gave the examples of the "pedagogical year," the work organization of the coming week, and added that it would then be the case that she would have to say the same thing four times. Gudrun informed everyone that where they had tried "board meetings" the employees agreed that decisions were made much faster and they felt more involved. Kristina added that Lean was about streamlining so as to have more time with the children, but also to get everyone more involved in the organization of work. Sigrid concluded that she felt that everyone was involved at her preschool. Gudrun answered back: "I can almost say for certain. Humans want to feel competent, important, belonging to a community. With Lean we turn the organizational hierarchy upside down. Management should only support improvement work. We could miss out on valuable ideas. Can we afford it?" Sigrid insisted and said that these types of meetings weren't the same as a weekly meeting. In the end Gudrun's solution was to have both the Lean "board meetings" and the weekly meetings, which was surprising, since it hardly meant more time with the children. At the same time, it was a classic example of how bureaucratization processes lead to more bureaucracy (Niskanen 1971), or how meetings produce more meetings (Schwartzman 1989).

The two preschools where I did my fieldwork had slightly different versions of the Lean board, but what they had in common was that they both measured the employees' "joy at work." At one of the preschools the whole staff had to put colorful dots—modeled on the green, yellow, and red dots used to measure the status of production in the car industry—to their name to signal how their day had been, while at the other preschool it was only the management group that did this.

One day I attended a management meeting at one of the preschools. Present in the room were the Head of Unit, the pedagogist, the four workplace heads, and myself. On the table were yellow/orange dots with smiling/non-smiling faces. They had stopped using the green, yellow, and red dots with smiling/non-smiling faces. It was the same at the other preschool where they instead used green, blue, and red. The green, yellow, and red modeled on the traffic light indicated that "yellow" meant warning and they wanted it to have a more neutral color, in this case blue. At this meeting all the dots were yellow/orange and instead the smiling/non-smiling faces on the dots signaled the mood, the "joy at work." Kristina, the Head of Unit, asked the management to go to the board and put a dot beside each of their names. Nina put a dot with a neutral face beside her name. Kristina asked why. Nina answered that it had been both this week. Kristina wondered if there was something that they could do [to change her dot into a smiling dot]. Nina informed us of the staff at her preschool, who were unhappy because there had been many out sick and they couldn't use substitutes [because of the need to save money within the municipality]. Kristina wondered if there was anything they could do with the "super-structure" [the written routines that organize work in the Unit]. She continued and said that we would have to live with the fact that we couldn't bring in substitutes in the way we liked since the municipality must save. It's important to nip it in the bud. It's important to have a dialogue, she concluded. Nina responded and said: "Well, we'll see after today. If I tried to talk to them about this, I'd probably get a reply like: 'You must know it's been a crap day but we have made it work, of course we have.'"

The dots are way of surfacing problems within the organization, but the ultimate goal is to have green/smiling dots. It is also something that the employees learn. If Elisabeth one week wonders if her division in the pre-school has a different standard for what is good, neutral, or bad because all the other divisions have lots of green on the board while her division is blue, by the week after she already has lots of green dots beside her name and positive formulations of what has been good about the week. The evalu-ation of a workday or a workweek by placing dots of different colors or smiling/non-smiling faces was not uncontroversial. And within other areas of the municipality, such as in departments of elderly care or social services, they had stopped using them altogether. One of the employees told me that in her department the manager abused the dots: "If you put a red dot, she could come up to you in the hallway and say that you had misunderstood. Things like that. So we don't use the dots." Another employee told me that they were also about to remove the dots from the board. Another staff told me that they had ended up with the board being all yellow all the time. The Lean Strategist, Susan, also warned us in a Lean Forum Meeting: "You need to pay attention if there is someone who always puts green dots. You need to ask them to explain why." Are they really as satisfied with their work as they portray or are they just trying to escape being responsible for "improvements" was the underlying implication.

There are certain practices circulating at the Lean "board meetings" which are instigated by the Lean model and how the model is performed. And the Lean "board meetings" are framed in particular ways pointing to particular solutions when management wants to create more "joy at work." The "board meetings" are set up to gently force staff to be involved in the organization of work. It is an active employee with entrepreneurial capabili-ties that is nurtured, the *entrepreneurial self* (Miller and Rose 1995). It is an employee that is encouraged to put red and blue/yellow dots and con-tinuously suggest improvement, while staff at the same time learn that the ultimate goal is to have green units enjoying "joy at work" in organizations with "perfect" flows, without "bottlenecks" such as children on the run or staff out sick, creating a milieu that favors positive utterances at the expense of negative statements, irrespective of how well-founded they may be. There is no room for just doing one's job well.

Conclusion: Flows-focused, Improvement-oriented, Evaluative Preschool Teachers

This chapter examined how the Lean management model plays out in Swed-ish public preschools through Lean meetings. It shows the significance of meetings for the Lean model, which becomes visible in the model's meeting formats but also through the ideas and practices circulating in the Lean meetings. These ideas and practices set the agenda and frame the preschool staff and their work practices. The meeting format, the architecture, of the

Lean meetings determine what kind of work practices may be "improved" by Lean having short stand-up meetings that focus on evaluating the day or the workweek, or using "improvement group" meetings and making value-stream-mappings by showing the "flow" through post-its on brown paper, or by filling in the "moment of truth" document formatted to identify moments when the children and parents—read: actually parents—interact with the preschool.

Lean meetings also circulate ideas, resistance, acceptance, and decision-making about the organization. There are certain ideas that come with the Lean model that have to be handled in Lean meetings. Lean meetings can only "improve" work practices in certain ways, focusing on "flows," "continuous improvement," "efficiency," "evaluation," and "customer value." Some of the employees try to resist changes in the organization of meetings. They attempt to keep the weekly meetings and ignore the call for using Lean "board meetings," or subtly resist the evaluation of moods using the colors, or smiling/non-smiling faces, by turning green and smiling or giving it up altogether. But this meeting ethnography also shows the acceptance of the Lean tools and an ethics of evaluation where evaluative goals in numerical or color-coded categorical forms is not questioned but treated as a natural order of things (cf. Thedvall 2015).

Thus, Lean meetings operate as makers of particular ways of understanding work practices and work organization, encouraging "continuous improvements" but only by focusing on flows, encouraging flow-focused thinking, and putting evaluation at the center. Evaluations by number or colors determine what solutions can be made and what problems can be identified. The Lean meeting also makes certain types of employees, placing the active, evaluative employee at the pinnacle by evaluating "joy at work" supported by an assumed correlation between "joy at work" and active, responsible employees. The visualization techniques of the Lean "board" not only evaluate the mood, "joy at work," but also list who is responsible for what improvements so that it is plain to see for all the passing employees.

In other words, it is in the Lean meetings that work practices are instigated and ways of thinking and discussions are directed towards certain problems and solutions. It is through the Lean meetings that what it means to be a relevant, first-class employee in a Lean organization is produced. And the question is: Is it these flows-focused, improvement-oriented, evaluative preschool teachers we want taking care of our children? My answer would be no. Regardless, this chapter brings to light the significance of what we do in meetings and of what meetings make within organizations. It also demonstrates the rich and valuable material insights meeting ethnography can produce. These meetings reveal themselves to be condensed field sites for the examination of the kind of framework the Lean management model instantiates and in what ways it is set to impact organizations such as preschools.

Notes

1 I'm sure there are, there must be, but I haven't been able to find any.
2 The maximum fee each month in 2016 for a child between one and two years is 1313 SEK (approx. 175 USD or 140 euro) and for a child between three and five years is 875 SEK (approx. 115 USD or 90 euro).
3 This research is part of the research project *Managing preschool the Lean way. An industrial management model enters childcare* No. D0181501 funded by the Swedish Research Council. I am grateful to the funding agency for its generous support.
4 All the people appearing in the text are anonymized.
5 The concept of pedagogist (*pedagogista* in Italian – and in Swedish) is from the Reggio Emilia philosophy.
6 *Arbetsplatsträff* in Swedish, also known as "APT," may be translated into "workplace meetings," but they are more than workplace meetings. They are the result of collective agreements between unions and the employers and the so-called cooperation agreement where staff need to be informed and heard in dialogue on the important issues of the organization, preferably once a month.

References

Arlbjørn, Jan Stentoft, Per Vagn Freytag and Henning de Haas. "Service supply chain management: A survey of Lean application in the municipal sector." *International Journal of Physical Distribution & Logistics Management* 41(2011): 277–295.

Ben-Ari, Eyal. "State, standardisation and 'normal' children: An anthropological study of preschool." In *Family and Social Policy in Japan: Anthropological Approaches*, edited by Roger Goodman, 111–130. Cambridge: Cambridge University Press, 2002.

Bourdieu, Pierre. *Language and Symbolic Power*. Cambridge: Polity Press, 1991.

Chalice, Robert. *Improving Healthcare Using Toyota Lean Production Methods*. Milwaukee, WI: Quality Press, 2007.

Curriculum for the Preschool Lpfö 98, revised 2010. Skolverket: The Swedish National Agency for Education, 2010. http://www.skolverket.se/publikationer?id=2704.

Deming, Edwards W. *Out of the Crisis: Quality, Productivity and Competitive Position*. Cambridge: Cambridge University Press, 1988.

Foucault, Michel. "The political technology of individuals." In *Technologies of the Self: A Seminar with Michel Foucault*, edited by Luther H. Martin, Huch Gutman and Patrick H. Hutton, 145–162. Amherst, MA: University of Massachusetts Press, 1988.

Foucault, Michel. "Governmentality." In *The Foucault Effect*, edited by Graham Burchell, Colin Gordon and Peter Miller, 87–104. London: Harvester Wheatsheaf, 1991.

Garsten, Christina, Jessica Lindvert and Renita Thedvall. *Makeshift Work in a Changing Labour Market: The Swedish Model in the Post-Financial Crisis Era*. Cheltenham, UK: Edward Elgar, 2015.

Islamoglu, Huri. "Komisyon/Commission and Kurul/Board: Words that rule." In *Words in Motion: Toward a Global Lexicon*, edited by Carol Gluck and Anna Lowenhaupt Tsing, 265–285. Durham: Duke University Press, 2009.

Martin, Emily. "Managing Americans – Policy and changes in the meanings of work and the self." In *Anthropology of Policy: Critical Perspectives on Governance and Power*, edited by Cris Shore and Susan Wright, 239–257. London: Routledge, 1997.

Miller, Peter and Nicholas Rose. "Production, identity, and democracy." *Theory & Society* 24(1995): 427–467.

Modig, Niklas and Pär Åhlström. *This Is Lean*. Stockholm: Rheologica Publishing, 2012.

Niskanen, William A. *Bureaucracy and Representative Government*. Chicago: Aldine, 1971.

Oakes, Leslie S., Barbara Townley and David J. Cooper. "Business planning as pedagogy: language and control in a changing institutional field." *Administrative Science Quarterly* 43(1998): 257–292.

Pedersen, Rahbek Gjerdum Espen and Mahad Huniche. "Negotiating Lean: The fluidity and solidity of new management technologies in the Danish public sector." *International Journal of Productivity and Performance management* 60(6) (2011): 550–566.

Prounlove, Nathan, Claire Moxham and Ruth Boaden. "Lessons for Lean in healthcare from using six sigma in the NHS." *Public Money and Management* 28(2008): 27–34.

Radnor, Zoe. *Lean in the Public Sector*. London: Routledge, 2012.

Rose, Nicholas and Peter Miller. "Political power beyond the state: Problematics of government." *British Journal of Sociology* 43(2) (1992): 172–205.

Sahlin-Andersson, Kerstin. "Imitating by editing success: The construction of organizational fields." In *Translating Organizational Change*, edited by Barbara Czarniawska and Guje Sevón, 69–92. Berlin: Walter de Gruyter, 1996.

Schwartzman, Helen B. *The Meeting: Gatherings in Organizations and Communities*. New York: Springer Science, 1989.

Sense, Peter. *The Fifth Discipline: The Art and Practice of the Learning Organization*. London: Random House Books, [1994] 2006.

Shore, Cris and Susan Wright. *Anthropology of Policy: Critical Perspectives on Governance and Power*. London: Routledge, 1997.

Tamm Hallström, Kristina and Renita Thedvall. "Managing administrative reform through language: Implementing Lean in Swedish public sector organizations." Special issue *After NPM* edited by Kajsa Lindberg, Barbara Czarniawska and Rolf Solli. *Scandinavian Journal of Public Administration* 19(2) (2015): 89–108.

Thedvall, Renita. "Punctuated entries: Doing fieldwork in policy meetings in the EU." In *Organisational Anthropology: Doing Ethnography in and among Complex Organisations*, edited by Christina Garsten and Anette Nyqvist, 106–119. London: Pluto Press, 2013.

Thedvall, Renita. "Managing preschool the Lean way: Evaluating work processes by numbers and colours." Special issue edited by Cris Shore and Susan Wright. *Social Anthropology* 23(1) (2015): 42–52.

Urla, Jacqueline. "Total quality language revival." In *Language in Late Capitalism: Pride and Profit*, edited by Alexandre Duchêne and Monica Heller, 73–92. New York: Routledge, 2012.

Womack, James P., Daniel T. Jones and Daniel Roos. *The Machine that Changed the World: The Story of Lean Production*. New York: Rawson Associates and Macmillan, 1990.

Conclusion: The Meeting and the Mirror

Helen B. Schwartzman

In his famous book, *Mirror for Man* (1949), Clyde Kluckhohn suggested that:

> Ordinarily we are unaware of the special lens through which we look at life. It would hardly be fish who discovered the existence of water. Students who had not gone beyond the horizon of their own society could not be expected to perceive the custom which was the stuff of their own thinking. The scientist of human affairs needs to know as much about the eye that sees as the object seen
>
> (p. 16)

When *The Meeting: Gatherings in Organizations and Communities* was published in 1989, I hoped that it would encourage anthropologists to look at meetings as an important part of the "water" that makes up our everyday life. Over the next two decades, however, this did not happen but now more than twenty-five years later I am delighted and also gratified to see that a new generation of anthropologists is calling for the development of meeting ethnographies.[1] The chapters in this exciting volume, *Meeting Ethnography: Meetings as Key Technologies of Contemporary Governance, Development, and Resistance*, provide us with richly detailed studies of meetings in multiple contexts, including Argentina, Malawi, Switzerland, Sweden, Norway, the UK, and the United States. The authors argue that it is crucial for anthropologists to begin to theorize this "ubiquitous gathering" that may be used by executive boards to manage the operations of large-scale, multi-national corporations and at the same time employed by activists protesting the actions of these same corporations. What can we say about an activity that can be put to such diverse uses? Are the meetings of the corporation the same kind of event as the meetings of the activists? What are the important similarities and differences exhibited by these meetings? Does it make sense to try to define what a meeting is and how we "know" it as an event, or a ritual, a lens, technology, site, performance, etc.? How can (or can) we define what a meeting is, what it does, and how it does it? How should we

DOI: 10.4324/9781315559407-9

go about recognizing, defining, examining, and analyzing meetings and their social, cultural, and political economic contexts? These are just some of the issues that are taken up in the impressive group of papers presented in this volume.

I will begin my more specific comments about these papers by returning to Clyde Kluckhohn's use of the mirror image as a way to describe the value of anthropology for examining what "others," as well as the anthropologist, may not be able to see even when it is right in front of us. This brings me to the title of my chapter, which juxtaposes the meeting as an event with the mirror as an object—an object which sees and is seen. I suggest that there are important connections between mirrors and meetings especially in regard to the ability of mirrors to deflect, multiply, transform, and distort images, rendering some things visible and others invisible. These connections will be more apparent when we recognize two additional features of mirrors. First, in order to see the image that appears in a mirror it is necessary to look *at* it, not through, behind, or over it, but *at* the mirror. This is commonsensical, but there is something else about mirrors that is not so obvious and it is that the image we see in the mirror is a transformed image that *appears* to be a lateral reversal from left to right (and not a vertical reversal up/down) but actually is a reversal from front to back.[2] This ability to change the image of what we see in subtle and sometimes not so subtle ways (such as the ways that I have mentioned above) is one of the reasons that mirrors are so useful for magicians and illusionists who want to misdirect and deceive their audiences. In short, mirrors are not exactly what they seem to be and the same is true of meetings. I will return to these points at various times in my discussion of the chapters in this volume.

In *The Meeting* I suggested that sometimes it is necessary "to walk into a social system backwards in order to see it, and the forms that produce it, in a new way" (p. 4). This is one of the important connections that I see between mirrors and meetings as I have mentioned above because in order to understand the role that meetings play in social life it is necessary to first look *at* them and not *through* them or *behind* them, as if they are either not there or are hiding or masking something that we cannot see. However, when we do this we realize that meetings do not simply "reflect" or "reveal" the social order outside a meeting but in many important ways the social order is *made (produced, created, constituted)* in the act of the meeting and this, in turn, creates the possibility for challenging, inverting, and subverting it.

Meetings: Everywhere and Nowhere

One of the things that first struck me when I began to think about meetings was how they seemed to be everywhere in social life, and especially everywhere in academic life, but, oddly, almost nowhere in the research literature. As I have suggested above, it has taken anthropologists and other researchers some time to actually *see* meetings because the first image, and the dominant image, has been to look through them or behind them but not at them. In the introductory chapter to this volume, "Exploring the Boring: An Introduction to Meeting Ethnography," Jen Sandler and Renita Thedvall present a very useful overview of the history of studies of meetings, councils, committees, and political speech by anthropologists, and they depict how meetings have gradually come into view at least for a number of ethnographers. This view suggests that meetings should be examined "as a tool for ethnographic fieldwork and anthropological thought" because they enable us to see in "myriad contemporary shifts in global and local governance, development, and resistance through their everyday manifestations in the lives of activists, bureaucrats, civil servants, corporate players, politicians, and international development actors" (p. 2).

This chapter does a terrific job of tracing the history of anthropologists' "discovery" of meetings and with this discovery the need to think more critically about how to theorize meetings and their place in social life as well as the value of developing informative and innovative "meeting ethnographies" for anthropologists and many other researchers. Sandler and Thedvall suggest that the need for researchers to pay attention to meetings could not be more pressing now because of the increased attention that anthropologists (and others) are paying to the work, activities, and effects of multiple organizations (such as NGOs) as well as efforts to theorize and analyze "the state" and its bureaucratic operations (e.g., Sharma and Gupta 2006; Bernstein and Mertz 2011).[3] At the same time there is renewed interest in many fields in examining social movements and "grassroots" organizing processes and efforts to resist and challenge state oppression (such as the Arab Spring), economic globalization (the World Trade Organization protests in Seattle in 1999), economic injustice (Occupy movement in 2011), racial injustice and violence (Black Lives Matter).

The increasing concern that anthropologists have demonstrated with issues related to governmentality, democracy promotion/assistance, collective action, and direct democracy would seem to absolutely require that ethnographers pay more attention to the role of meetings in these efforts, and yet many contemporary researchers examining these issues have frequently ignored this important social form in their studies. To mention just one example, the 2012 AE Forum in the *American Ethnologist* (Volume 39) includes two articles examining the, at the time, very recent Occupy movements. One article by Razsa and Kurnick looks at the Occupy movement in Slovenia and the second article looks at #OccupyEverywhere and #OccupyBoston (Juris, 2012). The commentary on the two articles is by David Nugent (2012). Following the lead of their Occupy interlocutors, the authors of these articles portray the Occupy movement as producing an entirely new and experimental set of political relations. Although they suggest that their research makes contributions to the growing literature on the anthropology of democracy they contend that direct democracy or alternative democracies "have been relatively neglected in anthropology" (Razsa and Kurnick 2012: 240). What is surprising about just this one claim is that the authors do not seem to have even considered the possibility that previous research in the field of political anthropology, and specifically research examining the range of speech and decision-making styles and practices (including consensual as well as hierarchical models), might have something to offer them in their efforts "to extend the ways that direct democracy and direct action have been theorized to date" (Razsa and Kurnick 2012: 240). If they were to look at this literature they would find, I suggest, that much of it would lead them to recognize the need to begin their ethnographic accounts by theorizing 'the meeting' as the social form which is at the very center of these new "emergent practices." These researchers would do well to follow the approach of Christoph Haug (2013), who studies contemporary social movements in Europe, and has specifically focused on examining meeting styles, theorizing processes of meeting governance, and asking questions about how interorganizational collaborations are constituted in face-to-face meetings.

Recognizing and Defining Meetings

Once we notice meetings it does become important, if also quite difficult, to try to describe or define them. In *The Meeting* I attempted to specify what we are talking about when we describe an event as "a meeting." I was particularly interested in trying to clarify what is characteristic about the talk that occurs in a meeting, how it is regulated along with expectations about the goal of the event. I tried to combine the insights of Erving Goffman with the work of the ethnomethodologists Atkinson et al (1978) in developing my definition of a meeting as "a gathering of three or more people who agree to assemble for a purpose ostensibly related to the functioning of an organization or group . . . A meeting is characterized by multiparty talk that is episodic in nature, and participants develop or use specific conventions for regulating this talk . . . The meeting form frames the behavior that occurs within it as concerning the 'business' or 'work' of the group, or organization, or society" (1989: 61–62).[4]

The tension between developing a definition that tries to specify some of the generalities of a meeting as an event along with a recognition that meetings are, first and foremost, localized events with a historical foundation is crucial to keep in mind and I see my attempts at developing a definition as only a beginning, and in no way a final effort in this regard. Having said this I would also stress that we do need to think clearly about how it is that participants (including ourselves) "know" a meeting when we/they *see* it, *hear* it, even *feel* it. What is it about an interaction that informs us that we are "in" a meeting or we are "observing" a meeting? How is this event recognized, labeled, and accomplished in particular settings by the participants? What is it about interaction that informs other groups, societies, etc. that they are "meeting" (if this is even the right word)?

In their first chapter Sandler and Thedvall depict the October 2015 workshop group's discussion held during the last day of this gathering, and I believe that their presentation really captures the wide-ranging, challenging, and thoughtful nature of this conversation. Since it was the last day there was a strong feeling that we should begin to grapple more generally with a number of the issues that had been taken up more specifically in the papers presented on the previous two days. As Sandler and Thedvall report, there was a specific focus on several of the issues that I have mentioned above about how (or whether to) define a meeting/meetings, whether we should be limited in our definitions to only those encounters that the participants in our site(s) would label as a meeting, or do we (can we) go beyond this? An array of images were suggested for helping us to understand a meeting as "an ethnographic object." For example, we discussed meetings as a technology, a window, a site, a pulse, a ritual, a lens, a form of play (or play of forms), a performance. Wisely, we did not settle on one image but used this discussion to consider the range of approaches available to us.

One of the papers that we discussed on the first day of the workshop was by Christina Garsten and Adrienne Sörbom, "Small Places, Big Stakes: Meetings as Moments of Ethnographic Momentum" and it portrays the researchers' quest to gain access to "the meeting proper" at the World Economic Forum's Annual Meeting in Davos, Switzerland in 2011. Their chapter raises a number of important theoretical and methodological issues about how we define what a meeting is and also what happens if it seems like it is impossible to gain access to "the meeting" or, at least, the meeting(s) where we think the "action" is. In their search for "the meeting" Garsten and Sörbom traveled far and wide (from Switzerland to South Africa), staring at high-wired fences and talking to security guards with automatic weapons on their shoulders. Their recurring question was "Is there a meeting here?" And, also, what do we learn about Davos meetings by *not* gaining access to the meeting(s) itself?

These questions are important to consider especially in thinking about how we recognize and define meetings in multiple social systems. In the case of Davos it is possible to suggest that we gain more knowledge about meetings by not gaining access to them than if we had, somehow, made it over the fence or actually charmed the security guards to admit us to the event? I think that we learn a lot about meetings, especially so-called "high-level" meetings or difficult-to-access meetings, and even secret meetings in this chapter, and it is crucial for the development of meeting ethnographies to have an example of a study that shows us all of the circles, barriers, parties, other meetings, and events that surround a "meeting" or a "summit" like Davos. Perhaps the term summit is a more accurate description of what it takes to climb up the Davos hierarchy in order to gain entrance to the event as opposed to what we more commonly think of when we refer to Davos as a summit (i.e., a meeting between the heads of government). Perhaps the most important thing about these meetings is the way that the space of a meeting is configured and policed and "made private" and exclusive, allowing entry to only select participants and denying entry to everyone else. The status of being one of the "select few" who can enter and participate in the Davos meetings is conferred on the participants in multiple ways including the use of spatial, temporal, material, and social markers along with the deployment of a large-scale security apparatus (including 5,000 Swiss soldiers!). The production and reproduction of elite status that this process creates may be the most important thing about these meetings (as opposed to what might actually happen in the meeting/s itself). Certain people become certified, legitimated, and elevated by this process and once this happens everything else that the meeting produces (speeches, talks, deliberations, parties, chats, etc.) may be secondary. When you think about it, what kind of impact has Davos actually had on efforts to reduce climate change, food insecurity, nuclear proliferation, or reduce rising inequality (these are all themes that Davos meetings have addressed over the last few years)? Everyone who is drawn to Davos (including the protestors who set up their own Occupy camp outside the meeting ground in 2011) assumes that something important will be accomplished or decided at a Davos summit. No one seems to notice that this rarely happens.

Meetings: Makers and Breakers of Social Order[5]

In their introductory chapter, Sandler and Thedvall suggest that meetings operate as "makers of governance, resistance, discipline, development, re-articulations . . . Meeting, as a way of interacting, is what enables people to impose projects of collective reason and interaction upon others. Meeting is what produces structural violence, and it is what produces liberation" (p. 15). In other words, meetings play an important role in both creating as well as challenging the social order. This means that we should examine meetings as both *makers* and *breakers* of social order but this also requires asking what it is about meetings that allows them to *act* in this way. One answer must be the way that social structure and cultural values are "bred into" (see Ranson et al 1980) the meeting as a social form and the fact that we cannot "act" outside the social forms that we use to generate interaction as well as to interpret what it means.[6] This is another way of asserting that meetings are an important place for the production as well as reproduction of social systems and for connecting the local with the global. If meetings are where "power is produced and enacted, dynamics of identity and hierarchy are negotiated and organization is produced, determined, and challenged" (Sandler and Thedvall, p. 1), how does this happen? I believe that these are some of the most important questions that meeting ethnographers need to consider. Several of the papers in this volume take up this issue in interesting and productive ways, but three papers stand out for me in this regard and I will discuss their contributions below.

In Nancy Kendall and Rachel Silver's chapter, "Mapping International Development Relations through Meeting Ethnography" the authors use their research on international development projects to illustrate "the strengths and limitations of meeting ethnography in revealing how relations of power and authority are produced through international development discourses, policies, and practices" (p. 24). Their focus is on "partner meetings" held in the education sector in Malawi that bring together central actors in this field such as representatives of international donors or funders, government representatives from the specific state ministry, "middle" organizations involved in the implementation of a project such as NGOs based in the funder country, and "end recipients," which may also be NGOs that are based in the country (pp. 24, 27). Kendall and Silver are particularly interested in showing the value of meeting ethnography "for studies of globalized relations of power and authority" and clearly "partner meetings" are particularly good sites for examining these issues (p. 28).

What is most exciting about this chapter is that Kendall and Silver do not just assert that partner meetings play an important role in "supporting the radical disempowerment of the Malawian state and the empowerment of funder and international NGO actors" but they show us how this happens in specific meeting settings (p. 28). This is where the value of meeting ethnography really stands out because by presenting three different meeting vignettes they are able to show us how, for example, funder domination is enacted in the way the meeting is organized as well as in the flow of the actual discussions that take place between the funders in this setting with occasional interjections by the NGO representative (p. 30). The vignettes also illustrate how the Ministry staff representative engaged in subtle forms of resistance (not speaking during most of the meeting, slouching at his seat, no meeting materials in front of him) to the domination and inequitable relations on display in this meeting context. The three meeting vignettes also illustrate three different "observational styles and analytic vantage points" that can be employed by meeting ethnographers in recording and interpreting the significance of the meetings.

Kendall and Silver also argue for the importance of meeting ethnography in the field of international development because they suggest that it allows researchers to question what the authors believe is an over-reliance on "discursive data" (i.e., analysis of official discourse and limited interviews) in efforts to study "up" (when the focus is on policymakers, funders, government ministers, and bureaucrats) (pp. 25–27). In other words, because of issues of access as well as a lack of resources to conduct studies in multiple sites, the focus has typically been on what people *say* rather than on what they *do* (a classic contrast for all ethnographers). This approach tends to create "over-determined analyses of the power of global discourses to shape daily practices," which overlook opportunities for change as well as possibilities for resistance in the settings in which actors confront each other (pp. 25–27). This approach grants all power in these settings to the institutions and their representatives that produce this discourse and turns all recipients of these programs into powerless actors. In contrast, Kendall and Silver argue for an approach they refer to as "policy as/in practice" or "studying through," which enables linking micro and macro processes in order to understand "how official development rationalities themselves are socially produced, maintained, and transformed" as opposed to the more common assumption that these rationalities are "fixed, coherent, and cohesive at the funder level" (p. 26). What Kendall and Silver are very successful at doing in this chapter is to present a sustained argument for, and illustration of, the value of meeting ethnography as a rich methodological window into conducting practice-oriented research that examines the "how" of the development apparatus (p. 25).

In "Argentinian *Asamblea* Meetings as Assemblage: Presence in Emergence" Karin Skill and Susann Baez Ullberg employ "assemblage theory," along with their own ethnographic research conducted in two different regions in Argentina (in the small town of Andalgalá in the northwest and in Santa Fe City in the northeast of the country), to ask important questions about the emergence, experience and experimentation characteristic of Argentinian *asemblea* meetings in these contexts. They are concerned with how "heterogeneous elements like people, ideas, landscapes, knowledge, material and technologies" are assembled through a process of "social labor" and how these "specific temporal-spatial conjunctures" endow these meetings with "capacity" (p. 71). The answers they provide in their chapter are very useful for thinking about the agency of meetings.

One of the interesting points about this argument is the stress that is given to contingencies, heterogeneity, mixing, interminglings, and unpredictability in terms of understanding what is assembled in these meetings and how this influences what sorts of actions are (or are not) taken by the *asemblea*. Skill and Baez Ullberg use examples from their field work to illustrate how *asemblea* meetings mix contemporary global practices of protest (such as the Occupy movement and its direct democracy practices, see Graeber 2009) with long traditions of collective action in Argentina and Latin America more generally (see Salmenkari 2009) (p. 73). The authors also illustrate how important it is that while "the *asemblea* meeting as an assemblage can be described as a contingent configuration of different material and nonmaterial elements, it is also a social community. As such, *asambleistas* not only identify with the cause at stake, but also have a strong sense of belonging to the *asemblea* community" (pp. 73–74). In their terms it is the interaction between *belonging* to a social community (the *asemblea* community) and *becoming* an *asambleista* that endows the individual and the community with agency. This approach focuses attention on the role of another form of mixing in *asemblea* meetings, in this case it is the intermingling of experienced and inexperienced activists (like the example of Marta, a flood victim who became an activist in Santa Fe City) in the meetings that enables individuals to "learn *asemblea* meeting practices as well as practices of protest," and it is in this way that "people become activists and the *asemblea* becomes collective action in and through the meetings" (p. 85).

The importance of examining how people learn meeting practices is taken up also in the chapter by Simone Abram, "Learning to Meet (or How to Talk to Chairs)." Using research on the formalized meetings of local councils in Britain and Norway, Abram asks, how do participants "learn to enact the universalizing technology of government that I suggest meetings to be?" (p. 46). In this way Abram is looking at a similar process of "learning to meet" that Skill and Baez Ullberg illustrate in the case of how individuals becomes activists in *asemblea* meetings; however, the form of the municipal meetings discussed by Abram and what it takes to "master" this form is quite different, and in this way very revealing, about the issues I have discussed here in terms of understanding how meetings acquire agency or capacity.

The process of "doing meetings" in the local councils examined by Abram is both similar and different to the process of "doing" *asemblea* meetings.[7] What is similar is the power of the meeting form to transform the behavior of the individuals who are assembled (whether in a plaza or in a government office) from private, individual talk and chatting, to public and official discussion of particular issues. There are expectations about who speaks and when and what they are allowed to say for both groups, although what these expectations are, how they have developed, how they are enforced, and what forms of standardization exist are different. I have already mentioned the practice of "direct democracy" in *asemblea* meetings where there is, for example, the assumption that no particular member or group should take on a leading role and everyone should be able to express their opinions (Skill and Baez Ullberg, p. 77, this volume). In contrast in the council meetings in Abram's study there is always a leader who controls the order and the flow of discussion and there are clear sanctions for violating these practices as Abram's research illustrates.

Abram's specific focus is on understanding how governmental meetings have become standardized "with agendas, minutes, apologies, items, other business, etc." and in this way how they have become "a navigable system that can be used and adapted around the globe" (p. 47). Historically this standardization or "meetingization" (see van Vree 1999) has been traced to colonial administrative practices as well as the circulation of meeting rulebooks (like the *ABC of Chairmanship* produced by Sir Walter Citrine in 1939 in the UK discussed by Abram or, I would add, *Roberts Rules of Order*, published originally in 1875 by General Henry Martyn Roberts in the United States). However, Abram is not concerned with analyzing the specifics of these guidebooks but, instead, she wants to understand how the bureaucratic meeting form has become so successful and ubiquitous and therefore how it is that "different people in particular places come to learn the varied skills that are needed to master the art of managing meetings. The basic rules may appear simple, but they are further reaching than they may appear at first encounter, are largely tacit, and their mastery is complex"

(p. 47). Abram shows us, using examples from her ethnographic research, how these tacit meeting rules and practices are made explicit in different types of meeting encounters. In one example we see how a new member of the district council in western Norway is corrected for engaging in direct crosstalk with another member without addressing her comments to the chair of the meeting (who in this case is the mayor of the community). Secondly, Abram shows us how youth learn the intricacies of meeting practices by "playing" at meetings. In Norway many municipal governments create youth councils that provide students with opportunities to learn and practice "municipal meeting style" by formulating specific project proposals (which may actually be funded) and then presenting them and engaging in a debate about which ones might be worthy of support.

What I find most interesting about Abram's chapter is her emphasis on the importance of considering "bureaucratic meetings as a technology of government, *which both enables and is, itself, government*" (p. 46, my italics). In this way she directly addresses the problematic assumption that we must look through, or possibly behind, meetings in order to clearly see the actions and the power of the "state." In this view the meeting is either a neutral form that has no effect on what transpires within it or it is a façade that disguises the role of the state. Abram suggests the reverse of this view by proposing that "the state is not the reality which stands behind the mask of council meetings, it is itself the mask which prevents our seeing the meetings as they are" (p. 46). She wants to understand "the role of council meetings in creating the local state" (p. 46) but she pushes this point further when she asks how it is that the bureaucratic meeting has become so ubiquitous that it is virtually invisible (p. 47). I have suggested in other publications that the meeting frame itself contributes to this disappearance process by directing us to look at the topic of the meeting, but not the meeting itself. This is only one way to think about what I believe are the important questions about meeting invisibility that Abram raises here. How is it that meetings have come to be perceived as standardized, neutral, and rational decision-making forms? Is this just a matter of, to invoke Kluckhohn here, fish not being able to perceive water, or is this perhaps a way to answer one of our questions about how meetings acquire agency? Is it actually the invisibility of meetings that provides these events with force or capacity?

The Material Meeting

At some level social anthropologists have always been concerned with the materiality of everyday life in terms of describing the environments, objects, artifacts, and things that are an important part of the worlds that individuals and groups inhabit. Generally, however, attention has been given to the description of the uses and meaning of particular "things" within the cultural setting in which they were observed. Until recently, there was very little attention given to the place of artifacts and other forms of material culture in bureaucratic settings. This changed in the late 1990s with the publication of Richard Harper's *Inside the IMF: An Ethnography of Documents, Technology and Organizational Action* (1998) and it really blossomed after the volume, *Documents: Artifacts of Modern Knowledge*, edited by Annelise Riles, appeared in 2006. Several chapters in this book (e.g., Don Brenneis, Adam Reed, Marilyn Strathern) offer incisive analyses of the role of documents, such as recommendation forms, prison intake records, and university mission statements in the social life of the groups these ethnographers studied. The anthropology of documents has now become an important topic of research for many anthropologists and a number of sophisticated analyses of these "modern" artifacts have appeared over the last ten years (e.g., Elyachar 2006; Feldman 2008; Hull 2008, 2012a, 2012b). What is most exciting to me in this regard is that I believe this relatively recent turn toward documents is at least partly responsible for the even more recent turn towards meetings, illustrated by this volume as well as other upcoming publications.[8]

In his article "Documents and Bureaucracy" (2012a) Matthew Hull makes a very important point about the need "to restore analytically the visibility of documents" because, and here the parallel with meetings should be very obvious, the tendency has been to look through them rather than at them (p. 253). He suggests that one important way to do this is to treat documents as "mediators, things that 'transform, translate, distort, and modify the meaning or the elements they are supposed to carry' (Latour 2005: 39). Just as discourse has long been recognized as a dense mediator between subjects and the world, newer anthropological scholarship on bureaucratic documents treats them not as neutral purveyors of discourse, but as mediators that shape the significance of the signs inscribed on them and their relations with the objects they refer to" (2012: 253). The parallels between documents as mediators and meetings as mediators are striking in my view and I believe that I was hinting at this view of meetings as a mediating form when I suggested that meetings at the Midwest Community Mental Health Center were "sense makers" and *the* form, in this context, "that generates and maintains the organization as an entity, and one that also influences business in ways that may be totally unanticipated and unintended by its members" (1987: 290). What this means for meeting ethnographers is that we need to be able to show how meetings may "transform, translate, distort, and modify" the actions taken within as well as outside the meeting context. I think that attempts to do this in our research will be another important way to examine how meetings acquire force and the consequences they produce (even when the consequences may be unintended or directly contradictory to the intentions of the meeting participants).

Renita Thedvall's chapter, "Meeting to Improve: Lean[ing] Swedish Public Preschools," speaks to several of the issues I have mentioned here in regard to how meetings acquire agency and how this agency may be related to the way that documents and meeting artifacts co-produce each other in particular settings. I believe these points are dramatically illustrated in Thedvall's study as she examines what impact the "Lean management model" has had on public sector programs in Sweden. In the case presented here the focus is on public preschools and their adoption of this model and how it has been applied in these childcare settings. It is stunning to see how an array of fairly simple artifacts like colored post-it notes, white boards, brown paper, and the aesthetics of their presentation and visualization come to structure the activities of the childcare workers in these settings. In particular, this includes the introduction of what seems like a multitude of meetings—whiteboard meetings, "moment of truth" meetings, improvement group meetings, reflection meetings—which are used to monitor, improve, and evaluate the performance and satisfaction of the workers in these settings.

Most importantly, the Lean model has been introduced in order to improve the documentary practices (referred to as "pedagogical documentation") required by the state in order to systematically record "each child's learning and development . . . [and] how it changes over time" (p. 148). The paradox of implementing the Lean model, which was adapted from an approach to create more efficient "workflow" in the auto industry, in a preschool context is discussed by Thedvall as "staff need to find ways to fit their work activities into the labels and tools of the model" (p. 146). In particular, rather than improving the "workflow" of childcare staff, this approach seems to contribute to continued interruptions of their "workflow" or "workday." Contrary to the intent of the Lean program, what this illustrates is how this program, designed to produce a more efficient and satisfying workday for employees, can become so "thick" (dare I say "fat") with meetings and mood evaluations and post-it note requirements, etc. that the goal of the setting (caring for children) is almost lost. Thedvall describes a management meeting at the preschool, which includes the "Lean Strategist" (Gudrun), who is responsible for making sure that this school becomes a Lean organization. "Gudrun asks if all employees take part in the weekly meetings. One of the workplace heads, Sigrid, responds that it is one from each division in the preschool. Gudrun continues and asks if it is possible to have everyone join. Sigrid says with a bit of irony in her voice that someone needs to take care of the children" (p. 152).

Space, Place, Time and Attention in Meetings

All meetings take place in some type of space and they also require some type of time commitment from participants. This may be "real" space and time or virtual space and time but it is necessary to take account of the important role that space and time/temporality plays in the construction of an event as a meeting. The space may already have been set aside in particular settings or reconfigured from other activities and, in some instances, appropriated from other uses, especially when public space is used for gatherings (e.g., a plaza, a square, a park). The time commitment required of participants may be voluntary or it may be a required part of one's job and this may entail balancing other time commitments, which are often other meetings (see my discussion of "Meetings, Time, and Attention" in *The Meeting*, pp. 145–167). All of the chapters in this volume illustrate important aspects of the role of meeting time and space in their ethnographic projects but two of the chapters, Jen Sandler's "Meetings All the Way Through: U.S. Broadbased Reform Coalitions and the Thickening of American Democracy" and Japonica Brown-Saracino and Meaghan Stiman's "How to Avoid Getting Stuck in Meetings: On the Value of Recognizing the Limits of Meeting Ethnography for Community Studies," are particularly important to consider in terms of considering the role of meetings in time and space in the development of meeting ethnographies.

All the Time

Jen Sandler begins her chapter with this description:

> After the Team A meeting of the Coalition for Local Initiatives, twenty-five supervisory and administrative staff members file out, most chatting. I make a split-second decision as to who to follow through the post-meeting meetings that will take place over the next half hour. I participate in one or two semi- and informal debrief meetings, and sometimes initiate debrief meetings of my own with key players. Then I hurry to the next meeting on my schedule, which is most often some form of a pre-meeting or project development meeting, wherein staff or leaders are strategizing to organize or produce products for an upcoming meeting
> (p. 106).

This is what it is like to conduct "meeting-saturated fieldwork" and Sandler uses her research with a broad-based urban reform coalition in a city in "Middlestate, USA" to show us how these settings lead both participants and researchers inexorably to meetings, or, as she describes it "meetings all the way through" (p. 106). In discussing the reform coalition that is the focus of her study, Sandler makes an important distinction between this group (which she calls the Coalition for Local Initiatives or CLI), which is centered on a population (poor people in a racially and economically diverse metropolitan area), and "niche" activist organizations, like the Alzheimer's Association, where the focus is on one specific issue (e.g., curing the disease). Of course, meetings figure prominently in both types of organizations but in coalition formations there is the need to "bring together political and economic elites with an 'organic' base of some sort; elites bring political and capital power, and the base brings political legitimacy" (p. 108). Because these types of organizations reach across a much more diverse set of groups, they are "inherently unstable" and this requires that they "constitute themselves continually through projects, through the *doing*. They *become* through their collective constitution" (p. 107, my italics). Sandler illustrates how this "collective constitution" is created and orchestrated by the participation of Coalition members in an array of meetings, such as 1-on-1 meetings, site council meetings, demonstration meetings, planning meetings, meetings with "elites." She shows us with richly detailed descriptions of particular meetings, as they occur in specific spatial settings (a room in a one-story wing of a large black evangelical church, a room in a neighborhood elementary school), how this process works, and the amount of time that it takes to create these meetings.

Tucked into her analysis of the significance of meetings for CLI are a number of important recommendations for how more generally to conduct meeting ethnographies. For example, she shows us how meetings serve "as a technology of relationship-building" and how this requires understanding all of the different types of meetings (nonformal and formal meetings, as mentioned above) that are crucial for this process of "relationship-building." In other words, ethnographers working in "meeting-saturated" settings need to produce a kind of meeting scan that will help them evaluate all (or most) of the possible meeting sites that it may be important to attend. At the same time the meeting ethnographer will want to review this "scan" with participants to compare viewpoints on these "meeting worlds." In my view one of the most important research recommendations that Sandler makes relates to issues of meeting space and time. She advises researchers to never leave a meeting alone right after it has adjourned (p. 106). Why? Because after every meeting there will be post-meeting analyses or "debrief" meetings by participants and this is crucial information for the ethnographer. This illustrates an extremely important point that is central to Sandler's ethnography and, really, to all meeting ethnographies and that is that one of the first goals of the researcher should be to try to understand how the participants in the setting are themselves interpreting their meetings (or any other activities in which they are engaged with each other). As Sandler notes that nearly everyone she speaks with wants to interpret a meeting for her, to help her understand the various backstories of why so-and-so said what she did while another person said nothing, why it was interesting that two people came in together, the history of that particular meeting or site that might help her make sense of the project. In helping the researcher "make sense" of what is happening in meetings we are also, obviously, learning incredibly important information about how the participants themselves are "making sense" of these events.

Too Much Time

There is a long-standing concern in the fields of business and management studies with how much time individuals and groups in work settings spend in meetings. It is now standard practice to begin any popular discussion of meetings with estimates of the amount of time individuals, groups, organizations, and communities spend in meetings. The current estimate is that 11 million meetings take place every day in the United States. It is not clear on what basis this estimate was made but the assumption always seems to be that most of the time American workers spend in meetings is wasted time.[9]

Japonica Brown-Saracino and Meaghan Stiman are also concerned with the amount of time spent in meetings but their focus is on the amount of time researchers spend in meetings and the reasons why they may be drawn to these events. In their chapter, "How to Avoid Getting Stuck in Meetings," they use their own research in a number of different community settings in the United States (for example, communities undergoing gentrification in Chicago and in New England, a tourist village in Maine) to examine the risks and the benefits of meeting ethnography for community studies researchers. They suggest that ethnographers need to carefully evaluate why they may be spending so much time observing and/or participating in community meetings. Is it because the site itself is overwhelmed with meetings, as Sandler's study illustrates so well, or is it because these are the events that are the easiest to access, the most comfortable and practical to observe or participate in? What else is going on in the setting and what might the researcher be missing by getting "stuck" in meetings?

The authors draw on their numerous hours of meeting observations and participation to develop a series of "good practices" for community studies researchers to follow. These practices include suggesting important ways to conceptualize what a meeting does (not just revealing but also constituting social systems, p. 103) and the methods a meeting ethnographer should use to make sure that they extend their research outside of meeting contexts. Here Brown-Saracino and Stiman stress that it is important to: (1) sample a "broad range" of the meetings that may occur in a particular setting to get "the lay of the land"; (2) extend their observation of meetings to include the events, activities, and conversations that take place both before and after the meeting itself; and (3) note carefully who attends the meetings they observe, whose voices are heard, whose voices are not heard, and who does not even attend these events (p. 103). I think that the bottom line here is something that several of the authors in this volume have stressed and that is that a researcher engaged in meeting ethnography must not stop at the meeting event. These events will only be intelligible when they are considered together with the entire range of material that a good ethnographer will produce in the course of their study. Nancy Kendall and Rachel Silver put it this way: "A full analysis requires bringing meeting observations into dialogue with other data collection methods: interviews, participant observation, document analysis, budget flow analysis, and other data . . . a robust meeting ethnography methodology combines institutional and global ethnographic methods that situate and connect the meeting to the macropolitical, economic, and social environments in which the meeting comes to make sense" (p. 42).

Mirrored Meetings

A powerful argument is presented in this book for why we can no longer take meetings for granted and continue to assume that we can somehow look *through* them unhindered by their presence. Meetings are interactional events that need to be confronted and theorized and this means asking the kinds of questions that all of the contributors in this volume are asking about what produces meetings along with what their presence produces in particular settings, how this influences what we see, and how we can examine this in our studies? I suggested earlier that there is an important connection between meetings and mirrors and I will draw this point out here in two ways. First, unless a mirror is functioning as a portal to another world or reality (as in Lewis Carroll's *Through the Looking-Glass and What Alice Found There* (1871), a mirror presents itself as an object that requires users to look directly *at* it in order to see the image that it "reflects." However, as I have also mentioned earlier, the image that one sees in a mirror is an image that has been reversed and therefore transformed. This ability to change the image of what we see in subtle, and sometimes not so subtle ways, is one of the reasons that mirrors are so useful for magicians, conjurers, illusionists, and tricksters who want to misdirect and deceive their audiences. Classic magic tricks such as Pepper's Ghost,[10] Houdini's disappearing elephant,[11] simple tricks to produce the appearance of someone levitating, and many, many others all rely on the careful placement of mirrors, lighting, and stage design in order to create their illusions. What I am suggesting here, by making this association, is that in our attempts "to explore the boring," as Jen Sandler and Renita Thedvall encourage us to do in their introductory chapter, we might want to look at how an ordinary event like a meeting might work in some extraordinary, even magical, ways.

When meetings act as mediators (in the way described by Matthew Hull earlier in relation to his discussion of bureaucratic documents) they display some of the features of mirrors: to deflect, multiply, transform, and distort images. This produces some surprising but also very consequential effects in the social systems that the researchers in this volume discuss, and it is another reason that a meeting should never be looked at as a neutral or unimportant medium. Meetings display mirror-like qualities in several of the papers in this volume. For example, Christina Garsten and Adrienne Sörbom show us how the meetings at Davos can be viewed as a world of "smoke and mirrors"; but this is not a world where smoke and mirrors disguise what is *really* happening because, I would argue, smoke and mirrors are what is really happening here, and all that is happening. The exclusivity and also multiplicity of the meetings conjures a feeling of importance and action, but if we were able to climb over the fences, or go behind the guards and pull up the "curtain" (so to speak) I think that we would only see more smoke and mirrors or, perhaps, it would be "smoke and meetings." In thinking about this case I was reminded of the *The Wizard of Oz* books by

L. Frank Baum and especially the character of the "Wizard" who turns out to actually be a con man from Omaha, Nebraska.

There are many other ways that meetings in the settings discussed in this volume illustrate mirror-like features. In Simone Abram's study of council meetings in Norway and the UK she illustrates how common it is to think that meetings are "masks" for the state, whereas it is the state (and our ideas about it as an entity) that "is itself the mask which prevents our seeing the meetings as they are" (p. 46). The role of misdirection is important to consider here and the meeting frame contributes to this process by suggesting that it is what goes on within the event (the meeting topic) that is important and not the event of the meeting itself. In other words, as in a magic show— "look over here" and "don't look here" and so the meeting disappears. Perhaps, as I mentioned earlier, it is this ability to disappear or be erased that is one of the very important ways that meetings acquire force in social systems because they are not what they seem to be.

Renita Thedvall's chapter shows us what happens when a type of meeting, and the materials and objects that accompany it, are introduced into a context where it is not clear that the form "fits" the setting. In this case Lean meetings seem to act like the distorting mirrors one sees at carnivals, producing modifications, shifts, and even some contortions by staff in order to adapt their everyday practices, as well as the overall goals of the preschools, to the Lean model of meetings. Jen Sandler's chapter shows us what it is like to work and conduct research in a setting where there is an almost infinite regress of meetings. Working in this context must feel in some ways like walking into a "house of mirrors," or "house of meetings," all reflecting on each other and making it difficult to navigate a path through the maze-like pattern of the meetings that are constantly calling for both the participant's and the researcher's attention. In contrast, Japonica Brown-Saracino and Meaghan Stiman urge us to look outside the frame of the mirror with its multiple repeating and reflecting meetings. They call attention to and underline an important point, which is that meeting ethnographers must always ask, what else is in the picture as well as what is outside the picture that I may have missed?

As I come to the end of my comments I realize that one of the things that I have focused on throughout my review is a point raised by Sandler and Thedvall in their introduction. It is a point that should not be missed: meetings "make things happen" (p. 15). This volume would not exist if it were not for the meetings that happened in Stockholm and in Amherst. All of the chapters in this volume have moved us forward in addressing a series of important theoretical and methodological issues in the ethnography of meetings. I am particularly interested in the question, how do meetings "make things happen?" but there are an abundance of questions for researchers engaged in meeting ethnography to consider. At the risk of being seen as someone who spends too much time in meetings I think that we need another meeting to make more things happen in this exciting new field.

Acknowledgements

I would like to thank Jen Sandler and Renita Thedvall for organizing the series of three workshops on Meeting Ethnography that occurred in Stockholm and in Amherst that led to the publication of this impressive volume. I was able to participate by Skype in the 2014 workshop and in person at the October 2015 workshop held at the University of Massachusetts, Amherst. I think that this workshop was an amazing experience for all of the participants; I know that it was for me. Everyone came together having read all of the papers in advance and we were able to productively and critically discuss all of the issues raised by each paper, and then in the final day we engaged in a remarkable conversation about the theoretical and methodological challenges of making meetings an object of ethnographic inquiry. The collegiality created by the workshop organizers as well as all of the participants was exceptional and created the perfect context for our discussions. Special thanks go to my fellow commentator at the workshop Don Brenneis and to all of the participants for helping us move the study of meetings and the conduct of meeting ethnography many steps forward. Thanks to: Simone Abram, Celeste Alexander, Susann Baez Ullberg, Japonica Brown-Saracino, Christina Garsten, William Girard, Krista Harper, Nancy Kendall, Gregory Duff Morton, Kysa Nygreen, Jen Sandler, Rachel Silver, Adrienne Sörbom, and Renita Thedvall.

Notes

1 I want to note here that during these decades, from 1989 to now, meetings did become a more common topic of research in the fields of communication studies and organizational research as evidenced by a number of articles and I am pleased to say that many of these studies drew on my work in *The Meeting*. A recent volume edited by Joseph A. Allen, Nale Lehmann-Willenbrock, and Steven Rogelberg, *The Cambridge Handbook on Meeting Science*, was published in 2015 and includes a very useful collection of chapters that illustrate the approach taken towards meetings by this group of researchers. I was invited to contribute the concluding chapter to this volume (see Schwartzman 2015).

2 There is much discussion, and even controversy, about why this occurs and one standard explanation is that, in fact, a mirror reverses front to back and not left to right; see the excellent discussion of this by Chris McManus (2002: 307–312). I would like to thank my son-in-law, Raoul Röntsch, for helping me understand the physics of mirrors.

3 It took anthropologists some time to return to the study of institutions, organizations, and bureaucratic settings even though this was a major focus of interest for the entire first generation of American applied anthropologists, researchers such as Conrad Arensberg, Eliot Chapple, Burleigh Gardner, Solon T. Kimball, F. L. W. Richardson, Leonard Sayles, and W. Lloyd Warner (see Schwartzman 1993 for a discussion of this research).

4 As I mention in the text my definition was an attempt to begin to conceptualize some of the general characteristics of a meeting. It was meant as a starting point and not an ending point. There are a number of reasons to question my specification that a meeting should involve at least three or more people. In his article

examining meetings and language ideology in Brazil's MST landless movement Duff Morton (2014) suggests that a meeting must be situated in a historical context and he identifies a "modern meeting . . . as a concept and practice developed inside the language ideology endemic to democratic modernity" (p. 729). He relates his argument about modern meetings to the work of Wilbert van Vree (1999).

5   I have adapted the title of this section from the excellent book, *Makers and Breakers: Children and Youth in Postcolonial Africa* (2005), edited by Filip De Boeck and Alcinda Honwana.

6   Anthony Giddens's theory of structuration (see 1984) and his focus on the relationship of human agency and social structure as these are expressed in "the routines of daily life" has been an important resource for me in thinking about the issues discussed here and I have also been influenced by the work of Deirdre Boden (1995).

7   For a discussion of the idea of "Doing Staffings" see David Buckholdt and Jaber Gubrium (1979).

8   Hannah Brown, Adam Reed, and Thomas Yarrow are editing a special volume of the *Journal of the Royal Anthropological Institute* on the topic "Meetings: Ethnographies of Organizational Procedure, Bureaucracy and Assembly."

9   A recent article in the *New York Times Magazine* entitled "Meet Is Murder" begins with this statement: "They're boring. They're useless. Everyone hates them. So why can't we stop having meetings?" (Heffernan 2016: 29). The mandatory time estimate follows: "Fifteen percent of an organization's time is spent in meetings, and everyday, the transcontinental conference room known as the white-collar United States plays host to 11 million meetings, according to research collated by Fuze, the telecommunications company. . . . One study mysteriously calculates that the nation wastes more than \$37 billion in 'unproductive meetings' " (p. 30). An entire genre of books, as well as web articles, now exists focused on "reforming" meetings in organizational settings and especially cutting back on the time spent in meetings.

10 Pepper's Ghost is an illusion technique used in theaters, amusement parks, museums, and other contexts. It was invented by Henry Dirks in 1862 and popularized by John Henry Pepper. Using a carefully designed stage set, controlled lighting, a sheet of glass, and mirrors, ghost-like people or objects are made to appear as if they are fading in and out of existence. It is sometimes referred to as a reflected illusion. The Haunted Mansion at Disneyland in California uses multiple Pepper's Ghost effects as does the Hogwarts Express attraction at Universal Studios Florida. Teleprompters are a modern version of the Pepper's Ghost effect. (Source: https://en.wikipedia.org/wiki/Pepper%27s_ghost.)

11 Harry Houdini was famous for his escape acts but he also was a vaudeville performer and his most well-known stage illusion was making a full-grown elephant (known as Jennie) disappear at New York's Hippodrome Theatre on January 7, 1918. It was thought that the trick for doing this was lost but it turns out that the elephant was placed in a box and then moved to the side and a diagonally placed mirror was used to make it seem like the entire box was empty but actually what the audience saw was a half-empty box reflected to look whole. Pepper's Ghost effects and Houdini's elephant trick as well as many other tricks involving mirrors are discussed in Jim Steinmeyer's very informative book *Hiding the Elephant: How Magicians Invented the Impossible and Learned to Disappear* (2005).

References

Atkinson, M. A., E. C. Cuff and J. R. E. Lee. "The recommencement of a meeting as member's accomplishment." In *Studies in the Organization of Conversational Interaction*, edited by Jim Schenkein, 133–153. New York: Academic Press, 1978.

Bernstein, Anya and Elizabeth Mertz. "Introduction, bureaucracy: Ethnography of the state in everyday life." *PoLAR: Political and Legal Anthropology Review* 34(2011): 6–10.

Boden, Deirdre. *The Business of Talk: Organizations in Action*. Oxford: Blackwell, 1995.

Buckholdt, David and Jaber Gubrium. "Doing staffings." *Human Organization* 38(1979): 255–264.

Carroll, Lewis. *The Annotated Alice: Alice's Adventures In Wonderland & Through The Looking Glass* (Martin Gardner, introduction and notes). New York: Clarkson Potter, [1871] 1960.

De Boeck, Filip and Alcinda Honwana, eds. *Makers and Breakers: Children and Youth in Postcolonial Africa*. Lawrenceville, NJ: Africa World Press, 2005.

Elyachar, Julia. "Best practices: Research, finance and NGOs in Cairo." *American Ethnologist* 33(2006): 413–426.

Feldman, Ilana. *Governing Gaza: Bureaucracy, Authority, and the Work of Rule, 1917–1967*. Durham: Duke University Press, 2008.

Giddens, Anthony. *The Constitution of Society*. Berkeley: University of California Press, 1984.

Graeber, David. *Direct Action: An Ethnography*. Oakland, CA: AK Press, 2009.

Harper, Richard. *Inside the IMF: An Ethnography of Documents, Technology and Organisational Action*. New York: Academic Press, 1998.

Haug, Christoph. "Organizing spaces: Meeting arenas as a social movement infrastructure between organization, network, and institution." *Organization Studies* 34(2013): 705–732.

Heffernan, Virginia. "Meet Is Murder." *New York Times Magazine*, February 28, 2016, 28–32, 70.

Hull, Matthew. "Ruled by records: The expropriation of land and the misappropriation of lists in Islamabad." *American Ethnologist* 35(2008): 501–518.

Hull, Matthew. "Documents and Bureaucracy." *Annual Review of Anthropology* 41(2012a): 251–267.

Hull, Matthew. *Government of Paper: The Materiality of Bureaucracy in Urban Pakistan*. Berkeley: University of California Press, 2012b.

Juris, Jeffrey S. "Reflections on #Occupy everywhere: Social media, public space, and emerging logics of aggregation." *American Ethnologist* 39(2012): 259–279.

Kluckhohn, Clyde. *Mirror for Man*. Boston: McGraw Hill, 1944.

Latour, Bruno. *Reassembling the Social: An Introduction to Actor-Network-Theory*. Oxford: Oxford University Press, 2005.

McManus, Chris. *Right Hand, Left Hand: The Origins of Asymmetry in Brains, Bodies, Atoms and Cultures*. Cambridge, MA: Harvard University Press, 2002.

Morton, Gregory Duff. "Modern meetings: Participation, democracy, and language ideology in Brazil's MST landless movement." *American Ethnologist* 41(2014): 728–741.

Nugent, David. "Commentary: Democracy, temporalities of capitalism, and dilemmas of inclusion in Occupy Movements." *American Ethnologist* 39(2012): 280–283.

Ranson, Stewart, Bob Hinings and Royston Greenwood. "The structuring of organizational structures." *Administrative Science Quarterly* 25(1980): 1–17.

Razsa, Maple and Andrej Kurnick. "The Occupy Movement in Žižek's hometown: Direct democracy and a politics of becoming." *American Ethnologist* 39(2012): 238–258.

Riles, Annelise, ed. *Documents: Artifacts of Modern Knowledge*. Ann Arbor: University of Michigan Press, 2006.

Salmenkari, Taru. "Political opportunities and protest mobilization in Argentina." *El Norte-Finnish Journal of Latin American Studies* 4(2009): 1–18.

Schwartzman, Helen B. *The Meeting: Gathering in Organizations and Communities*. New York: Plenum Press, 1989.

Schwartzman, Helen B. *Ethnography in Organizations*. Qualitative Research Methods Series, Volume 27. Newbury Park, CA: Sage, 1993.

Schwartzman, Helen B. "There's something about meetings: Order and disorder in the study of meetings." In *The Cambridge Handbook on Meeting Science*, edited by Joseph A. Allen, Nale Lehmann-Willenbrock and Steven Rogelberg, 735–745. Cambridge: Cambridge University Press, 2015.

Sharma, Aradhana and Akhil Gupta. *The Anthropology of the State: A Reader*. Oxford: Wiley-Blackwell, 2006.

Steinmeyer, Jim. *Hiding the Elephant: How Magicians Invented the Impossible and Learned to Disappear*. New York: Carroll & Graf Publishers, 2005.

van Vree, Wilbert. *Meetings, Manners and Civilization: The Development of Modern Meeting Behavior*. Leicester: Leicester University Press, 1999.

Notes on Contributors

Simone Abram is Reader in the Department of Anthropology at Durham University (UK). Her work on government and planning has been published in journals and books, including *Culture and Planning* (2011) and *Elusive Promises* (2013). She is currently a Director of the Durham Energy Institute.

Susann Baez Ullberg is a social anthropologist, currently a postdoc scholar at the School of Global Studies at the University of Gothenburg. She also works at CRISMART Crisis Management Research and Training at the Swedish Defense University in Stockholm. Her fields of research are primarily environmental, disaster, and development anthropology, focusing theoretically on issues such as time, knowledge, morality, and materiality, with a regional focus on Latin America. She is an affiliated researcher at different international research institutes and one of the founders of DICAN (Disaster and Crisis Anthropology Network) within EASA (European Association of Social Anthropologists).

Japonica Brown-Saracino is associate professor in the Department of Sociology at Boston University. Relying on ethnographic methods, Brown-Saracino studies gentrification, identity, community, and residential choices. She is the author of *A Neighborhood That Never Changes* (2009) and editor of the *Gentrification Debates* (2010). Her recent articles on place, identity, and sexualities have appeared in *American Journal of Sociology*, *Social Problems*, and *Qualitative Sociology*.

Christina Garsten is Professor of Social Anthropology at the Department of Social Anthropology, Stockholm University, and Chair of the Executive Board of SCORE (Stockholm Centre for Organizational Research, Stockholm University and Stockholm School of Economics). Her research interests are focused on organizational anthropology, with a special emphasis on globalization processes and transnational dynamics. Recent research has focused on transparency and accountability as forms of governance articulated in labor market policy and the field of corporate social responsibility. Her current research explores the role of think tanks in emerging new forms of transnational governance, i.e., in the shaping of policy processes, in the diffusion of policy-relevant knowledge and ideology, and in the fashioning of society at large.

Nancy Kendall is associate professor of Educational Policy Studies at the University of Wisconsin-Madison. She is a comparative ethnographer who examines the consequences of education policies on the life experiences of marginalized girls, boys, families, and communities in Southern Africa and the United States. Her research has examined children's sense-making and experiences with gender and education, political democratization, sexuality and HIV/AIDS education, orphanhood, and school fee policies. She is currently conducting research in Malawi on adolescent girls' economic, social, and communal survival strategies, and in the United States on low-income students' experiences of college affordability.

Jen Sandler is Lecturer in Anthropology and Director of the UMass Alliance for Community Transformation at the University of Massachusetts Amherst. Sandler's research and teaching is focused on the politics of knowledge in urban social reform activism. She is interested in how a wide range of reform activists develop and disseminate ways of thinking about social change. Sandler's publications include participatory ethnographic studies of evidence-based policy and practices, popular education, and community organizing, primarily in the United States.

Helen B. Schwartzman is Professor Emerita of Anthropology at Northwestern University. She is a psychological anthropologist with interests ranging from the study of children at play to the examination of adults at work, especially at work in meeting contexts. She is the author of several books and articles about children, organizations, and communities including: *Transformations: The Anthropology of Children's Play* (1978); *Children and Anthropology: Perspectives for the 21st Century* (2001); *The Meeting: Gatherings in Organizations and Communities* (1989); and *Ethnography in Organizations* (1993).

Rachel Silver is a PhD Candidate in Anthropology and Educational Policy Studies at the University of Wisconsin-Madison. Her research explores the relationship between discourses on girls' education and sexuality in international development and the lived experiences of young women. Rachel's dissertation is an ethnographic examination of the diverse meanings attached to schoolgirl pregnancy in Malawi, and the consequences of these on girls' post-pregnancy opportunities. She is co-author of *Educated for Change? Muslim Refugee Women in the West* as well as chapters in edited volumes on globalization in education and forced migration across the global South.

Karin Skill holds a PhD in the multidisciplinary field of science and technology studies, and a master's degree in social anthropology. In 2010 she performed postdoctoral research at the University of California at Santa Cruz, at the Department for Anthropology. Her main research interests are political ecology and environmental anthropology, and she has done research on environmental politics and mobilization, knowledge production, sustainable development, gender, intercultural pedagogy, and ecofeminism, in Sweden and Latin America.

Meaghan Stiman is a PhD candidate in the Department of Sociology at Boston University. Her research broadly examines how communities and neighborhoods change and the groups of people who help to produce these changes. Using a combination of ethnographic and interview data, her dissertation traces the role, experience, and impact of second homeowners and second homeownership in rural and urban contexts: Rangeley, a rural four-season vacation destination in Northern Maine, and Boston, a growing site of urban second homeownership.

Adrienne Sörbom is associate professor of sociology, research leader at SCORE (Stockholm Centre for Organizational Studies), Stockholm University, and Stockholm School of Economics, and senior lecturer at Södertörn University. Her research interests may be termed political sociology and include the organization of global politics among different types of actors, such as trade unions, social movements, and global think tanks. Her work is published both in Swedish and English, in, for example, *Statsvetenskaplig tidskrift*, *Social Movements*, *Critical Sociology* as well as at Edward Elgar and Routledge.

Renita Thedvall is associate professor of social anthropology, senior researcher, and Deputy Director at SCORE (Stockholm Centre for Organizational Research) at Stockholm University and Stockholm School of Economics. She has a particular interest in how policies are shaped and presented in the form of models, indicators, and standards within the areas of employment policy, work life, and social issues. Her research is based in the field of policy and organizational anthropology as well as the anthropology of bureaucracy. Recent articles have appeared in *Journal of the Royal Anthropological Institute* (JRAI), *Scandinavian Journal of Public Administration*, and *Social Anthropology*.

Index

Abram, Simone 6, 15, 48ff
activism 1, 4, 6, 11, 17, 18, 69–85,
    106–124, 129, 158, 165–166, 170
agency 111, 165, 166, 167, 168
aid coordination 27
Andalgalá 69–85
architectural, meetings as 14–16, 144
arenas for articulation 11, 13, 19, 130
Argentina 69–85
asamblea meetings 69–85
assemblage 72–85, 130, 165

Bailey, F.G. 4
betwixt and between 133–136, 139
Brenneis, Don 5, 168
bureaucracy 2, 3, 4, 46–66, 77, 144,
    153, 160, 166, 167, 168

Chatham House rules 129
collective action 71, 72, 81, 84–85,
    116, 160, 165–166
communicative event 5, 132, 138–139
community 6, 11, 12, 17, 74, 106–124,
    128, 130, 131–132, 136, 137, 165,
    170, 172
community of practices 12, 13, 15
community studies 88–103
credentialing 12, 13

Davos 126–141
decentralization 3, 31–32, 35
democratic practice 58
development aid 24–43
disaster 70–71, 74, 76, 76–77, 78, 80,
    81, 84
discourse as/in practice 25
documents 14, 15, 17, 18, 42, 48,
    49–50, 52–53, 80, 84, 112, 144,
    148–151, 155, 168–169

education 18, 28–43, 58, 60–61, 78,
    84, 106, 107–108, 148, 164
emergence 69, 84ff, 165
equally available speech acts 7, 10, 13
ethnographic momentum 126–141
evaluate 150, 151–154, 155, 169
experiential and experimental sites 128,
    138–141
experiential learning 50, 52

Foucault, Michel 13, 14, 15, 16, 36,
    46, 52, 144

Garsten, Christina 128, 140
Goffman, Erving 4, 161
Graeber, David 4, 6, 73, 76, 77–78

Haug, Christoph 4, 6, 14, 161

infrastructure 13, 14, 53, 108, 112,
    115ff, 138
international development 2, 16,
    24–43, 164
interview 29, 42, 89, 90, 98, 116, 172
invisibility 14, 47, 52, 159, 167

jet-plane ethnography 139

knowledge 2, 6, 7, 9, 13, 17, 18, 48,
    50, 55, 56, 65, 71, 76, 82, 92, 107,
    111–112, 115, 117–123, 124,
    143, 145
Kuper, Adam 4, 56

Larkin, Brian 14
Latour, Bruno 14, 16, 46, 124, 168
lean 19, 143–155, 169, 174
learning 17, 37, 46–66, 166
literacy 29, 33–37

maker, meetings as 14–16, 111, 122, 144, 155, 163
Malawi 24–43
management model 14, 19, 143–155, 169
material(ity) 14, 15, 31, 46, 48, 52–53, 54, 55, 71, 72, 73, 80, 81, 84, 85, 115, 124, 144, 163, 165, 167, 172, 174
meeting(s), what is a 9–16, 162; 1-on-1 116–122, 171; board 96, 111, 143; ceremonial 111; committee 6, 19, 38, 48, 54, 56, 94, 111, 117, 160; council 4, 6, 46, 51–55, 58–64, 65, 94, 116–118, 160, 166; formal 16, 54, 56, 97, 129, 136, 138, 139, 140; informal 18, 116, 140; nonformal 116; partner 27–30, 37, 40, 164; post- 16, 18, 106, 171; pre- 18, 106, 117, 119, 121; project 37, 106, 111; staged 128–130, 132, 135, 140; team 56, 111, 143; town 90–91, 96; virtual 3, 6, 169
meeting ethnography 1–20, 24, 26, 29, 37, 41–42, 88, 89, 94–97, 102, 110, 124, 127, 129, 155, 164, 172
"meeting proper" 18, 129, 132, 138–139
meeting-saturated fieldwork 110ff, 124, 170, 171
method 16–19
microcosm 128–130
middle figure 25ff
mining 69ff
mirror 158–174
Myers, Fred 5

NGO 3, 24ff, 26, 28, 32, 33, 41, 75, 76, 140
non-political 81, 83
Norway 46–66

outsidedness 129
ownership 27, 37–38, 41, 88

para-ethnography 110, 124, 136
participant observation 18, 19, 29, 42, 73, 139, 172
participation 27, 42, 50, 71, 91, 129
partner meeting 27–30, 37, 40, 164, 167, 172
pedagogy 5, 58, 62–65, 79, 83, 84, 148–151
performance 36–37, 42, 50, 55, 57, 66, 130, 150, 158, 162

place-based populations 90, 93, 95, 102
policy 1, 6, 13, 25–43, 53, 106–124, 144, 165
political technology 13
Polletta, Francesca 4, 6, 18, 91, 100
polymorphous engagements 136
power 1, 4, 5, 8–9, 11, 13, 15–16, 18–19, 24–43, 53, 55, 56, 65, 80, 88, 92–94, 96, 103, 106–124, 138, 144, 163, 167
practice approach 25
practices of circulation, meetings as 14–16, 112, 115, 122, 144
preschool 143–155
presence 66, 69, 76, 84–85, 173
protest 4, 69–85, 158, 165
punctuated entries 19, 145, 147

Rabinow, Paul 78, 128, 138
reenactment 133
reform coalition 106–124
restricted access 127–129, 138
Richards, Audrey 4, 56

Sandler, Jen 4, 6, 106ff
Santa Fe City 69–85
Schwartzman, Helen B. 1, 2, 5, 7, 8, 19, 46, 48, 66, 89, 91, 92, 93, 96, 99, 132, 153, 158ff
social arena 127, 131
social change 17, 83, 123
social labor 71, 73, 79, 82–84, 165
social order 4, 159, 163
social process 14, 50, 128, 139
studying through 25–27, 37, 42
Sweden 143–155

technologies of government 46
technologies of meetings 110
technology 13–14, 17, 27, 42, 71, 81, 110, 116, 162
Thedvall, Renita 3, 6, 8, 19, 143ff
think tank 130, 140
Time and Space 82, 114, 127, 131, 138, 170
translocal 72, 140, 141

USA 88–103, 106–124

van Vree, Wilbert 7, 166
virtual meetings 3, 6, 169

World Economic Forum (WEF) 126–141

For Product Safety Concerns and Information please contact our EU
representative GPSR@taylorandfrancis.com
Taylor & Francis Verlag GmbH, Kaufingerstraße 24, 80331 München, Germany